DID THE SAVIOUR SEE THE FATHER?

DID THE SAVIOUR SEE THE FATHER?

Christ, Salvation and the Vision of God

Simon Francis Gaine

t&t clark

LONDON • NEW YORK • OXFORD • NEW DELHI • SYDNEY

T&T CLARK
Bloomsbury Publishing Plc
50 Bedford Square, London, WC1B 3DP, UK
1385 Broadway, New York, NY 10018, USA

BLOOMSBURY, T&T CLARK and the T&T Clark logo are
trademarks of Bloomsbury Publishing Plc

First published in Great Britain 2015
Paperback edition first published 2018

A catalogue record for this book is available from the British Library.

ISBN: HB: 978-0-56766-443-3
PB: 978-0-56768-213-0
ePDF: 978-0-56766-440-2
ePub: 978-0-56766-442-6

Library of Congress Cataloging-in-Publication Data
Gaine, Simon.
Did the Saviour see the Father? : Christ, salvation, and
the vision of God / by Simon Francis Gaine.
pages cm   ISBN 978-0-567-66443-3 (hardback)
1. Jesus Christ–Knowledge of his own divinity. 2. Jesus Christ–Person and offices. I. Title.
BT216.5.G35 2015   232'.8–dc23
2015017461

Typeset by Fakenham Prepress Solutions, Fakenham, Norfolk NR21 8NN

To find out more about our authors and books visit
www.bloomsbury.com and sign up for our newsletters.

CONTENTS

ABBREVIATIONS

AAS	*Acta Apostolicae Sedis*
AS	*Augustinian Studies*
AT	*Annales Teologici*
BLE	*Bulletin de Littérature Ecclésiastiastique*
CBQ	*Catholic Biblical Quarterly*
CCCM	Corpus Christianorum, Continuatio Mediaevalis
CCSG	Corpus Christianorum, Series Graeca
CCSL	Corpus Christianorum, Series Latina
CPG	Clavis Patrum Graecorum
CSCO	Corpus Scriptorum Christianorum Orientalium
CSEL	Corpus Scriptorum Ecclesiasticorum Latinorum
DC	*Doctor Communis*
DH	H. Denzinger, P. Hünermann, R. Fastiggi and A. E. Nash, *Enchiridion symbolorum definitionum et declarationem de rebus fidei et morum, Compendium of Creeds, Definitions and Declarations on Matters of Faith and Morals* (San Francisco: Ignatius, 43rd edn, 2012)
DTC	*Dictionnaire de Théologie Catholique*
ETL	*Ephemerides Theologicae Lovanienses*
GCS	Die griechischen christlichen Schriftsteller der ersten drei Jahrhunderte
HJ	*The Heythrop Journal*
ITQ	*Irish Theological Quarterly*
JJT	*Josephinum Journal of Theology*
LC	*Sancti Thomae de Aquino Opera Omnia iussu Leonis XIII P. M. edita* (Rome and Paris: Leonine Commission, 1882–)
LS	*Letter & Spirit*
MJLS	*Method: Journal of Lonergan Studies*
MTZ	*Münchener Theologische Zeitschrift*
NB	*New Blackfriars*
NRT	*Nouvelle Revue Théologique*
NT	*Novum Testamentum*
NTS	*New Testament Studies*
NV	*Nova et Vetera* (English edn)
OLA	Orientalia Lovaniensia Analecta
PE	*Pro Ecclesia*
PG	Patrologia Graeca
PL	Patrologia Latina
PTS	Patristische Texte und Studien
RB	*Revue Biblique*
RSPT	*Revue des Sciences Philosophiques et Théologiques*
RSR	*Recherches de Science Religieuse*

RT	*Revue Thomiste*
SC	Sources Chrétiennes
TJ	*Trinity Journal*
TQ	*Theologische Quartalschrift*
TS	*Theological Studies*
TTh	*The Thomist*
VC	*Vigiliae Christianae*
ZKT	*Zeitschrift für Katholische Theologie*

FOREWORD AND ACKNOWLEDGEMENTS

This is not a work of purely historical theology, and it is not my intention to ask simply what Thomas Aquinas or any other theologian thought about the question of whether Jesus Christ possessed the beatific vision during his earthly lifetime. Nor is this a work of systematic theology as such, in the sense that it does not treat this question of Christ's knowledge in anything like the ordered 'way of presentation' exemplified by Aquinas's *Summa Theologiae*. Again it is not a work of speculative exegesis, which would explain the Gospels and other texts most fruitfully in the light of such a systematic theology, as Aquinas does for example in his commentary on John's Gospel. It is instead an attempt to follow what Bernard Lonergan in one place called the 'way of theological discovery', where a theological question raised by a reading of Scripture in the light of Tradition leads us to a theological conclusion, in this case to conclude that the earthly Christ enjoyed the heavenly knowledge of the vision of the blessed.

It is more than ten years since I first thought of writing this book, and I am grateful to many people who have discussed the project with me or read part or all of earlier drafts. I would especially like to record my thanks to James Arthur, Nicanor Austriaco OP, Richard Conrad OP, John Emery OP, John Farrell OP, David Goodill OP, Andrew Hofer OP, Peter Hunter OP, Oliver Keenan OP, Jo Moyle, Robert Ombres OP, Richard Joseph Ounsworth OP, Connie Svob, Robin Ward and Thomas Joseph White OP. I would like to thank Prof. William Carroll, Prof. Sarah Coakley and Prof. Paul Murray for their invitations to deliver presentations on Christ's knowledge for, respectively, the Aquinas Institute's seminar at Blackfriars, Oxford, for the D Society at Cambridge and at the conference of the Catholic Theological Association of Great Britain in Durham.

Simon Francis Gaine OP

Part I

Chapter 1

'NO ONE THINKS THAT ANYMORE!'

Did the Saviour see the Father? I ask this question not merely of Jesus as he is believed to be now, seated in glory at the Father's right hand, but I ask it of him suffering and dying on the cross, of him teaching the crowds and instructing his disciples, of him obedient to Mary and Joseph as a youth and even as unborn in his mother's womb. In other words, was the Word made flesh blessed from the very first moment of the incarnation with the vision of the essence of the triune God in his human mind? Did Jesus Christ, even before his resurrection and entrance into heaven, possess on earth that clear beatific vision of 'God himself, three and one, just as he is,'[1] which his disciples hope to enjoy one day in heaven?

The importance of this question lies partly in its close relation to a whole series of questions about Jesus, his intellect, knowledge and self-consciousness.[2] Was his human knowledge very different from ours, or much the same? Was it very extensive or somewhat limited? Did it include the fact that he was the Jewish Messiah or that he was divine? How much did he know of his saving mission, and in what kind of terms? What future did he envisage for his followers? All of these issues are linked to a basic question about our salvation: is the Saviour we need one who is altogether like us or one who is in some ways *unlike* us? In particular, has God given us a Saviour of superior knowledge who can enlighten us in our darkness, or one who has become like us in our obscurity of vision? A Saviour who possessed the clear vision of God is surely a Saviour who in at least one important respect is very *unlike* us indeed.

The question's importance is also illustrated by the extent to which the answer given to it by Roman Catholic theologians underwent a dramatic change during the twentieth century. Up to the end of the 1950s there was a general unanimity among these theologians that the answer was 'Yes'. According to this consensus, Christ did indeed contemplate God with the vision of heaven, even during his time on earth. This was the view, for example, of the two pre-eminent Catholic theologians of the first half of the twentieth century, Louis Billot and Réginald

---

1. Council of Florence, *Laetentur Caeli*. Cf. Pius XII, *Mystici Corporis Christi*, 80. All translations in this book, unless otherwise indicated, are my own.

2. For an introduction to the wider issues, see R. Moloney, *The Knowledge of Christ* (London and New York: Continuum, 1999).

Garrigou-Lagrange. Among Billot's theses on Christology was one containing the following: 'There was in Christ from the first moment of his conception that blessed knowledge (*scientia beata*) by which the divinity is seen in itself. Moreover, this knowledge was in him according to the highest degree of perfection there can be in the actual order of things.'[3] And Garrigou-Lagrange, asking whether the Saviour was deprived on earth of that light by which the saints in heaven see God face to face, replied: 'The theologians answer in unison: Jesus saw what He taught in the light of the beatific vision … The contemplation of Jesus even here on earth was not inferior to that which the saints enjoy in heaven.'[4] By this blessed vision of the divine essence Christ also contemplated *all that God wills to be*. Thus Billot adds that Christ in his human soul sees all that God knows by what is called the divine 'knowledge of vision' (*scientia visionis*), and Garrigou that he 'already knew all creatures, all souls, all that they have done, are doing, and will do'.

However, from being a point of common agreement, the theological situation was radically altered to one where the answer 'No' became increasingly common and 'Yes' altogether unusual. In a lecture given at Trier in 1961, the distinguished theologian Karl Rahner had said of the traditional teaching on Christ's beatific knowledge: 'Such statements sound almost mythological today when one first hears them; they seem to be contrary to the real humanity and historical nature of Our Lord.'[5] Rahner proposed instead a theory of Christ's knowledge of God based on self-consciousness, an explanation he had already suggested in a programmatic article on Christology published in 1954.[6] The notion of a direct or immediate rather than beatific vision quickly made an impression.[7] Over the next few decades, theologians would treat Christ's knowledge in terms not only of self-consciousness, but also of ordinary human knowing, faith, prophecy and mysticism, while the beatific vision fell by the wayside. Bernard Lonergan, who died in 1984, was almost the only truly prominent theologian not to have given it up.[8] By 1978, another distinguished Catholic theologian, Hans Urs von Balthasar,

---

3. L. Billot, *De Verbo Incarnato* (Rome: Gregorian, 7th edn, 1927), pp. 223–4.

4. R. Garrigou-Lagrange, *Our Savior and his Love for Us* (trans. A. Bouchard; St Louis and London: Herder, 1951), p. 162.

5. K. Rahner, 'Dogmatic Reflections on the Knowledge and Self-Consciousness of Christ' in *Theological Investigations*, vol. 5: *Later Writings* (trans. K.-H. Kruger; London: Darton, Longman & Todd; Baltimore: Helicon, 1966), pp. 193–215 (194–5).

6. K. Rahner, 'Current Problems in Christology' in *Theological Investigations*, vol. 1: *God, Christ, Mary and Grace* (trans. C. Ernst; London: Darton, Longman & Todd; New York: Seabury, 1961), pp. 149–200 (168–71).

7. See, e.g. E. Gutwenger, *Bewusstsein und Wissen Christi: Eine dogmatische Studie* (Innsbruck: Felizian Rauch, 1960); J. Ratzinger, 'Bewusstsein und Wissen Christi', *MTZ* 12 (1961), pp. 78–81; H. Riedlinger, *Geschichtlichkeit und Vollendung des Wissens Christi* (Quaestiones Disputatae, 32; Freiburg, Basel and Vienna: Herder, 1966); E. Gutwenger, 'The Problem of Christ's Knowledge', *Concilium* 1 (1966): 48–55.

8. See Moloney, *The Knowledge of Christ*, p. 98.

could boldly state that 'Jesus does not see the Father in a *visio beatifica*'.[9] Rahner's hesitations had prevailed. Gerald O'Collins and Daniel Kendall wrote of the older teaching: 'For many people it would seem to inject a strong element of make-believe into the whole of [Jesus'] life story and cast doubt on his authentic humanity.'[10] To anyone who spoke of Christ's beatific vision, it could now easily be retorted: 'No one thinks that anymore!'

This shift among Catholic theologians was part of a much wider change that took place in Catholic theology during the twentieth century. The theological consensus still found in the time of Pope Pius XII had its roots in the highly influential revival of scholasticism in the previous century, which had been endorsed by his predecessor, Leo XIII. This 'neoscholastic' or 'neothomist' revival was focused on the thought of the medieval Dominican friar, Thomas Aquinas, and his later commentators. Aquinas had taught that Christ had various kinds of knowledge.[11] As God he knew the divine nature and all the things that lay in the power of God to do, not only what God had done but all he *could* do. In addition to this infinite divine knowledge, Christ also had various kinds of knowledge in his single finite human mind. The first was the intuitive vision that the blessed have of the divine essence, which we commonly call the 'beatific vision'; the second a further supernatural but more conceptual knowledge divinely 'infused' and 'imprinted' on to his mind, the kind of knowledge had naturally by angels; and the third an ordinary acquired knowledge based on human experience, such as we all have. With respect to the beatific vision, Aquinas taught that Christ possessed it from the first moment of his conception,[12] and by it saw not only the essence of God but also all that was, is or will be, in any way whatever, done, thought or said by all, at any time.[13] Aquinas made sense of the presence of this beatific knowledge in Christ with respect to its role in his saving mission: since his goal was to bring us to the beatific vision, it was necessary that he should have this knowledge himself – his blessed vision was the cause of ours.[14] That Christ's beatific vision exercises this causal role in heaven after his bodily glorification has never really been in doubt among Catholic theologians, though it has hardly been the object of much recent theological interest. What came to be questioned was whether Christ possessed this cause of the vision of the saints *before his death and bodily glorification*, during his earthly lifetime.

With Aquinas's authority behind it, the picture of Christ's fourfold knowledge – one divine and three in his humanity – had become the conventional framework for theological accounts of Christ's knowledge given not only by the nineteenth-century theologians responsible for the Thomist revival, but also by their successors

9. H. U. von Balthasar, *Theo-Drama: Theological Dramatic Theory*, vol. III: *Dramatis Personae: Persons in Christ* (trans. G. Harrison; San Francisco: Ignatius, 1987), p. 200.

10. G. O'Collins and D. Kendall, 'The Faith of Jesus', *TS* 53 (1992): 403–23 (409).

11. *Summa Theologiae*, 3a., q. 9.

12. Ibid., 3a., q. 34, a. 4.

13. Ibid., 3a., q. 10, a. 2.

14. Ibid., 3a., q. 9, a. 2.

in the first half of the twentieth century, theologians like Billot and Garrigou. Moreover, while Aquinas's principles and teachings had already received a general approval from the Church's 'Magisterium' or teaching authority, the thesis that Christ had enjoyed the beatific vision on earth also began to receive its own particular measures of ecclesiastical approbation. This came about at a time when the position of scholasticism was being strengthened throughout the Catholic Church in the wake of Pius X's condemnation of 'Modernism'. Despite the fact that the Church's response involved the rejection of any doubts about the reality of Christ's extraordinary knowledge,[15] the worry that a purely scholastic framework was somehow inadequate had not gone away, and signs of fresh thinking on the development and limits of Christ's natural knowledge were emerging.[16] In the background there also lay the proposal made towards the end of the nineteenth century that Christ had a non-beatific but perfect consciousness of himself, the inner life of the Trinity and the plan of salvation.[17]

On 5 June 1918, a decree was issued by the Holy Office – the Roman body which dealt with doctrinal issues and the predecessor of today's Congregation for the Doctrine of the Faith – as an answer to some queries raised by the Sacred Congregation on Seminary and University Studies. The third of the three questions raised indicates the decree's immediate background in the growing interest among theologians in limitation and development in Christ's human knowledge. The reply nowhere denied that there were such aspects to Christ's knowledge, but dealt with the level of acceptance in teaching in Catholic institutions that recent theological opinions could be awarded. The actual question put to the Holy Office was whether it could be 'safely taught' that the opinion of certain more recent theologians on the limited knowledge of Christ's soul was to be received *no less than* the teaching of older theologians on Christ's 'universal knowledge'.[18] The answer was that this could not be safely taught: the older and more established teaching, which was linked in scholastic theology to Christ's beatific vision, must have a higher level of acceptance in the teaching of Catholic theology.

The first two questions were more explicitly linked to the beatific vision. The first was whether it might be 'safely taught' that Christ did *not* possess the knowledge had by the blessed (that is, the inhabitants of heaven) while on earth.[19] In other words, could it be safely taught that Christ did not during his earthly lifetime possess the beatific vision? The Holy Office replied that such a proposition

15. Cf. Holy Office, *Lamentabili*, 32–5.

16. For a contemporary impression, see J. Rivière, 'Le problème de la science humaine du Christ: Positions classiques et nouvelles tendances', *BLE* 7 (1915–16): 241–61, 289–314, 337–64. On comparable concerns in Anglican theology, see M. M. Adams, *Christ and Horrors: The Coherence of Christology* (Cambridge: CUP, 2006), pp. 60–6.

17. H. Schell, *Katholische Dogmatik: Kritische Ausgabe*: vol. 3: *Menschwerdung und Erlösung, Heiligung und Vollendung* (eds H. Petri and P.-W. Scheele; Paderborn etc.: Schöningh, 1994), pp. 120–40.

18. Holy Office, *Circa Quasdam Propositiones de Scientia Animae Christi*, 3.

19. Ibid., 1.

could *not* be safely taught. To the contrary, then, the safe teaching endorsed by the Holy Office was that Christ *did* so possess the beatific vision. The second question was whether the opinion could be safely taught that *denied* the possibility of being certain of the teaching that Christ knew all that God knows, past, present or future, in the Word, that is, all that God knows by the 'knowledge of vision', and was ignorant of nothing.[20] In other words, could it be safely taught that the thesis that Christ had knowledge of all that God had actually caused to be by the knowledge of the beatific vision was in fact an uncertain thesis? The answer was again negative. The safe teaching was rather that Christ's possession of the 'knowledge of vision' could be dubbed certain. The expectation was evidently that seminary professors would stick to what Billot, whose influence was at his height, had been teaching in Rome for some years.

While such a disciplinary measure, though approved by Benedict XV, gave Christ's possession of the beatific vision a relatively low degree of magisterial force, it was subsequently to appear in ordinary papal teaching. Pius XI's encyclical of 1928, *Miserentissimus Redemptor*, took as its topic reparation made to the Sacred Heart of Jesus by the faithful, that is, compensation made by believers for a kind of debt incurred by some offence. The Pope asks, though, how solace can be brought to Christ by such reparation, when he is now reigning in heaven. Thinking of Christ in the Garden of Gethsamene, he writes:

> But if the soul of Christ became sorrowful unto death on account of our sins, which were in the future but yet were foreseen, there is no doubt that he also already derived something of solace from our reparation, which was likewise foreseen, when 'there appeared to him an angel from heaven' (Lk. 22.43), in order that his Heart, weighed down by weariness and anguish, might be consoled.[21]

The reality of this consolation presupposed that Christ in his agony had knowledge not only of our sins but of our reparation also. The fact that Pius wrote at a time when the theological consensus was in favour of Christ's possessing the beatific vision makes it easy for us to see that the Pope was making use of the same scholastic teaching on Christ's knowledge, if only implicitly. In his blessed knowledge, Christ knew both our sins and our acts of reparation.

Teaching about Christ's heavenly knowledge on earth then made an explicit appearance in 1943 in Pius XII's *Mystici Corporis Christi*. Pius emphasizes Christ's beatific knowledge of all God wills to be, teaching that he possesses the 'knowledge of vision' to a degree that surpasses the heavenly knowledge of all the saints as regards both extent and clarity.[22] The purpose of this encyclical was to treat of the Church as Christ's Mystical Body, and of the relationship of the Body's Head and members, and so the Pope speaks of Christ's vision extending not only to the divine essence but to all who were to be united to him in the Church:

20. Ibid., 2.
21. Pius XI, *Miserentissimus Redemptor*, 13.
22. Pius XII, *Mystici Corporis Christi*, 48.

The most loving knowledge by which the divine Redeemer has pursued us
from the first moment of his incarnation utterly surpasses all the searchings
of the human mind; for by that blessed vision (*beatam illam visionem*), which
he enjoyed as soon as he was received into the womb of the Mother of God, he
has continuously and perpetually had present to him all the members of his
Mystical Body, and embraced them with his saving love.[23]

Then, thirteen years later, he again made use of Christ's possession of the beatific
vision in another encyclical letter, *Haurietis Aquas*, the subject this time being the
Sacred Heart. Pius taught that this Heart is a symbol of the love that was infused
into Christ's soul and directs its acts in the light of his most perfect knowledge,
which included a 'blessed' knowledge.[24] The teaching of these encyclicals was by no
means an extraordinary definition of Catholic dogma. Nevertheless, these letters
had considerable weight for Catholics as expressions of the ordinary teaching of
the Vicar on earth of the Head of the Mystical Body. When the Second Vatican
Council (1962–5) was first called, the Holy Office expressed the (unrealized)
expectation that Christ's beatific vision would be among the Council's explicit
teachings, and bishops at the Council made appeal to this vision in order to argue
that the Council should explicitly teach that Christ was exempt from ignorance.[25]
Thus the common teaching of Catholic theologians was in clear continuity with
the teaching of the Catholic Magisterium.

What consensus there was among Catholic theologians some half a century
after *Mystici Corporis* was quite different from the once confident Thomism that
lost its dominance in Catholic theology around the time of Vatican II. Although
the Council reaffirmed the importance of Aquinas for theology, the influence of
Thomism had already begun to wane in the middle of the century and after the
Council it collapsed almost altogether. With Thomism's effective loss of its privileged position went the conventional theological discussion of Christ's earthly
knowledge in terms of the beatific vision, except as a point of historical reference.
When one of the most recent critics of Aquinas's teaching on Christ's blessed
vision has been one of Aquinas's most eminent students, Jean-Pierre Torrell,[26]
one could be forgiven for concluding that only the most diehard of Thomists
would dare defend the older teaching. Yet, when a group of mainly Italian- and
French-speaking theologians did mount a defence of it in 1983,[27] Jean Galot felt

---

23. Ibid., 75.

24. Pius XII, *Haurietis Aquas*, 56.

25. See J. A. Riestra, 'La scienza di Cristo nel concilio Vaticano II: Ebrei 4, 15 nella
Costituzione Dogmatica "Dei Verbum"', *AT* 2 (1988): 99–119 (100, 110).

26. See J.-P. Torrell, 'S. Thomas d'Aquin et la science du Christ: Une Relecture des
questions 9–12 de la "Tertia pars" de la Somme de Théologie' in S.-T. Bonino (ed.), *Saint
Thomas au XXe siècle: Actes du colloque du centenaire de la "Revue Thomiste"* 25–28 mars
1993 – *Toulouse* (Paris: St Paul, 1994), pp. 394–409. It is reprinted in Torrell, *Recherches
thomasiennes. Études revues et augmentées* (Paris: Vrin, 2000), pp. 198–213.

27. See *DC* 36 (1983). One of these articles, which had first been published in 1977,

obliged to answer them with a thorough critique that neatly summed up a new post-conciliar consensus against the older view.[28] Likewise, when a number of theologians, including this time English-speaking theologians, began to speak up for it more recently,[29] Thomas G. Weinandy expressed his discomfort with the teaching more than once.[30] The fact that each of these critics is notable for his orthodoxy further underscores the extent to which Aquinas's teaching had fallen from theological favour.

General agreement on parting company with the older view did not mean that a single agreed theory of Christ's knowledge had taken its place. However, if there was any point of convergence among Catholic theologians on the knowledge of Christ in the decades after Vatican II, it seems to have been that, despite whatever extraordinary knowledge he might possess, he shared the same ordinary processes of knowledge as any other human being. More recent theologians could claim an important *continuity* with Aquinas on this point, because it was part of his own theological development that, in contrast to his contemporaries, he had come to appreciate the reality of Christ's actually acquiring intellectual knowledge from the world around him through experience.[31] The overall picture, however, is hardly one of simple continuity between Aquinas and more recent theologians. In terms of Aquinas's wider portrayal of Christ's knowledge, there was a far greater *discontinuity* in Catholic theology in the middle of the twentieth century, a departure from the teaching of Aquinas. From now on, some other kind of knowledge was called upon to 'do duty' for the role previously played by the beatific vision.

---

was translated as B. de Margerie, *The Human Knowledge of Christ: The Knowledge, Fore-knowledge and Consciousness, Even in the Pre-paschal Period, of Christ the Redeemer* (Boston, MA: St Paul's, 1980).

28. J. Galot, 'Le Christ terrestre et la vision', *Gregorianum* 67 (1986): 429–50.

29. R. Cessario, 'Incarnate Wisdom and the Immediacy of Christ's Salvific Knowledge' in *Problemi Teologici Alla Luce dell'Aquinate* (Studi Tomistici, 44:5; Vatican: Vaticana, 1991), pp. 334–40; T. J. Tekippe, 'Towards a Systematic Understanding of the Vision of Christ', *MJLS* 11 (1993): 77–101; G. Mansini, 'Understanding St. Thomas on Christ's Immediate Knowledge of God', *TTh* 59 (1995): 91–124; M. Levering, *Christ's Fulfillment of Torah and Temple: Salvation according to Thomas Aquinas* (Notre Dame: Notre Dame, 2002); J. Saward, *Cradle of Redeeming Love: The Theology of the Christmas Mystery* (San Francisco: Ignatius, 2002); G. Mongeau, 'The Human and Divine Knowing of the Incarnate Word', *JJT* 12 (2005): 30–42; T. J. White, 'The Voluntary Action of the Earthly Christ and the Necessity of the Beatific Vision', *TTh* 69 (2005): 497–534; B. M. Ashley, 'The Extent of Jesus' Human Knowledge according to the Fourth Gospel' in M. Dauphinais and M. Levering (eds), *Reading John with St. Thomas Aquinas: Theological Exegesis and Speculative Theology* (Washington, DC: CUA, 2005), pp. 241–53.

30. T. G. Weinandy, 'Jesus' Filial Vision of the Father', *PE* 13 (2004): 189–201; T. G. Weinandy, 'The Beatific Vision and the Incarnate Son: Furthering the Discussion', *TTh* 70 (2006): 605–15.

31. *Summa*, 3a., q. 9, a. 4.

It is important to note that the Magisterium itself appeared at the time to be implicated up to a point in this theological shift. Rahner had initially been careful to claim that his theory of Christ's 'immediate vision' did not fall short of what was taught by Pius XII in *Mystici Corporis*. He suggested that the encyclical could be interpreted to teach not that Jesus enjoyed a *blessed* knowledge, strictly speaking, but only the same knowledge that the blessed also had.[32] On that basis he held that understanding Christ's vision in a non-beatific way did sufficient justice to the authority of the encyclical. Later theology, however, was not so scrupulous, and was prepared to admit that Rahner's was a significant departure from the older Magisterial teaching. Moreover, the confidence of theologians that their loyalty was not compromised by exploring alternatives to Pius's teaching was not officially contradicted.[33] Alluding in 1969 to Rahner's theory, one author noted approvingly how the thesis of Christ's beatific vision had been 'considerably modified by important theologians without protest from the magisterium'.[34] Not only, though, were alternative theses effectively tolerated, but no absolutely explicit reference to Christ's possessing the beatific vision was made in any document of the Magisterium or its official advisory bodies during the remainder of the century. For example, questions of Christ's knowledge of himself and his mission were treated in documents of the Church's International Theological Commission in 1979, 1981 and 1985.[35] The documents produced by the Commission, while not being authoritative Church teaching, nonetheless indicate something of Catholic theological mood at the highest level, since its role is to advise the Magisterium on theological matters. It did not go unnoticed that the three documents discussed Christ's knowledge without any reference to the beatific vision at all. Raymond Moloney observes that what is 'most significant in this 1985 statement is that not a word is said about the beatific vision', adding that it 'leaves open the question of the special human knowledge of the beatific vision'.[36] However, while this reticence need indicate no more than that the theologians were not as a group able to endorse any single theological account of Christ's knowledge, or at least that they had no intention of attempting one,[37] such reticence inevitably contributed to an impression that the Magisterium had withdrawn its former endorsement of the earthly Christ's heavenly vision.

32. 'Knowledge and Self-Consciousness of Christ', p. 203 n.10; cf. pp. 213–14 n.12.

33. Cf. Riedlinger, *Geschichtlichkeit und Vollendung des Wissens Christi*, pp. 136–7; C. Duquoc, *Christologie: Essai Dogmatique*: vol.1: *L'Homme Jésus* (Paris: Cerf, 1968), pp. 158–63.

34. P. Schoonenberg, *The Christ* (London and Sydney: Sheed & Ward, 1972), p. 126.

35. For the English versions, see 'Select Questions on Christology' in M. Sharkey (ed.), *International Theological Commission: Texts and Documents 1969–1985* (San Francisco: Ignatius, 1989), pp. 185–205; 'Theology, Christology, Anthropology' in ibid., pp. 207–23; 'The Consciousness of Christ concerning Himself and his Mission' in ibid., pp. 305–16.

36. Moloney, *The Knowledge of Christ*, p. 124.

37. International Theological Commission, 'Consciousness of Christ', p. 307.

There was moreover no explicit mention of Christ's beatific vision in the *Catechism of the Catholic Church*, which was promulgated in 1997 by Pope John Paul II as an authoritative guide for all catechesis. When the *Catechism* came to treat of Christ's knowledge, its first emphasis was not on any extraordinary supernatural knowledge within his soul, but was rather on the *ordinary* human conditions of his knowing.[38] Only then does the text go on to say that Christ's human knowledge is an expression of his divinity. However, although this knowledge is first of all an 'intimate and immediate knowledge that the Son of God made man has of his Father', while also showing a 'divine penetration' into the secret thoughts of human hearts and including 'the fullness of understanding of the eternal plans he had come to reveal', none of this is explicitly interpreted by the text itself in terms of the 'beatific vision'.[39] The language of beatific vision is certainly used by the *Catechism*, but only in regard to heaven itself, and is nowhere applied to Christ's knowledge while on earth.[40] Given this context, it was not easy to conclude that Pope John Paul was definitely referring to the beatific vision when he spoke in his apostolic letter, *Novo Millennio Ineunte* (2001), of the 'knowledge and experience of the Father' which Christ alone had, and of his seeing the Father and rejoicing in him, still experiencing that union with the Father which was of its very nature a source of beatitude and happiness, even as he clearly saw the gravity of sin and suffered in a moment of darkness on the cross.[41] Nor did the actual quotations from the saints the Pope used as analogies in illustration of this knowledge speak explicitly of the 'beatific vision', but only of blessedness of soul and joy.[42] Had Pius XI said all this in an earlier theological context, it would doubtless have been quickly deduced that he meant the beatific vision, but at the turn of the twenty-first century in the pontificate of John Paul II, matters were hardly so clear for theologians, who would be able to interpret the apostolic letter according to their own theories of Christ's knowledge and blessedness, human and divine.

Reviewing the more recent teaching of the Magisterium, O'Collins understandably concluded in 2002 that Aquinas's view of 'the earthly Jesus' knowledge no longer enjoyed official endorsement'.[43] In such a situation, Catholic theologians in general hardly felt any obligation to follow the older Magisterial teaching. Older papal encyclicals could be taken to reflect an outmoded theology used in the expression of their more primary points of teaching. The Holy Office's declaration that the absence of the beatific vision from Christ could not be safely taught was even regarded not as dealing with particular questions relating to the limitations of Christ's human knowledge but as aimed more broadly against Modernism, in particular against those who denied that Christ had knowledge of his divinity.

38. *Catechismus Catholicae Ecclesiae* (Vatican: Libreria Editrice Vaticana, 1997), 472.

39. Ibid., 473–4.

40. Ibid., 1023.

41. John Paul II, *Novo Millennio Ineunte*, 26.

42. Ibid., 27.

43. G. O'Collins, *Incarnation* (London and New York: Continuum, 2002), p. 84.

These also denied Christ's *beatific* knowledge, but it was now asserted to be their denial of knowledge of his divinity that had been fundamentally at issue.[44] In contrast to the Holy Office's decree, O'Collins and Kendall opined: 'Today, in a changed ecclesial, theological, and cultural climate, to teach that during his earthly life Christ enjoyed the knowledge which the blessed have in heaven might itself not be such "safe" teaching.'[45] As theologians and Magisterium had once been in concert in strongly asserting Christ's possession of the beatific vision, so they now seemed to be in concert in holding back from the idea. If it was true that no one thought the earthly Christ had had the beatific vision anymore, that at least seemed to hold good for the Magisterium too.

It was in this context that I first conceived of writing a book that would gather together the results of the more recent defences of Aquinas' teaching and address the criticisms generally made of it, asking whether there might be a form in which the Thomist view was still viable.[46] However, before I had the opportunity to make a start on this book, the situation was altered by a new statement from the Magisterium. In 2006, with the approval of Pope Benedict XVI (who in his younger days as Joseph Ratzinger had been no defender of Christ's beatific vision), the Congregation for the Doctrine of the Faith released a 'notification', which was occasioned by two books by Jon Sobrino,[47] and whose content took many by surprise. It drew attention to a number of Sobrino's propositions that were said to be 'not in conformity with the teaching of the Church', some of which were connected to Christ's 'self-consciousness'. The notification charged that Sobrino reduced Jesus to the category of a prophet and mystic, missing the intimate and immediate knowledge of the Father, which is said by the Congregation to be a 'vision' beyond that of faith.[48] The document illustrates this intimate knowledge

44. J. Galot, *Who is Christ?: A Theology of the Incarnation* (trans. M. A. Bouchard; Chicago: Franciscan Herald, 1981), pp. 357–58 n.33.

45. 'The Faith of Jesus', p. 409.

46. During my period of writing, Christ's beatific vision has also been defended by E. T. Oakes, *Infinity Dwindled to Infancy: A Catholic and Evangelical Christology* (Grand Rapids, MI and Cambridge: Eerdmans, 2011), pp. 210–21; E. Durand, *L'Offre universelle du salut en Christ* (Paris: Cerf, 2012), pp. 156–68; J. Wilkins, 'Love and Knowledge of God in the Human Life of Christ', *PE* 21 (2012): 77–99 (an excellent article based on the work of Lonergan); and W. L. Brownsberger, *Jesus the Mediator* (Washington, DC: CUA, 2013). See also the extensive critique of von Balthasar's rejection of Christ's beatific vision by A. L. Pitstick, *Light in Darkness: Hans Urs von Balthasar and the Catholic Doctrine of Christ's Descent into Hell* (Grand Rapids, MI and Cambridge: Eerdmans, 2007), pp. 171–90. For what appears to be an attempt to rework Christ's beatific vision in the context of Balthasar's Trinitarian theology, see N. J. Healy Jr., 'The Filial Mode of Christ's Knowledge', *NV* 11 (2013): 341–55.

47. *Jesus the Liberator: A Historical–Theological Reading of Jesus of Nazareth* (trans. P. Burns and F. McDonagh; Tunbridge Wells and New York: Burns & Oates, 1994); *Christ the Liberator: A View from the Victims* (trans. P. Burns; Maryknoll, NY: Orbis, 2001).

48. Congregation for the Doctrine of the Faith, *Notificatio de Operibus P. Jon Sobrino, S. I.*, 5.8.

of the Father by quoting Pius XII on Christ's possession of the beatific vision from the first moment of the incarnation. It then goes on to cite John Paul II's *Novo Millennio Ineunte* and the *Catechism*, neither of which, as we have seen, makes explicit mention of the 'beatific vision'. The notification, however, asserts that John Paul was in fact insisting on the same vision of the Father of which Pius XII spoke in *Mystici Corporis*, and by implication it asserted the same of the *Catechism* also.

Most recently, Christ's vision of the Father has been touched on by Pope Francis in his encyclical on faith, which was largely prepared by his predecessor, Pope Benedict. Francis speaks there of Christ's 'vision' of his Father taking place 'in a human way' (*humana ratione*) in the course of time, on account of the incarnation. As with John Paul II and the *Catechism*, there is no explicit identification of this vision as the *beatific* vision, and one can imagine a theologian thinking to interpret it too in some other way, perhaps as the 'vision of faith' of which the encyclical often speaks. However, given the context of the notification concerning Sobrino not many years before, it would seem that we definitely have in a recent papal teaching an attribution of the vision of heaven to the earthly Christ. To interpret it otherwise must surely suppose that the notification of the preceding pontificate no longer stands, and that Sobrino's views are no longer considered problematic.

What we see at work in the notification with regard to the teaching of John Paul II and the *Catechism* is an approach to earlier magisterial pronouncements that finds in them a significant continuity with yet earlier teaching. This reflects to some degree the hermeneutics for interpreting the work of Vatican II, which had been publicly approved by Benedict XVI at the end of 2005. In a speech to the Roman Curia he contrasted a hermeneutics of the Council that treated it as a rupture in discontinuity with previous Catholic teaching with a hermeneutics that placed the Council's reform within a deeper continuity with Tradition.[49] In a not entirely dissimilar way, the more recent magisterial teachings of John Paul II and the *Catechism* are interpreted by the Congregation for the Doctrine of the Faith not in continuity with more recent theology but in continuity with the older Magisterium of Pius XII. In contrast to the more recent theological consensus that is loathe to attribute beatific knowledge to Christ, the Magisterium seems in the notification to have reaffirmed its commitment to just that position. And so, whereas it had seemed that there had been a certain continuity between Magisterium and theologians throughout the twentieth century, whatever the shifts in Church teaching and theology might have been, this clarification of *continuity* in the Magisterium seems to have left something of a *discontinuity* between today's Magisterium and more recent, even contemporary, theology.

However, if theologians were now to apply to this issue the same hermeneutics as does the Magisterium, this would raise the question of the theological reformulation of the thesis of Christ's vision, since the hermeneutics in question is not simply one of continuity but one of renewal in continuity, a hermeneutics

---

49. Benedict XVI, *Ad Romanam Curiam ob omina natalicia*.

of reform. The task of theology is more than mere repetition, and so it is in this context that we shall draw together recent defences of the Thomist position and attempt to reformulate a case that it makes best theological sense to hold that Christ did indeed possess the beatific vision during his earthly lifetime. Since this thesis can only be made truly thinkable for theologians once more by addressing those reasons why so many theologians have ceased to think it convincing, we shall approach it principally by way of examining the various arguments that have been customarily put against the thesis by its critics, suggesting in each case that it has been too easily dismissed. As we have already seen, there is a general perception that the Thomist view of Christ's knowledge undermines the reality of his humanity. It is often argued that, while Scripture and Tradition present Christ's humanity as real, they do not support Christ's enjoyment of the beatific vision. In Chapter 2 we shall address the claim that this teaching cannot be found in the Bible, and in Chapter 3 the argument that nor is it found in the Fathers of the Church. Then in Chapter 4 we shall turn to the contention that the theory of Christ's earthly beatific vision is just bad theology, without a firm foundation of any kind in Scripture and Tradition upon which the theory can be properly constructed.

While those three chapters, which comprise the remainder of Part One of the book, test the claim that there is nothing explicit or implicit in Scripture, Tradition and sound theology that positively favours the thesis, Part Two will address the claim that there is much that *is* found in Scripture and Tradition that necessarily excludes this vision for theology. It has been argued that Christ's possessing the beatific vision is incompatible with the human reality of his faith, his defective knowledge, his freedom of will, his negative emotions, suffering and death. Chapter 5 will address the argument that says that Christ, while on earth, exercised faith, and so could not have seen the Father. Chapter 6 reckons with the claim that, since Christ's knowledge was imperfect in various ways, he could not have enjoyed the beatific vision. Chapter 7 examines the notion that Christ was free, and that this was incompatible with his possessing beatifying knowledge. Chapter 8 will then deal with the argument that Christ's psychological and physical suffering excluded his seeing the divine essence. Moving in these later chapters from Christ's extraordinary knowledge, through his ordinary knowledge, to his will, emotions and bodily life, I hope to sketch an outline of the extraordinary Saviour God has in fact given us and who is indeed the Saviour humanity truly needs.

Chapter 2

'IT'S NOT IN THE BIBLE!'

Critics of Jesus' beatific vision have not hesitated to point out its absence from the pages of Holy Scripture. 'Nothing in scripture', declares Avery Dulles, 'indicates that Christ continuously had the beatific vision.'[1] This is not a claim that the Bible anywhere explicitly rejects the notion, but only that it is nowhere there asserted. Yet this cannot be anything but a most significant point, so long as it is supposed that the contents of the Bible have some positive relevance to the claim that Jesus saw the Father in his human mind. Without this crucial supposition, the objection would appear to be little more than an argument from silence, proving nothing. After all, there are many things we may suppose to be true, even of Jesus, that are not mentioned in the pages of the Bible, and we could imagine that his vision of God might turn out to be one of them. Before searching the Scriptures for indications of Christ's beatific vision, then, we need to enquire further into how far the Bible's witness is relevant to this debate among Catholic theologians. If its relevance were marginal, and Christ's vision of God thus freed from the necessity of any appeal to the contents of Scripture, the objection would lose much of its force. But if Scripture's relevance is not so easily dismissed, we can hardly avoid taking the objection very seriously indeed. Determining the seriousness of this objection will be the first task of this chapter. Then, in the remainder of the chapter, taking the objection in its full force, we intend to show that, while Christ's beatific vision may make no incontrovertible appearance in Scripture, there *is* something definitely present in Scripture that demands a theological explanation, one that might be provided by the thesis of his beatific vision.

Some theologians may suppose it to be a mistake even to look for an indication of Christ's vision in Scripture, and hence theology can legitimately leave its witness to one side. Something of this kind made an appearance in Rahner's lecture of 1961. As we noted in the first chapter, Rahner wished to replace the conventional doctrine of Christ's *beatific* vision with a vision of God that was merely immediate or direct, explained in terms of self-consciousness. Instead of

---

1. A. Dulles, 'Jesus and Faith' in D. Kendall and S. T. Davis, *The Convergence of Theology: A Festschrift Honoring Gerald O'Collins, S.J.* (New York and Mahwahs, NJ: Paulist, 2001), pp. 273–84 (278).

drawing Christ's vision from a reading of Scripture, Rahner based his new interpretation on the scholastic practice of making logical deductions from dogmas,
in this case from that of the hypostatic union, that is, the union of Christ's
human and divine natures in one person. He noted how in his time there had
arisen a certain tension between biblical exegetes and dogmatic theologians on
how they treated Christ's knowledge.[2] But rather than attempt to bridge the gap
that had opened up between exegesis and dogmatics, Rahner opted for a theory
of Christ's human vision that allowed exegetes and dogmaticians to feel they
could go their own separate ways in good conscience.[3] This he did by relegating
Christ's immediate vision to the level of a pre-reflective, unthematized, unobjectified self-consciousness, a level to which the thematized, objectified expressions
of Scripture do not as such bear witness.[4] Without his wishing to dictate any
particular exegetical conclusions to biblical scholars, Rahner's theory effectively
removed Christ's vision from their normal competence. He agreed that the
dogma of the hypostatic union itself was derived out of reading Scripture, but
Christ's human vision becomes in his theology a 'purely dogmatic'[5] necessary
inference from the fact of the union and is not offered as a theological explanation of anything about Christ's knowledge that appears in the Gospels. By
an argument about self-consciousness based on metaphysical necessity, Rahner
had liberated himself from 'appeal to the testimony of the Scriptures and of
Tradition', on which he said the theory of Christ's *beatific* vision must needs be
more dependent.[6] He thus insulated his own theory from an objection to which
the theory of Christ's beatific vision remained vulnerable, namely, that it made no
appearance in Scripture.

Was Rahner correct to put such clear water between the basis of his own
theory and that of the one he hoped to displace? Other critics of the thesis of
Christ's beatific knowledge have had different perceptions, supposing it too to be
based on arguments from metaphysical necessity.[7] But, if that were the case, it too
could be declared free of an appeal to Scripture and the objection that it cannot
be found there. However, it has been only a minority of theologians, such as the
nineteenth-century neoscholastic Matthaias Joseph Scheeben, who have argued
dogmatically from the proximity of divinity and humanity in the incarnation to
the absolute necessity of Christ's beatific vision, and their arguments are hardly

2. 'Knowledge and Self-Consciousness of Christ', p. 195.

3. Ibid., pp. 198–9. Cf. A. Vögtle, 'Exegetische Erwägungen über das Wissen und
Selbstbewusstsein Jesu' in J. B. Metz, W. Kern, A. Darlapp and H. Vorgrimler (eds), *Gott
in Welt: Festgabe für Karl Rahner* (2 vols; Freiburg, Basel and Vienna: Herder, 1964), vol. 1,
pp. 608–67.

4. 'Knowledge and Self-Consciousness of Christ', pp. 199–201. Cf. p. 212.

5. Ibid., p. 198.

6. Ibid., p. 204.

7. Galot, 'Le Christ terrestre et la vision', pp. 433–4; J. P. Galvin in F. Schüssler Fiorenza
and J. P. Galvin (eds), *Systematic Theology: Roman Catholic Perspectives* (Dublin: Gill &
Macmillan, 1992), p. 293 n.89; Weinandy, 'Jesus' Filial Vision of the Father', p. 196.

conclusive.[8] Aquinas takes this proximity to make even the sanctifying presence of the habit of grace in Christ's soul only 'most fitting' and no more, while its necessity was clinched by the fact that this perfection was there for the purpose of our *salvation*, which includes its role in enabling Christ to make the act of beatific knowledge for our benefit.[9] For Aquinas, the relevant necessity is salvific rather than metaphysical. More recently, William G. Most has to the contrary treated this habitual grace, along with the hypostatic union, as part of Christ's 'very metaphysical structure', arguing via grace's fullness to the absolute necessity of Christ's beatific vision.[10] He thus conflated the presence of the Word in the hypostatic union and the presence of the Word as the object of knowledge, while Aquinas saw these unions as definitely unconfused, one in the order of being and the other in the order of knowledge.[11] As Marie-Joseph Nicolas has observed, a 'more rigorous theology of the incarnation' allows for the theoretical possibility that God *could* cause there to be a hypostatic union in the order of being without a union in the order of (beatific) knowledge.[12] The recognition of this possibility would deprive theologians of an argument for Christ's beatific vision based on metaphysical necessity and leave them more reliant on the particular witness of Scripture and Tradition, and so exposed to the objection that Christ's beatific vision makes no appearance in the Bible.

Sometimes, however, Aquinas himself has been taken as arguing from metaphysical necessity, but this reading of his texts has been thoroughly refuted.[13] Like other scholastics of his time, Aquinas understood the Word not only to assume what was essential to human nature, but also to 'co-assume' both perfections of his humanity and defects in it, according to soteriological require-ment.[14] In some matters of co-assumption, then, Aquinas thought it necessary for the Saviour of the human race to excel. With regard to knowledge, Anselm of Canterbury had already set the tone for scholasticism by stating that it was knowledge rather than ignorance that divine wisdom judged 'useful' to Christ's teaching mission.[15] Aquinas too held that it was right for Christ's humanity to be

---

8. *The Mysteries of Christianity* (trans. C. Vollert; St Louis MO and London: Herder, 1947), pp. 325–6. See also R. M. Schmitz, 'Christus Comprehensor. Die "Vision Beatifica Christi Viatoris" bei M. J. Scheeben', *DC* 36 (1983): 347–59.

9. *Summa*, 3a., q. 7, a. 1.

10. W. G. Most, *The Consciousness of Christ* (Front Royal, VA: Christendom, 1980), pp. 166–68.

11. *Quaestiones Disputatae de Veritate*, q. 26, a. 10 ad 8.

12. 'Voir Dieu dans la "condition charnelle"', *DC* 36 (1983): 384–94 (385).

13. L. Iammarrone, 'La visione beatifica di Cristo Viatore nel pensiero di San Tommaso', *DC* 36 (1983): 287–30 (303–5); and L. Bogliolo, 'Strutture Antropologiche e visione beatifica dell'anima di Cristo', *DC* 36 (1983): 331–46 (345) are among those who make this claim. Their interpretation is refuted by Mansini, 'St. Thomas on Christ's Knowledge of God', pp. 92–5.

14. *Summa*, 3a., qq. 4–15.

15. *Cur Deus Homo*, 2.13.

perfected in respect of knowledge of its own, distinct from the divine knowledge: only so, he argued, could Christ's humanity have the perfection that befitted its saving role in bringing the human race to perfection.[16] He then went on to state that it was because of our need to receive the beatific vision from our Saviour that the knowledge in his humanity had to include this same vision, as we noted in the previous chapter.[17] Aquinas thus argues from the heavenly goal of biblical salvation history to the necessity of the Saviour's beatific vision, and from his beatific vision to the necessity of the grace of the Holy Spirit in him to enable this act of vision. Aquinas's argument depends ultimately on the nature of salvation, as he takes it to be portrayed in Scripture, rather than on metaphysical necessity.

We must conclude from this that Rahner was justified in judging his own theory to be more independent of appeal to the biblical narrative than the Thomist one. However, whether the liberation of theology from the witness of Scripture and Tradition is something desirable in itself is questionable. Without detracting from the general value of making theological deductions, it seems to me that there is hardly any advantage in making too strong a separation between biblical exegesis and dogmatic theology, as Rahner seems to have done, and that any theological discourse about Christ's knowledge should ideally be an attempt to seek a deeper understanding of what we draw from the Bible. From this perspective we can see why the objection to Christ's beatific vision on the basis of its absence from the pages of the Scriptures is so fundamental. The Bible cannot but be an important court of appeal in the debate over Christ's beatific vision among Catholic theologians, precisely because their community of faith grounds its belief and teaching about Jesus Christ in the Scriptures, and particularly in the Gospels, writings it believes to be divinely inspired. The Gospels, according to Vatican II, 'faithfully hand on what Jesus, the Son of God, while living among men, really did and taught for their eternal salvation'.[18] Whatever their authors' methods of composition and use of sources might be, however the evangelists shaped their materials in view of their own theological ends, the Gospels nevertheless tell us 'the honest truth about Jesus',[19] while the other writings of the New Testament 'confirm those things which concern Christ the Lord'.[20] On this Catholic view, the theological creativity of the inspired authors in no way nullifies the surety of their substantial witness to the essential truth about Jesus Christ.

It is worth noting that if, to the contrary, these writings were instead considered unreliable guides to the reality of Jesus, their use for establishing the truth about his knowledge would be in serious doubt. At best they would provide historical evidence of what the authors or perhaps their communities professed to believe about Christ or wanted others to believe, all of which may then be taken to be at odds with the reality of the historical Jesus. The more sceptical critic would

16. *Summa*, 3a., q. 9, a.1.
17. Ibid., 3a., q. 9, a. 2.
18. *Dei Verbum*, 19.
19. Ibid.
20. Ibid., 20.

hardly be willing to base a firm conclusion about any vision of God Jesus might have enjoyed on the contents of the Bible. A milder critic, however, would no doubt be willing to test claims about Jesus' knowledge on the basis of the biblical witness up to a point. In that case, criteria would need to be adduced for distinguishing which passages could be regarded as reliable witnesses to the historical Jesus who is taken to lie behind the biblical texts, and which cannot. However, the criteria used in such circumstances are often in danger of being loaded against any passages that would grant even more fundamental doctrines, such as the divinity of Christ and his divine knowledge, let alone the beatific vision. Many passages that would otherwise be considered relevant to the question of Christ's having extraordinary knowledge of any kind are thus consigned to irrelevance.[21] And once the reliability of passages that attest to an extraordinary knowledge of God on the part of Jesus is dismissed, it becomes practically impossible to argue from Scripture about the nature of any such extraordinary knowledge Jesus might have had.

While views of this sort may prevail in much New Testament scholarship, we shall here be concerned with what is at issue between theologians who agree among themselves within their community of faith that the Bible does indeed give substantially reliable access to the truth about Jesus. As a matter of fact, the most articulate and trenchant critics of the thesis of Christ's beatific vision have been theologians of this kind, such as Galot and Weinandy.[22] The assumption of Scriptural reliability, common both to them and to those they oppose, makes everything Scripture has to say about Christ's possession of extraordinary knowledge relevant to guiding them through the dispute about his beatific vision or lack of it. Any theologian in the debate may of course have something to add on historical-critical grounds in favour of the reliability of the particular biblical passages on which he draws, taking issue on historical grounds with the objections of those who deny their authenticity.[23] Some prefer to base themselves as far as possible on texts from the three Synoptic Gospels on account of the fact that, despite significant support being given by some scholars to the historicity of John, the historicity of the Synoptics has in general been more widely accepted by critics.[24] Such moves, however, are inevitably something of an ancillary strategy. This is because the central theological arguments and conclusions rest on the assumption of the essential reliability of Scripture for informing us about Jesus Christ, whatever the particular histories of the formation of its texts might be. Given this assumption, we can hardly blame a theologian for wanting to look into the Scriptures to test the claim that Christ enjoyed the beatific vision. If the

21. See, e.g. A. T. Hanson, 'Two consciousnesses: the modern version of Chalcedon', *SJT* 37 (1984): 471–83 (477–81), who rejects the historical authenticity of Mt. 11.27 and the Gospel of John.

22. E.g. Galot, 'Le Christ terrestre et la vision'; Weinandy, 'Jesus' Filial Vision of the Father'.

23. E.g. de Margerie, *The Human Knowledge of Christ*, pp. 14–16.

24. E.g. Mansini, 'St. Thomas on Christ's Knowledge of God', pp. 101–9.

Scriptures are the guide for our knowledge of Christ, they must surely be our first port of call to unlock the secret of his own knowledge. This is why the objection that Christ's beatific vision is *not* found in the Scriptures is so fundamental for a Catholic theologian.

A further complication, however, is raised by the suggestion that, while Scripture is relevant in a more general way to establishing the truth about Jesus Christ, those passages which may *appear* to make claims about him possessing extraordinary knowledge do not in fact do so. This proposal has been justified on the basis of principles endorsed during Vatican II by the Church's Pontifical Biblical Commission, namely, that the evangelists wrote from the post-resurrection perspective of a clear perception of Christ's divinity, and that they proclaimed this faith through a variety of literary forms customary at the time and suited to their immediate audience.[25] Writing that the Gospels are thus not 'literal accounts' of Jesus' ministry but employed 'post-resurrectional theological insights' read back from Christian preaching, the distinguished exegete Raymond Brown went on to assert that a Catholic may therefore 'maintain that a true post-resurrectional insight into Jesus' extraordinary identity as Son of God has been given expression in the Gospels in terms of extraordinary knowledge during the ministry'.[26] In other words, whatever appears in the Gospels' accounts of Jesus' ministry to involve a claim about him possessing such knowledge could instead be a claim about his identity *only*, meaning that the theologian is hindered from basing his reflections about Jesus' knowledge on any such texts, which are thus irrelevant to the question of whether or not Jesus possessed the extraordinary knowledge of the beatific vision.

We should be wary, however, of driving a wedge between Jesus' identity and his knowledge, as though a reliable claim about his identity will not at least contain within it some further claim about his knowledge. In fact, should Scripture in any way express the claim that Jesus enjoyed the extraordinary identity of the divine Son of God, as the Church's reading of Scripture holds to be the case, then a claim to an extraordinary knowledge appropriate to this Son is surely implied. Moreover, unless we suppose that the Gospels' narrative portrayals of Jesus as a teacher sent from God propose no more than his extraordinary identity to the exclusion of any actual engagement in teaching, the fact that they highlight his teaching role tells in favour of the accounts of his extraordinary knowledge being meant to be just that. A Christ who is the herald of the kingdom of heaven sits easily with a Christ who possesses extraordinary knowledge of God: such an extraordinary teacher must doubtless know something extraordinary to teach. It would seem in any case difficult to prove the hypothesis that the evangelists were making no claims at all about Jesus enjoying extraordinary knowledge in narratives that exhibit him possessing such knowledge, as Brown himself seems to recognize.[27] To make a convincing case that the evangelists were concerned

25. Pontifical Biblical Commission, *Instructio de Historica Evangeliorum Veritate*, 2.
26. R. E. Brown, *The Critical Meaning of the Bible* (London: Cassell, 1982), p. 87 n.8.
27. *Jesus God and Man* (London and Dublin: Chapman, 1968), pp. 47–9.

only with Jesus' identity to the exclusion of his knowledge requires one to bring forward convincing arguments to show that attributing knowledge to someone in narrative form was a customary way of making claims about that person's identity *to the exclusion of* any claims about his knowledge. Until such a case can be made, it would seem more prudent for a theologian not to discount in advance the possibility that passages that attribute extraordinary knowledge to Christ do indeed propose that he enjoyed such knowledge. Having determined to remain open to this possibility ourselves, and conscious of the true seriousness of our opponents' objection, we are now in a position to take on that objection as it stands, and begin our enquiry into whether the Bible anywhere ascribes the beatific vision to the earthly Christ.

On turning to the Scriptures, our first result is that we can find no statement that Jesus saw 'the divine essence with an intuitive vision and even face to face, without the mediation of any creature by way of object of vision'.[28] These words were used in 1336 by Pope Benedict XII to describe the beatific vision enjoyed by the souls of the blessed in heaven. No biblical author applies such words to Jesus, and no biblical author even speaks of him possessing the 'beatific vision'. This fact would certainly close the debate, if we supposed that these are the kind of statements we might find in Scripture. Such modes of expression, however, belong to a later age, including the medieval scholastic '*visio beatifica*', which not even Aquinas used. Aquinas lived in a century where it had been debated among theologians exactly *what* was seen in the vision of heaven and *how* it was known. Benedict XII was closing a debate in the following century about *when* the vision was ordinarily granted to souls, whether before the resurrection of the body or only at the resurrection, which he resolved in favour of the former.[29] These controversies were accompanied by the development of a complex terminology we can hardly expect to find in Scripture without being guilty of serious anachronism. This means that not only does Scripture not contain such words as 'Christ enjoyed the beatific vision', but it does not even contain such words as 'the saints in heaven will possess the beatific vision'. But if we cannot think to find such later modes of expression in the pages of the New Testament, how could anyone possibly hope to trace the presence of *either* doctrine there?

One line of enquiry is suggested by the fact that there are Christian teachings far more fundamental than the character of Christ's knowledge that are not found in Scripture in precisely the same words as were formulated in later times, and yet are traditionally held to be 'in' Scripture. Two examples are the doctrines of the Trinity and the incarnation. One need only compare what the New Testament has to say about the Father, the Son and the Holy Spirit, with the formulae employed in the creeds of later centuries to grasp the point. As disputes about the interpretation of Scripture arose, its meaning was clarified for believers by

---

28. Benedict XII, *Benedictus Deus*.

29. On these debates, see C. Trottmann, *La Vision Béatifique: Des disputes scolastiques à sa définition par Benoît XII* (Bibliothèque des Écoles Françaises d'Athènes et de Rome, 289; Rome: École Française, 1995).

new formulations of doctrine, which drew on the conceptual and terminological apparatus of Greek philosophy. Those who accepted the formulations with all their apparent novelty believed that they correctly articulated what Scripture had always taught in other terms. Re-expressing the teaching of Scripture in the very act of intending fidelity to its meaning, they developed a doctrinal reading of the Bible which thus provided the Church with a more refined, common orthodox framework for Scriptural interpretation in general.

One major dispute was how to interpret what was said in Scripture about the Son's relationship with the Father: was he equal to the Father, or was the Father greater than he? Given that Christ says he is less than the Father (Jn 14.28), should this not be understood to mean that the Word of God is not true God as the Father is, but that he is even a creature, however perfect or in some sense 'divine'? Against the latter reading of Scripture, which was taken up by Arius and the later 'Arians' who were associated with him, those who rallied to the Council of Nicaea (AD 325) maintained that the Son is co-equal with the Father, sharing the same divine essence. The Son is 'consubstantial' (ὁμοούσιον) with the Father, as the Council's Creed put it.[30] Though this word is not found in Scripture, it came to be accepted as distinguishing the orthodox view from the heretical, reading what Scripture says of the unity of Father and Son in this more profound way, rather than making the Son a lesser creaturely divinity. When Jesus says 'The Father and I are one' (Jn 10.30), this unity is no less than a unity in being, essence or substance, manifesting the persons' equality. Thus, on a Catholic account, although 'consubstantial' and many other formulae used in the orthodox reading of Scripture do not themselves appear in Scripture, that is not to say that the truths they express are thought by the orthodox not to be found there, but rather they are understood to be expressed there *in some other way*.

Since Catholic theologians are committed to some such doctrinal view where the more fundamental doctrines of God and Christ are concerned, they are bound to ask whether Christ's human knowledge and the beatific vision of the saints might not be similar cases. Merely because Scripture does not make the statement that 'Christ had the beatific vision', Catholic theologians cannot conclude without further ado that the teaching is not contained there in any way at all. Likewise they cannot conclude *without further ado* that the doctrine of the beatific vision of the saints in heaven is absent, just because it does not appear in those words. What we need to do, at the outset of our investigation, is to ask how Scripture expresses the doctrine later theology will call the beatific vision of the saints. Once we have established that, we shall be able to go on to ask whether Christ's possession of the beatific vision might not be expressed there in the same or equivalent terms. However, at the outset of this procedure, we need to distinguish carefully those texts in which we may find this eschatological vision of God enjoyed by the saints from the wider context of a whole host of biblical passages that speak in varying ways of 'seeing God'. In this way we shall assess how *Scripture* marks off

---

30. First Council of Nicaea, *Symbolum Nicaenum*.

the eschatological vision of God from all others, thus equipping ourselves to ask whether *this* vision (rather than any other) is in any way attributed to the earthly Christ.

As with words for 'know', there is more than one word for 'see' or 'look' in the Hebrew and Greek (Gk: ὁράω/εἶδον, βλέπω) of the Bible. Sometimes these words are distinguished in context by their intensity and are better translated into English by 'look at', 'gaze on' or 'behold'. The Greek θεάομαι has its own nuances of attentiveness and can mean behold or observe. Though βλέπω seems more often tied to the function of the eyes, all these words are by no means used exclusively of physical sight.[31] They are also used of perception and experience in a more general sense, of prophetic visions, of receiving information and coming to know and understand, and are sometimes linked in the latter case with an extended use of 'hear'. In Deuteronomy 29.2–4, the fact that the Israelites had seen with their own eyes what God had done to the Egyptians is contrasted with the fact that God had not given them 'eyes to see or ears to hear'. That this extension of the language of hearing and sight in particular should be so prominent can be of no surprise from an anthropological point of view, since human beings seem generally more conscious of the extent of their reliance on these two senses, and especially on sight. In some ways sight is privileged by human beings most of all, and it has been estimated that some three-quarters of the information we receive about the world comes through our sight. We commonly use sight to check on what we have otherwise perceived, and we prize what we have seen for ourselves at least over what we have merely heard about from others, as was evident in the methods of ancient historians and arguably in those of the Gospel writers.[32] Furthermore, it is a fact that we do easily speak of knowledge in terms of sight. Thus, when God himself is said to see something, this means that he has knowledge of it (e.g. Mt. 6.14; Acts 7.34). And just as God is said in Scripture to speak his word and be heard, so he is also said to appear and be seen.

The theme of seeing or beholding God finds its own context in the wider biblical theme of the special presence or indwelling of God. This dwelling in holy places becomes focused during the Scriptural narrative in the tabernacle and in the Jerusalem temple, but is then definitively located in Jesus and derivatively in the Church united to him, both of which are described in the New Testament in terms of the temple (Jn 2.21; 1 Cor. 3.16; 1 Pet. 2.4–5). There are several strands to the biblical theme of seeing God in this developing context of divine presence. The first contains what scholars call 'theophanies', of which there are several examples early on in the Old Testament, where God is said to have appeared in

---

31. On the various Greek words, see G. Friedrich (ed.), *Theological Dictionary of the New Testament* (trans. G. W. Bromiley, 10 vols; Grand Rapids, MI: Eerdmans, 1964–76), vol. 5, pp. 315–67.

32. See S. Byrskog, *Story as History – History as Story: The Gospel Tradition in the Context of Ancient Oral History* (Leiden: Brill, 2002); and R. Bauckham, *Jesus and the Eyewitnesses: The Gospels as Eyewitness Testimony* (Grand Rapids, MI and Cambridge: Eerdmans, 2006).

a holy place and sometimes to have been seen.[33] This seeing is associated with a visible appearance to the human eye, such as something we might identify as the physical manifestation of an angelic figure closely associated with God (e.g. Gen. 32.30). Again, in prayer, Moses recalls that it has been heard abroad that God, who is in the midst of his people in the wilderness, is seen 'eye to eye' (Num. 14.14). A second strand is the pilgrim who 'seeks the face of God' in the Jewish temple (e.g. Ps 27.8; 42.2). Israelite legislation directed all males 'to appear before the Lord' three times a year, and it may be that the Hebrew should be read 'to see the face of the Lord' (Exod. 23.17). It has been further speculated that 'seeing the Lord' may be bound up with seeing the temple itself, its sacred contents and liturgy.[34] A third strand is that of prophetic visions,[35] which may be construed as visions of God interior to the mind or imagination of the prophet, whether awake or asleep (though later Jewish tradition generally seems to have thought in terms of a bodily admission of the seer into heaven[36]). One such prophetic vision is that of Isaiah 6, which is set in the temple: 'I saw the Lord sitting upon a throne, high and lifted up' (v. 1). The precise object of these visions becomes more qualified in later biblical and other Jewish mystical texts. The prophet Ezekiel, for example, claims to have seen only 'the appearance of the likeness of the glory of the Lord' (1.28). Among the Wisdom literature, ben Sirach sounds a warning note about whether God himself had ever truly been seen: 'Who has seen him and could make him known?' (43.31). The incarnation then provides a response within the overall Scriptural narrative to ben Sirach's question (cf. Jn 1.18), as well as a certain climax to the whole theme of divine presence and human vision, when seeing Jesus is declared somehow to be seeing God: he says, 'To have seen me is to have seen the Father' (Jn 14.9; cf. 12.45). Christians claim to see Jesus in some sense now, despite his passing through the heavens (Heb. 2.9), and hope to 'see the Lord' at his Second Coming when he appears again in glory (e.g. Heb. 12.14; cf. 9.28).

Theologians are able to explore connections between the earthly Christ and this array of different kinds of Scriptural vision and presence. That he was a prophet, experiencing theophanies and visions of some kind during his earthly lifetime, is attested by Scripture clearly enough (e.g. Mk 1.10; 6.4). However, the details of the precise relationship between Christ and the temple, or how he saw his Father in seeing himself humanly, are not our concern here. We are asking whether Jesus experienced a further kind of Scriptural vision, a final vision beyond those we have already enumerated: Might Christ, in whose incarnate humanity revelation,

---

33. See T. Hiebert, 'Theophany in the OT' in D. N. Freedman et al. (eds), *The Anchor Bible Dictionary* (6 vols; New York and London: Doubleday, 1992), vol. 6, pp. 505–11.

34. On all these suggestions, see G. A. Anderson, 'To See Where God Dwells: The Tabernacle, the Temple, and the Origins of the Christian Mystical Tradition', *LS* 4 (2008): 13–45.

35. See J. Barton, *Oracles of God: Perceptions of Ancient Prophecy in Israel after the Exile* (Oxford: OUP, new edn, 2007).

36. C. Rowland, *The Open Heaven: A Study of Apocalpytic in Judaism and Early Christianity* (London: SPCK, 1982), p. 383.

temple, prophecy and wisdom came to fulfilment, have also experienced in his earthly lifetime a distinct ultimate, eschatological vision of heaven? That there is in Scripture a general doctrine of this further and final heavenly vision of God (and not simply of the glorified Christ), distinct from the various 'visions' we have already mentioned, we shall first illustrate with a number of texts which have conventionally been drawn in its support, arguing that together they propose for the saints a heavenly vision of the Father of Jesus Christ.

We should note that not even seeing the incarnate Son was considered by Christians as equivalent to inhabiting the *final* state of heaven. A vision of God on the last day already seems to have been an aspect of Jewish hope (cf. Job 25.25–27), and even those who saw Jesus during his lifetime on earth awaited a further eschatological divine vision. The concluding chapters of the Apocalypse of John at the very end of the canon of Scripture picture a 'new heaven and a new earth', succeeding the old earth and its temple and the heavenly temple, in which a 'new Jerusalem' descends from heaven to earth and a loud voice from the throne of God declares his dwelling to be with men (21.1–3).[37] The identification of the city by the angel as 'the Bride, the wife of the Lamb', that is, of Christ, indicates that the new Jerusalem in which God is present is the glorified Church. The further identification of the city with the eschatological temple is suggested by the measurements and composition of the city (21.15–21), which recall those of the temple sanctuary (1 Kgs 6.20), meaning that there is no distinct place of God's dwelling within the city. In fact the seer testifies that there was no separate temple, but does still more than identify city and temple. There is no separate temple, he says, because 'the Lord God the Almighty and the Lamb are its temple' (21.22).

Within this context of a climactic level of divine presence unmediated by any separate temple, we now find mention of the vision of God: 'they shall see his face (ὄψονται τὸ πρόσωπον αὐτοῦ)' (22.4). Here we have a definite example of an eschatological vision that theologians have come to identify as 'the beatific vision'. Now while this text certainly recalls the wider tradition of seeking God's face, it alludes in particular to Moses to whom God 'used to speak face to face (LXX: ἐνώπιος ἐνωπίῳ), as a man speaks to his friend' (Exod. 33.11). It was in this established context of intimate conversation that Moses asked for more, namely, to *see* God's glory. God responded positively that he would make his goodness pass before him and proclaim before him the glory of his name, but adds in v. 20 that Moses cannot see his 'face' (LXX: πρόσωπον). What Moses saw with his eyes in the theophany granted him is described as God's 'hinder parts'. While the Apocalypse is thus implying that the inhabitants of the new Jerusalem are given a privilege not granted to Moses, in doing so its author seems unperturbed by the reason Moses himself had been refused it. After all, why should that same

37. On this vision, see E. F. Lupieri, *A Commentary on the Apocalypse* (trans. M. P. Johnson and A. Kamesar; Italian texts and studies on religion and society; Grand Rapids, MI and Cambridge: Eerdmans, 2006), pp. 327–63; I. Boxall, *The Revelation of Saint John* (Black's New Testament commentaries; London and New York: Continuum, 2006), pp. 292–315.

principle of refusal not apply to the inhabitants of the new Jerusalem? God's reason why *Moses* could not see his face was that 'man shall not see me and live' (v. 20). This takes up a general theme in the Old Testament. Jacob (Gen. 32.30), Gideon (Judg. 6.22) and Manoah and his wife (Judg. 13.22) all express surprise that they remain alive, despite experiencing theophanies. The story of Moses appears to imply a distinction between such theophanies, where the recipients can in fact remain alive, and a vision of God's face, which was not even granted to Moses, a vision incompatible with mortal life. This notion is continued in the New Testament. 1 Tim. 6.16 speaks of God 'who alone has immortality and dwells in unapproachable light, whom no man has ever seen or can see'. The latter wording is clearly based on Exod. 33.20 and its immediate context is divine immortality, the mention of which connotes human *mortality*. This suggests the reason why the Apocalypse, or any New Testament text, can state without concern that the face of God will indeed be seen in the new Jerusalem: God is now himself the light of the city and the Lamb is its lamp, and the humanity that sees him will be mortal no more (21.4, 23). Humanity has now passed beyond that mortal state where sight of the face of God could not have been granted.

What though, more precisely, is the object of this vision attested by the Apocalypse? The text says that they shall see '*his* face', but to whom does 'his' refer?[38] Immediately before this we read that the 'throne of God and the Lamb' will be in the city, and that 'his servants shall worship *him*' (22.3). Now the 'Lamb' plainly refers to Jesus, the incarnate Son, and 'God' (θεός) to his Father – indeed all the authors of the New Testament seem to use θεός for the most part to denote the Father. It is the author's purpose to associate God the Father and Jesus Christ as closely as possible, not only by assigning them a single throne but by speaking of them jointly in the singular pronoun as the object of divine worship. The beatific vision of 'his face', as it is presented in the Apocalypse, is thus a gaze that takes in *both* the Father and the incarnate Son, something more than simply seeing the Father in seeing his incarnate Son, as had been granted during Christ's earthly life (cf. Jn 14.9). This point is crucial.

In addition to the concluding chapter of the Apocalypse, three other New Testament texts have stood out for Christians as bearing witness to the promise of an ultimate heavenly vision that takes in God the Father directly. This hope is most explicitly expressed in 1 John:

> And now, little children, abide in him, so that when he appears we may have confidence and not shrink from him in shame at his presence. If you know that he is just, know that everyone who does what is just is born of him. See how great is the love the Father has given us, that we should be called children of God; and so we are. The reason why the world does not know us is that it did not know him. Beloved, we are God's children now, and it has not yet appeared what we shall be. We know that when he [*or* it] appears we shall be like him, for we shall see (ὀψόμεθα) him just as he is. (2.28–3.2)

38. Cf. Lupieri, *Apocalypse*, pp. 355–6; Boxall, *Revelation*, pp. 311–12.

It is perhaps possible that the 'him' who is seen is both Father and Son, as in the Apocalypse, since Father and Son belong closely together in the Epistle (e.g. 5.20), just as they do in the Apocalypse. However, interpreters have often taken the 'him' who is seen here to be more likely the glorified Christ, the same incarnate Word who had been seen in this life (1.1),[39] while others have taken 'him' as referring to God the Father,[40] and yet others remain undecided.[41] I suggest that the Father is the more likely referent here. Of course it is natural to suppose that the one who is seen, whom we shall be like, is the same as the one who has appeared: 'we know that when *he* appears we shall be like *him*' (3:2). However, not only do these words not make it clear whether it is the Father or the Son who will appear, but it is not evident that φανερωθῇ even means *he* appears. It could also mean *it* appears, thus recalling the preceding 'it has not yet appeared (ἐφανερώθη)', in which case the translation would read: 'It has not yet appeared what we shall be. We know that when it does appear we shall be like him …' Nevertheless, whether we translate φανερωθῇ as 'he appears' or 'it appears', there is still the 'him' whom we shall be like, the one we shall see, and this I would argue is not Christ but God the Father.

When the author speaks of the future vision, he has only just mentioned the fact that we are already *God's* children. As has already been pointed out, the New Testament authors normally use 'God' to refer to the Father. Indeed John's letter has already called the Father θεός (1.5–7). John's poetic imagination speaks easily of *children* in the Christian community having their knowledge focused on the Father, and *fathers* having their knowledge focused on the Son (2.13–14). In the passage we are discussing he calls the whole community 'children of God', by which he means children of the Father. The immediate context is his speaking of the love of the *Father* by which we are God's children (3.1). The one whom the world did not know is then naturally read as the Father, leading to the conclusion that the one whom we shall be like and see is the Father. The gist of the passage is then as follows: the *Father* has made us his children, and in the future this same Father will appear and make us like himself, for we shall see this Father just as he is. Not that John thinks all this has nothing to do with the Son; far from it. On this reading, he is simply making the careful choice of focusing in this passage on the Father.

Some of those who argue to the contrary say that, although it is the Father who has made us his children, the one whom the world did not know is the Son, and the one who appears, whom we shall be like and whom we shall see, is also the

---

39. E.g. J. L. Houlden, *A Commentary on the Johannine Epistles* (Black's New Testament commentaries; London: Black, 2nd edn, 1994), p. 91; R. Schnackenburg, *The Johannine Epistles: Introduction and Commentary* (trans. R. and I. Fuller; London: Burns & Oates, 1992), pp. 157–8; S. S. Smalley, *1, 2, 3 John* (Word Biblical Commentary, 51; Nashville: Nelson, 1984), pp. 144–7.

40. J. C. O'Neill, *The Puzzle of 1 John* (London: SPCK, 1966), pp. 31–3.

41. R. E. Brown, *New Testament Reading Guide: The Gospel of St. John and the Johannine Epistles* (Collegeville, MN: Liturgical, 1960), pp. 110–11.

Son.[42] Now although one 'whom the world did not know' could in itself be either Father or Son, the immediate context, we have argued, suggests that here it is the Father. The contrary argument for it being the Son rests on the one who appears being the Son, an identification which of course demands its own supporting argument. The latter appeals to the slightly wider context of the passage, asserting that this future appearing refers back to a future appearing of the Son in 2.28,[43] a connection that is made even by those who concede that the one who is not known here is the Father.[44] Now there is no doubt that it is the incarnate Son of whom John speaks *after* our passage when he says in the past tense that 'that man appeared' (ἐκεῖνος ἐφανερώθη) (3.4; cf. v. 8). Whose, however, is the *future* appearing in 2.28 is not so easily resolved: 'And now little children, abide in him, so that when he appears we may have confidence and not shrink from him in shame at his presence.'[45] It is not immediately evident from this in whom John is exhorting his audience to abide, for it is not long since he has spoken of abiding in both Son *and* Father (v. 24). The one in whom they must abide in v. 28 is certainly the 'Holy One' who has anointed them, but the latter again could be either Father or Son (vv. 20, 27). This future appearing has been interpreted as the Son's by taking it to be a reference to Christ's Second Coming, before which we should have confidence. John does, however, speak elsewhere in his letter of his readers having confidence before 'God', that is, the Father (3.21; 4.16–17).

Moreover, as John continues in the present passage, he says, 'If you know that he is righteous, you may be sure that every one who does right *is born of him*' (v. 29), before continuing with 'See what love the Father has given us ...' (3.1). Though John of course holds both Father and Son to be righteous (1:9; 2:1), the righteous one of whom John is speaking here is one *of whom we are born*. Though there is doubtless a sense in which Christians are born of the Son (cf. Jn 1:12), just as they are born of the Spirit (Jn 3.6), the one of whom we are born is surely here most easily interpreted as the Father, just as elsewhere in this letter we are said to be born of *God* (3.9; 4.7; 5.1). Hence it would seem that the Father, the one of whom we are born, is also the one who will appear in 2.28, the one before whom we must be confident, the one who is righteous. Some who hold that the righteous one who appears is the Son have concluded that the clause containing 'every one who does right is born of him' has been drawn from a source and 'clumsily appended'[46] by the author to the first clause. This unlikely theory is meant to explain what must otherwise be perceived by others who hold the

---

42. R. Bultmann, *The Johannine Epistles: A Commentary on the Johannine Epistles* (trans. R. P. O'Hara, L. C. McGaughy and R. Funk; Hermeneia – A Critical and Historical Commentary on the Bible; Philadephia: Fortress, 1973), p. 48.

43. Ibid.

44. Houlden, *Johannine Epistles*, p. 87; Schnackenburg, *Johannine Epistles*, pp. 152–3; Smalley, *1, 2, 3 John*, pp. 131–2.

45. For references to God's appearing (παρουσία) and boldness (παρρησία) before him in Jewish literature, see O'Neill, *Puzzle of 1 John*, p. 33.

46. Bultmann, *Johannine Epistles*, p. 45.

righteous one to be the Son as John simply slipping mid-sentence from Son to Father. But if that is John's habit, it surely makes it difficult to determine whether the author is speaking about Father or Son in 3.2 or at many points in the letter. A simpler solution is to recognize that it is God the Father who appears in 2.28, and who is seen in 3.2. On this reading the passage bears witness to a future vision of the Father for the saints.

The next passage for us to consider comes from Paul's famous discourse in 1 Corinthians on the gifts of the Spirit and love. Here he contrasts an obscure vision belonging to the Christian present with a clear vision belonging to the future:

> For we know in part and we prophesy in part. But when completion comes, the partial will pass away. When I was a child I spoke as a child, I reasoned as a child; when I became a man I did away with childish things. For now we see (βλέπομεν) through a mirror in a riddle, but then face to face (πρόσωπον πρὸς πρόσωπον). Now I know in part; then I shall know just as I am also known. (13.10–12)

Like John, Paul is contrasting the present life of Christian faith with a future and final vision or state of knowledge which Christians still await. Although Paul does not explicitly mention the *object* of this eschatological vision, focusing a little more on the *manner* of the vision, like John he no doubt thinks of its object as the Father.[47] That we are concerned with knowledge of God may be gleaned from the wider context, as well as from Paul's allusion to what God says of Moses in Numbers 12.8: 'With him I speak mouth to mouth, clearly, and not in riddles; and he beholds the figure [LXX: glory] of the Lord.'[48] We should note that, though recalling the language of Numbers, Paul is definitely saying something about the saints quite different from what Numbers says about Moses. For one thing Paul does not deal directly at all with Numbers' claim about Moses' *vision*, and presumably thought of that as a vision 'through a mirror in a riddle' in comparison with the vision to come. What Paul in fact does in this passage is to allude to what Numbers says of Moses' direct *conversation* with God, that it was 'mouth to mouth' and not 'in riddles', applying this *mutatis mutandis* to the future *vision* that is 'face to face' and not 'in a riddle', a vision Moses did not have but we will. My point is that the allusion to Moses' clear speech *with God* intimates that Paul is telling us about a future clear vision *of God*: God the Father is the object of this vision. Moreover, when Paul says 'just as I am also known', he means 'known *by God*', a familiar biblical use of the passive verb.[49] He is telling us then that we

---

47. Cf. C. K. Barrett, *A Commentary on The First Epistle to the Corinthians* (Black's New Testament Commentaries; London: Black, 2nd edn, 1971), p. 307.

48. Cf. H. Conzelmann, *1 Corinthians: A Commentary on the First Epistle to the Corinthians* (trans. J. W. Leitch; Hermeneia—A Critical and Historical Commentary on the Bible; Philadelphia: Fortress, 1975), pp. 226–9.

49. Cf. R. F. Collins, *First Corinthians* (Sacra Pagina, 7; Collegeville, MN: Liturgical, 1999), p. 487.

shall know *God*, just as we are also known by *God*, that we shall see *God* face to face and not in a mirror. In other words, we shall see the Father face to face in heaven.

A final text, yet more frequently referred by Christian tradition to the beatific vision, is the saying of Jesus from St Matthew's version of the Beatitudes: 'Blessed are the pure in heart, for they shall see God (θεὸν ὄψονται)' (5.8). Contemporary exegetes also tend to interpret it as pointing to a final seeing of the Father.[50] Though some have taken Jesus to be the object of this vision, since he is at 1.23 called 'Emmanuel, which is interpreted "God-with-us" (Μεθ᾽ ἡμῶν ὁ θεός)',[51] that the Beatitude's θεός refers instead to the Father should hardly be in doubt.[52] 'God' in Matthew's Gospel always refers to the Father. That he is the object of this vision is supported by what Jesus says elsewhere in the same Gospel: 'I tell you that their angels in heaven always look upon the face of my Father (βλέπουσι τὸ πρόσωπον τοῦ πατρός μοῦ) who is in heaven' (18.10). However, the fact that the Beatitude is on the mouth of Jesus in a Gospel rather than from the pen of the writer of an Epistle makes its reference to the future capable of more than one interpretation. In the case of Paul and John, there is no such ambiguity, since each writes from the later time of the Christian Church, and looks forward to a future vision that had not already been provided for them by the present activity of Christ and the Spirit. When Jesus utters the Beatitudes, however, the time of this Church is still future within the overall biblical narrative. This means that Jesus' words are open to be interpreted as referring not to the beatific vision at all but to the presence of the kingdom of heaven in the life of the Church.

Whatever difficulties there may be in the interpretation of these texts, we may conclude that there is, in the New Testament, belief in an eschatological future vision of God, which brings to its ultimate culmination the foregoing biblical tradition of seeing God. While he is by no means its exclusive object, the texts have this vision largely focused on the Father. If we are to ask whether Scripture ever assigns this heavenly vision of the Father to the earthly Christ, we need to be precise about what it is in Scripture that marks this vision off from all others. It would seem that the biblical authors never make this mark by a simple appeal to the fact that it takes place for us in the future beyond death. Were they to do so, implying that it is the *futurity* of the vision as such that makes it intrinsically different from any other vision, it would be extremely difficult even to raise the

---

50. W. D. Davies and D. C. Allison, *A Critical and Exegetical Commentary on the Gospel According to Saint Matthew* (International Critical Commentary on the Holy Scriptures of the Old and New Testaments; 3 vols; Edinburgh: T&T Clark, 1988), vol. 1, pp. 456–57; D. J. Harrington, *The Gospel of Matthew* (Sacra Pagina, 1; Collegeville, MN: Liturgical, 1991), p. 79; D. A. Hagner, *Matthew 1–13* (Word Biblical Commentary, 33A; Dallas, TX: Word, 1993), p. 94; R. T. France, *The Gospel of Matthew* (New International Commentary on the New Testament; Grand Rapids, MI and Cambridge: Eerdmans, 2007), pp. 168–69.

51. N. T. Wright, *The New Testament and the People of God* (Christian Origins and the Question of God, vol. 1; London: SPCK, 1996), pp. 388–9.

52. Davies and Allison, *Matthew*, vol. 1, p. 456 n.43.

question of whether Jesus enjoyed this vision during an earthly lifetime that is essentially *past*. However, if Scripture were formally to mark off the eschatological vision from all others in some way other than its futurity, we should be able to ask quite legitimately whether the earthly Jesus of the past already possessed it.

Given the diversity of visions of God in Jewish and Christian tradition, it could hardly be surprising if the New Testament authors had felt the need to distinguish the eschatological vision of heaven more precisely. However, not everything associated with the vision in their texts would seem to be something that definitively marks off the vision from any other. Though Revelation 22.4 speaks of the vision of 'his face', it must be admitted that the theme of seeing God's face is not unique to this vision in Scripture. In the case of Matthew's Beatitude (given that we interpret it as referring to the final vision), what Jesus says about the pure of heart helps us little better. His reference to the 'pure in heart' picks up on the purity that was required of those who sought the face of God in the temple (cf. Ps. 24). 1 John also mentions the requirement of purity, saying that all who hope to see God must purify themselves (3.3; Rev. 21.27; 22.3). Being pure of heart is certainly a disposition required for seeing God, a matter of preparation, but it does not itself formally mark off this particular ultimate vision from any other.

1 John does, however, provide us with a solution. While the letter never quotes the Old Testament directly, it does allude to it a number of times. One such allusion is to the wider biblical theme of 'seeing God': 'No one has ever beheld (τεθέαται) God' (4.12). We are meant to take it that, though it is often said in the Old Testament that people had seen God, they had not in fact seen him, not even Moses. However, it would be implausible to suppose that John was rejecting the claims and authority of the Jewish Scriptures, however little direct use he makes of them in his letter. Indeed he seems to be very much in line with the Scriptural warning note sounded by ben Sirach, which we mentioned above. It is surely more plausible to suppose that, in alluding also to what he has already said in his letter about the vision to come, John is saying that no one has ever beheld God *as we hope to see him in the future*. In this denial he seems to include even having seen the incarnate Word, since he had already mentioned that seeing in the very first verse of the letter. Not even having seen Jesus was equivalent to the vision of heaven.

How then does John mark off the heavenly vision from all that had gone before? It certainly cannot lie in the fact that we are 'like him', at least not without qualification. Likeness to God is a general mark of human beings at the creation (Gen. 1.26). There are arguably many ways in which creatures, including humans, may be said to be like God. Though heaven surely involves a consummate level of likeness, which would be uniquely associated with the beatific vision, John does not seem to be making any such point here, since he does not explicitly distinguish this particular likeness from any other. Rather the vision is distinguished from all others by what John says about the object of vision. God is seen 'just as he is' (καθώς ἐστιν). The implication is that all other 'visions' did not have for their object God 'just as he is' but God in some other way, not just as he is but somehow as he is not. Our question will be whether the earthly Jesus saw God 'just as he is'. But before posing this question, we need to ask what more we can make of this distinction.

Turning to Paul, we find that he does not put the contrast quite so sharply. Though the visions of the Old Testament can hardly be absent from his mind, his explicit purpose is to compare the Christian present and future. He contrasts these not as seeing and not seeing but as seeing in a mirror and seeing face to face, as knowing in part and knowing as one is known by God. Though he does not express the contrast between the future and other visions as sharply as does John, there seems to be no necessary contradiction between the two authors, especially because Paul is more concerned with the *manner* of the vision. Paul thus presents us with a way of interpreting John's implied contrast between seeing God just as he is and seeing God in some other (lesser) way. We can see God just as he is, because we see him face to face, that is, directly, which Paul implies is how God knows us. No other vision can attain to God just as he is, because every other vision sees God indirectly 'in a mirror', that is, as reflected in something else. Whatever examples of this the author might have had in mind, examples are not hard for us to suggest: God is 'seen' indirectly in creatures, in theophanies, in the temple, in prophecies and spiritual gifts, in images and concepts, in each other who are made in God's image. Moreover, for Paul, all the 'visions' of current Christian life were visions not only 'in a mirror' but 'in a riddle'. Thus the mirror image Paul has in mind is not a clear image but an obscure one.[53] This intimates that the vision of this life is not only indirect but also obscure – it lacks the clarity Paul implicitly ascribes to the future, and yields only a partial knowledge in comparison to the clear vision to come. Interpreting John in the light of Paul once more, we may say that we shall see God just as he is because we shall see him face to face and clearly and not in an indirect and obscure fashion, not in a riddle. The vision of heaven is distinguished then by its immediacy and clarity. Even to see the Father in his incarnate Son, as Philip was invited to see him in the Gospel of John, is not to see the Father clearly and directly, absolutely speaking – had Philip seen the Father immediately and without any obscurity, he would hardly have asked Jesus to show him the Father. Even to see the Father *in the humanity of his Son* is to see the Father in a way that is indirect and even somehow obscure in comparison with what is to come. The beatific vision is marked off then by the fact that the Father is seen 'just as he is', that God is seen 'face to face', known as he knows us. Reading the Scriptures thus as a whole in accordance with Catholic theological method,[54] we can see that in this way Scripture differentiates the beatific vision from all other visions of the divine.

From the foregoing we can conclude that, just as Catholic faith holds it to be the case of the doctrines of the Trinity and incarnation, the doctrine of the *visio beatifica* of the saints does indeed appear in Scripture, even if not expressed in the same terms as are found in post-biblical doctrinal development. Having seen precisely how Scripture gives expression to this doctrine, we are now in the position of giving full force to the objection of our opponents by inquiring whether this Scriptural doctrine of an eschatological vision is somehow applied in Scripture to the earthly Christ. Should we find it said in Scripture that the earthly

---

53. Barrett, *First Epistle to the Corinthians*, pp. 307–8.
54. Second Vatican Council, *Dei Verbum*, 12.

Jesus saw God 'just as he is' or 'face to face' or knew God as God knew him, then we would surely be able to conclude without further ado that Jesus possessed this vision. But a search of the New Testament reveals that nowhere are these exact words applied to Jesus, not even after the resurrection.

Another line of enquiry lies in possible equivalents to these expressions, different expressions that refer to the same reality. While 'see face to face' and 'see just as he is' may not have precisely the same sense, we have found that they refer in Scripture specifically to the same reality, namely, the beatific vision. Perhaps there are more such equivalent phrases in the New Testament, not so refined maybe, but which are applied to this vision as possessed by the earthly Christ? One such phrase could be what is said in Matthew's Gospel of the angels, that they 'look upon the face' of the Father, or another could be something like the explanations we have given of John and Paul, that the blessed see God directly, immediately, clearly or without obscurity. On investigation, however, we can only conclude that no such precise words are applied by the New Testament to a vision or knowledge possessed by Jesus. The nearest we can find are a set of sayings about Jesus' knowing and seeing the Father where, as we shall see, the opponents of Christ's beatific vision are forearmed to interpret these texts not of any vision in his humanity at all but of his divine knowledge alone. In following these skirmishes, we shall conclude that, while this inquiry cannot deliver one incontrovertible candidate for Christ's beatific vision, it does manifest that there *is* something present in Scripture that demands a theological explanation, which could be provided by the theory of the earthly Christ's beatific vision. And in the light of this we shall see how, for all its strength on its own terms, our opponent's argument can hardly be fatal to the thesis of Christ's heavenly vision on earth.

What we find in the Gospels is certainly a more complex and richer picture than merely narratives depicting extraordinary knowledge but in fact merely making claims about Christ's identity. As we noted above, Christ's knowledge is related not only to his identity but also to a very salient feature of his saving ministry, namely, his teaching. Jesus is portrayed as one sent by God as our Saviour, whose salvific mission includes his authoritative teaching about God, his creation and his people. In all the Gospels Jesus is presented as one who teaches with authority. For example: 'And immediately on the sabbath he entered the synagogue and taught. And they were astonished at his teaching, for he taught them as one who had authority, and not as the scribes' (Mk 1.22). Not only is Christ's teaching presented as more authoritative than that of the scribes, but the formula he uses in the Sermon on the Mount in Matthew implies an authority transcending even that of the prophets and on a level with divine or Scriptural authority. Instead of using the prophetic 'Thus says the Lord', he says, 'But I say to you' (e.g. 5.21).[55] Where, people want to know, does he get all this, and what is this wisdom he possesses? (cf. Mk 6.2). The readers of the Gospels

---

55. Cf. S. Byrskog, *Jesus the Only Teacher: Didactic Authority and Transmission in Ancient Israel, Ancient Judaism and the Matthean Community* (Stockholm: Almqvist & Wiksell International, 1994), pp. 294–6.

are evidently meant to conclude that the uniquely authoritative teaching of Jesus is rooted in his unique, intimate relationship with God his Father. Jesus bears witness to this profound relationship as the source of his revelatory power when he says:

> I thank you, Father, Lord of heaven and earth, for having hidden these things from the wise and understanding and having revealed them to babes … All things have been delivered to me by my Father; and no one knows the Son except the Father, and no one knows the Father except the Son and any one to whom the Son chooses to reveal him. (Mt 11.25–26; cf. Lk 10.21–22)

What Jesus has taught has its origin in the Father who has given it to him. It is as the Son of the Father that Jesus has received what he then communicates to others, enabling them to believe.[56]

This perfect mutual knowing of Father and Son as the basis of revelation is more extensively meditated upon in the Fourth Gospel, which provides a kind of commentary on that personal foundation of Christ's teaching activity which permeates all the Gospels. In John we meet not only the language of knowing, showing, hearing, learning and receiving words from the Father, but also the language of 'seeing', the nearest the words of the New Testament actually come to saying something like Jesus saw God 'face to face' or 'just as he is'. John attests that, in contrast to any other claim for a human being to have seen God, Christ has in fact seen the Father. Thus Jesus says, 'Not that any one has seen the Father except him who is from God: he has seen the Father' (6.46). It is this vision then that roots Christ's revelation of the Father to us.[57] The themes of vision and revelation are linked by John in his prologue: 'No one has ever seen God; the only-begotten God who is in the bosom of the Father, he has made him known' (1.18). More clearly than in 1 John, the Gospel gives an answer to the doubt expressed by ben Sirach. Unlike Moses, with whom the prologue contrasts Jesus, and Isaiah whom John seems to have thought foresaw the glory of *Christ* (12.41), Jesus has seen the Father himself and is in this way able to reveal him.

Not only though had he seen the Father, but his vision extended further. For one thing, knowing God as his Father is evidently bound up with knowledge of his own identity: he knows himself to be the Son of the Father, and also as one sent by the Father into the world on a saving mission. The scope of his knowledge thus extends further than a vision of the Father alone, and a sense of this is conveyed by John. When speaking with Nicodemus Jesus says, 'Truly, truly, I say to you, we speak of what we know, and bear witness to what we have seen; but you do not receive our testimony. If I have told you earthly things and you do not believe, how can you believe if I tell you heavenly things?' (3.11–12). Later on in the same chapter, we read: 'He bears witness to what he has seen and heard, yet no one

---

56. France, *Matthew*, pp. 441–3.

57. A. Feuillet, 'La science de vision de Jésus et les Évangiles. Recherche exégétique', *DC* 36 (1983): 158–79.

receives his testimony' (v. 32). And later still in the Gospel we learn that the basis of what Jesus has seen is a vision in the Father's presence: 'I speak of what I have seen with my Father' (8.38). John doubtless means us to understand that Jesus' powerful vision experienced in the presence of the Father underlies his knowledge of his saving mission, his extraordinary knowledge of human beings (2.25; 13.11) and the knowledge of everything attributed to him by the disciples (16.30; 21.27).

However, given that Christ has seen the Father and with the Father, can we take this to be the beatific vision? The answer is at first sight by no means clear, especially when we recall how Catholic theology reads such sayings to do with Christ in the light of the development of Christian doctrine. Christians were early on able to cite different passages in Scripture against both those who denied the reality of his humanity and those who denied his divinity. Then, through the Arian controversy some were able to develop a way of referring both sets of passages to the single subject or person of Christ, attributing them to him *as God* or *as man*.[58] This doctrinal reading triumphed over a rival tendency, which became associated with Nestorius. This was to attribute the divine and human words and actions of Christ to one of *two* subjects or persons, one divine and the other human. A miracle might be attributed to the Word, while an ordinary human action would be attributed to 'the human being', as though to a second person. However, according to the tradition championed by Cyril of Alexandria and favoured at the Council of Ephesus (431), which condemned Nestorius, the same person of the Word of God was the single subject of whatever he did according to his divinity and whatever he did according to his humanity. In the terms approved by the Council of Chalcedon (451),[59] a saying or action or some aspect thereof would be attributed to the *single* person of Christ either in his divine nature or in his human nature. This procedure has sometimes been known as 'two-nature exegesis'.[60]

According to this doctrinal reading of Scripture, the same Son of God is, does and says some things according to his divine nature, and others according to his human nature. For example, *as God* Jesus Christ (this name denoting the single *person* of the Word) creates and sustains the universe, and *as man* the very same Jesus Christ eats and drinks. Again, it is *as God* that Jesus exists with the Father 'before' the incarnation (the humanity of Jesus does not pre-exist his conception in his mother's womb) and *as man* that he goes through the processes of enunci-ating human words and thinking human thoughts. It is as God that he is one (in substance) with the Father, and as man that he is less than the Father (and of one substance with us). What though of the extraordinary knowledge attributed by Scripture to Christ? Are we to read this as attributed to Christ according to his humanity or according to his divinity? He might be saying, for example, that he

58. L. Ayres, *Nicaea and its Legacy: An Approach to Fourth-Century Trinitarian Theology* (Oxford: OUP, 2004), pp. 32–7.

59. Council of Chalcedon, *De duabus naturis in Christo*.

60. M. Wiles, *The Spiritual Gospel: The Interpretation of the Fourth Gospel in the Early Church* (Cambridge: CUP, 1960), pp. 137–8.

has seen the Father in his divine mind, being one in essence and knowledge with the Father; or he might be saying that he has seen the Father in his human mind. If a human reading were accepted, we should have a testimony to a vision that could be interpreted as the beatific vision. But if only the divine is allowed, we would have a direct testimony only to divine knowledge, to Christ's divinity, and nothing more.

One option might be to suppose that, if there is no sign of any distinction being made here between Christ's divinity and his humanity, we are free or even obliged to allow Christ's vision of both natures.[61] One suggestion might be that we can attribute Christ's vision to both natures because of the fact that John wrote before the emergence of the Chalcedonian formula of two natures, which thus played no part in his conscious intention in writing. However, we should respond to such a suggestion with caution, if only because there are clearly cases when a manifestly correct interpretation can be reached without there necessarily being any relevant conscious intention on the part of the author. Though John may have had nothing like the Chalcedonian formula articulated in his mind, it is hardly difficult to conclude that when he describes Christ as eating and drinking, this must be interpreted according to his human nature alone – this is not on account of discerning any conscious authorial intention but because taking in nutrition is just not proper to the non-bodily divine nature but is to bodily human nature. Likewise, it is not difficult to conclude that Christ creates not as man but as God, if only we take into account that the infinite power required to make something exist out of nothing just cannot exist in finite human nature. However, in the case of Christ's vision and knowledge of the Father, we have nothing so clear cut as with the instances of creation and nutrition. It is not so easy in this respect to opt for one or other nature, since Christ must both know as God and know as man – each nature is (in a very different way) intelligent.

Given that knowing as such is proper to both natures, we are left far from clear how to assign claims to extraordinary knowledge in Christ between the two hypostatically united natures. Even knowing *God* can be assigned to either nature. It is hardly controversial to attribute knowledge of God – or of anything else – to the divine nature, given the Christian doctrine that God is omniscient. Moreover, human beings are credited with knowledge of God of various kinds throughout the Scriptures, knowledge which is sometimes quite extraordinary and evidently beyond ordinary human powers, including the final vision of God in heaven. Thus it is difficult to know whether to assign Christ's knowledge of God to his divinity or humanity. This is true, for example, of Paul's claim that in Christ 'all the treasures of wisdom and knowledge are hidden' (Col. 2.3). What concerns us especially is that it is true of Christ's 'vision' of the Father in John's Gospel: is there anything in the text itself to suggest that his vision is to be associated with one nature or another?

61. Cf. B. Leeming, 'The Human Knowledge of Christ', *ITQ* 19 (1952): 135–47, 234–53 (242–9).

There are two arguments that suggest that John's Gospel deliberately associates Christ's vision of the Father with his 'pre-existence' and thus, in Chalcedonian terms, with the divine nature. If persuasive, either of these arguments would then prevent us from interpreting this vision as referred also to Christ's human mind, at least on the level of the text's literal sense. The first argument was not, as far as I am aware, advanced until the twentieth century, and is based on John's use of the *perfect* tense (which includes a reference to the *past*) of the Greek ὁράω for Jesus' vision of the Father. John does use the present of βλέπω when speaking of Jesus seeing what the Father is *doing* (5.19). Βλέπω is a verb John employs for physical seeing, and it seems that its object here is the *works* God has done in creation. Ὁράω, however, he never uses in the present tense. Jesus does not say that he *sees* the Father, but that he '*has* seen' (ἑώρακεν) him. The Catholic exegete Marie-Joseph Lagrange suggested that the use of the perfect tense in 6.46 indicates that we have here a vision of the Father already possessed by the Son *before* the Word became flesh.[62] Since, on an orthodox view of the incarnation, the human mind of Jesus can hardly pre-exist his assumption of human nature, this would mean any vision he had 'before' the incarnation could only be a *divine* knowledge. Given divine eternity, the priority implied by the perfect tense could not of course be a strictly *temporal* priority, as though this vision had taken place or begun at an earlier point in created time, but the priority would be the non-temporal priority of eternity over time itself. That this vision existed eternally would be true at any point of worldly time, whether before or after the incarnation. The use of the perfect would point to the vision being beyond time – divine and eternal – rather than a vision that could be construed as human or temporal in any sense. Galot cites this use of the perfect against any suggestion that Jesus' vision in 6.46 is the beatific vision. According to Galot, the present tense would have been more appropriate for a beatific vision, but this is a tense John never uses for the Son's vision of the Father.[63]

An older argument in favour of referring such passages to divine knowledge is the link John makes in his Gospel between Jesus' vision and knowledge and his divine origin. For John, Jesus' unique vision of the Father is bound up with the Son's *heavenly origin* as the basis on which he can reveal the Father to us. It is this divine origin that is thus the ultimate vindication of what Christ reveals. When Jesus says in 6.46 that no one has seen the Father except himself, he is answering to complaints that he is claiming to have come down from heaven, and in response he describes himself, the exception, as 'one who is *from God*'. The importance of divine origin is also implied in the prologue, when the Son, who makes the Father known and by implication has seen him, is identified as the Father's only Son 'who is in the bosom of the Father' (1.18; cf. v. 14). The link is clear in Jesus' words to Nicodemus. After saying that he bears witness to what he has seen, and asking how Nicodemus will believe if he tells him of heavenly things, he goes on: 'No one has gone up into heaven except the one who came down from heaven, the Son of

62. M.-J. Lagrange, *Évangile selon Saint Jean* (Paris: Victor Lecoffre, 1927), pp. 181–2, n.46.

63. 'Le Christ terrestre et la vision', pp. 441–4.

Man [who is in heaven]' (3.13).[64] Jesus is able to reveal heavenly things precisely because of his heavenly origin in the Father. It is the origin of Jesus as divine that is at stake here. Jesus' humanity does not pre-exist his earthly life, but comes into existence in time when the Word becomes flesh. Put in Chalcedonian terms, the divine nature is received by the Son in his being eternally begotten by the Father. It is in this heavenly origin that the Son receives divine knowledge of the Father, which then underwrites his revelation of the Father and of all that he has seen in the Father's presence. It is thus precisely *as divine* that he has the *vision* of the Father to which John's Gospel explicitly attests.

As we shall recall in the next chapter, the divine interpretation of Christ's knowledge was already found among the Fathers of the Church, who were keen to argue from John's Gospel to Christ's divinity in opposition to the Arians. Though Aquinas's practice was to allow for several possible literal readings of a biblical text, and he spoke often of the beatific vision in his commentary on John,[65] he does appear to exhibit a certain preference for a divine interpretation of these passages. For example, he concluded that the vision implied in 1.18 can only be ultimately explained by a divine knowledge received through being begotten by the Father, a knowledge which alone is sufficient to vindicate the competence of Christ as revealer.[66] Though he allowed for interpreting the vision in 6.46 as in Christ's human mind, he seems to prefer a divine interpretation where the Son alone receives a truly comprehensive knowledge through a uniquely perfect reception of the Father's divine nature that comes by his eternal generation.[67] Likewise, the Son's seeing in 8.38 he says must be understood of a most certain knowledge that he equates with the Son's knowledge of the Father in Matthew 11.27, a passage he interprets in terms of divine knowledge.[68] That Christ 'bears witness' (Jn 3.32) to what he has seen and heard is referred to his humanity to be sure, but his actual seeing and hearing to his divinity.[69] And of his words to Nicodemus 'what we know … what we have seen' (v. 11), Aquinas refers 'know' to Christ's humanity but 'seen' to his divinity.[70]

Some neoscholastics, such as Paul Galtier, a major contributor to the debate on Christ's consciousness, happily accepted that there was no single biblical text that could be produced as definitive 'proof' for the thesis of the earthly Christ's vision.[71] We have seen that while it is possible to produce texts that easily

64. R. E. Brown, *The Gospel According to John* (New York: Doubleday, 1966), p. 129, is among the minority supporting the longer text.

65. See P.-Y. Maillard, *La Vision de Dieu chez Thomas d'Aquin: Une lecture de l' "In Ioannem" à la lumière de ses sources augustiniennes* (Paris: Vrin, 2001), pp. 238–42.

66. *Lectura super Ioannem*, 1.11.217–19.

67. Ibid., 6.5.947.

68. Ibid., 8.4.1216; cf. 1.11.219 and *Lectura super Matthaeum*, 11.9.965–66.

69. Ibid., 3.5.534–35.

70. Ibid., 3.2.462.

71. P. Galtier, *De Incarnatione ac Redemptione* (Paris: Beauchesne, 9th edn, 1947), pp. 258–9.

establish a heavenly vision of God for the blessed as a matter of Christian faith, those texts that might be brought forward in favour of *Christ's* earthly possession of it are more problematic. In the absence of a solemn magisterial definition comparable to that of Nicaea, it is difficult for a Catholic theologian just to claim that the doctrine is in Scripture, since arguments can always be adduced against any particular text, as we have seen. Even allowing for differences of expression, nothing in Scripture seems to inform us in any straightforward way that Christ enjoyed heavenly knowledge in his humanity. What I am suggesting, however, is that though Christ's beatific vision as such may not be thus openly attested Scripture, there *is* something in Scripture that can invite us to suppose by way of further theological reflection that Christ possessed this vision after all. It is in this way that the witness of Scripture proves its positive relevance to the claim that the earthly Christ possessed the vision of heaven.

To vindicate Christ as revealer must surely involve not only establishing the divine origin of what he reveals but also its human term or destination. As we have already seen, the New Testament presents Jesus not just as having knowledge by way of his origin from the Father, but as proclaiming the Father's kingdom with authority to those who hear his message. We find him not only possessed of divine knowledge, but as communicating knowledge in a human way. Again John's Gospel provides us with a kind of commentary on what takes place in the teaching activity of Christ throughout the Gospels. For example, speaking to his opponents in John, Jesus identifies himself as 'a man who has told you the truth which I heard from God' (8.40). Later he cries out, 'What I say I say as the Father has spoken [to me]' (12.50). To the disciples on one occasion he says, 'Everything that I have heard from my Father I made known to you' (15.15). And to the Father he says, 'I have given them the words which you gave me' (17.8). We are here concerned with the communication to the disciples of teaching set in human words, images and concepts, including teaching about the Father and the relationship between Father and Son. Though the ultimate origin of this teaching may be divine, it is human in its mode of expression, able to be received in the human minds of the disciples, whatever their difficulties in understanding it.

It is crucial to note that none of the Gospels leaves the impression that Christ's human mind had no role to play in this transmission. The disciples learn in a human way about heavenly things through the agency of the human mind of Christ their teacher. Though Christ's human mind was not the ultimate *source* of his extraordinary knowledge of the Father, it was nevertheless involved in the *passing on* of this knowledge to those who accepted his teaching. Human teaching presupposes knowledge in the human mind of the teacher. Were it otherwise, Christ's human mind would in some important respect be redundant. We surely do not suppose that Christ taught like a recording machine of some kind that merely transmits sounds without understanding, but by first humanly grasping the sense of what he had received from the Father before transmitting it by his human voice.[72]

---

72. Cf. Billot, *De Verbo Incarnato*, p. 227 n.

However, to vindicate Christ as revealer in theological terms must surely involve not only establishing the divine origin of his revelation and its human term, but also the pathway from origin to term. Christ could hardly teach authentically about God, unless his humanly communicable knowledge of God at term had in some way received the benefit of his source of divine knowledge, through his human mind having some mode of access to his divine mind, so to speak. For those who think that Scripture explicitly testifies to Christ's beatific vision, the search for this mode of access is already over.[73] However, even if Scripture is taken to make no explicit testimony to any such particular mode, it remains true that, if the human mind through which Christ teaches were deprived of some such access, the whole picture of Christ we find in Scripture of Christ the revealer would lose all plausibility. His role as teacher thus requires him to have not only a source in divine knowledge as well as humanly communicable knowledge, but also a kind of continuity between his divine mind and his human mind rather than isolation of one from the other. Now to suppose that Christ merely knew in his human mind the bare fact *that* he knew the Father in his divine mind, but without knowing the Father in any real way in his human mind itself, would again be to make the human mind redundant in an important respect. Instead we must surely suppose that Christ had a knowledge of the Father in his humanity that would, in its own order, imitate the perfection and intimacy of his divine knowledge, a kind of impression of divine knowledge on the human mind. Without such a profound and intimate knowing of the Father in Christ's humanity, we should have isolation rather than continuity between the divine and human minds. And in this continuity we may discern something of the path by which Christ's human teaching had the benefit of his divine knowledge, an access to the divine mind that would play a crucial part in bringing his humanly communicable teaching to fruition.

It is possible that there may be some passages in the Gospels that bear witness to such a profound and intimate knowledge of the Father in Christ's human mind. For example, to the Pharisees Jesus says, 'Even if I do bear witness to myself, my testimony is true, for I know (οἶδα) whence I have come and whither I am going' (8.14). Later he says of the Father, 'I know (οἶδα) him ... I know him and I keep his word' (8.55). Need such verses be referred only to Christ's divinity, as has been asserted of those that say Christ 'has seen' the Father? They certainly could not be referred exclusively to divine knowledge merely on the basis of the tense of the verb, since οἶδα is always used with the present meaning of 'I know'. This knowledge cannot be thus assumed to be merely divine, as might Christ's 'having seen' the Father in John, but could easily be knowledge of God in the human mind. It must be admitted that in his commentary on John, Aquinas again referred both these verses to Jesus' *divine* knowledge and *origin*.[74] Nevertheless, in favour of a 'human' interpretation, it could be urged that since their context is that of human acting – Christ bears witness in his humanity, keeps the Father's word in his

---

73. Leeming, 'The Human Knowledge of Christ', pp. 251–2; de Margerie, *The Human Knowledge of Christ*, pp. 22–4.

74. *Super Ioannem*, 8.2.1149; 8.8.1284.

humanity – that might lead us to suppose that we have here a knowing in Christ's humanity. Jean Poinsot, Aquinas's great seventeenth-century interpreter, known as 'John of St Thomas', thought Aquinas was implying such an argument when in the *Summa* he presented 8.55 (in contrast to his position in the *Commentary*) as knowledge of the Father *in Christ's humanity*.[75] On the other hand, someone working on Galtier's principles could allow the possibility that Christ is here witnessing and so on in his humanity but speaking (in an admittedly human way) about knowledge he in fact possessed only in his divinity. However, even if no particular verse can be absolutely tied down to extraordinary knowledge of God in Christ's human mind, it is still entirely implausible that no such powerful and intimate knowledge existed in the human mind of the one who humanly teaches human beings about the Father. The picture presented of Christ in Scripture as a whole cannot make real sense without some such continuity between his divine and human minds. To deny this would be to evacuate his identity as revealer of any meaning.

Guy Mansini has argued from scattered references in Aquinas's commentary that he traced a path by way of discovery from such a picture of Christ's teaching in the Gospel back to his possession of the beatific vision.[76] In the remainder of this book we shall examine how far the impression of divine knowledge in Christ's human mind required by this biblical picture can be theologically interpreted in terms of the knowledge enjoyed by the saints. If this attempt is successful, then the silence of Scripture on Christ's beatific vision, or at the very least the difficulty in interpreting his vision of the Father as being present in his human mind, will lose any crucial role it may have had in defeating the thesis. However, since a Catholic theology can only attempt such a theological explanation by reading Scripture in the light of Tradition, in the next chapter we shall investigate how far the Fathers of the Church interpreted Christ's human knowledge in terms such as these.

75. *Cursus Theologicus in Summam Theologicam D. Thomae* (10 vols; Paris: Vivès, 1883–86), vol. 8, p. 294. See Aquinas, *Summa*, 3a., q. 9, a. 2.

76. 'St. Thomas on Christ's Knowledge of God', pp. 98–101.

Chapter 3

'IT'S NOT IN THE FATHERS!'

Opponents of Christ's possession of the beatific vision protest not only that the doctrine is absent from Scripture – they also object that it cannot be found in the teachings of the Church Fathers. As Torrell puts it, the question was 'unknown to patristic tradition'.[1] The witness of the Fathers is relevant because of the key role they have traditionally played as authorities in Catholic theology. It was during the patristic period that the outlines of orthodox interpretation of Scripture were established, including the Chalcedonian understanding of Christ we followed in the last chapter. Even during antiquity itself, the force of their authority was felt. Later, the profession of faith adopted after the Council of Trent and then Vatican I laid down that Scripture could not be interpreted contrary to the unanimous consent of the Fathers.[2] Were a moral unanimity to have emerged during the period either that the earthly Christ possessed the beatific vision or that he did not, the whole question of how to read Scripture on the point in an authentically Catholic way would be settled. No side, however, has ever dared claim an explicit patristic *consensus* in support of either point of view, as we shall see. Nevertheless one opponent of Christ's beatific vision has instead brought forward a charge of the utmost seriousness, namely, that the thesis properly belongs not in the tradition of the orthodox Fathers at all but in a heretical, Nestorian context. This charge we shall address before turning to the patristic evidence itself and the question of what we can legitimately expect from its witness.

Weinandy, a keen student of Cyril of Alexandria, the chief opponent of Nestorius, has said he is convinced that the whole question of whether Jesus possessed the beatific vision is a 'Nestorian' one.[3] He is appealing here to the contrast between Chalcedonian orthodoxy, where what belongs to Christ's human nature and what belongs to his divine nature are both attributed to a single personal subject, and Nestorian heresy, where whatever is divine is attributed to the person of the Word and whatever is human to a second distinct human person, a much weaker presentation of the personal unity of Christ. To claim Christ's beatific vision as Nestorian is to charge that it inevitably involves the

---

1. 'S. Thomas d'Aquin et la science du Christ', p. 402.
2. Pius IV, *Iniunctum Nobis*; First Vatican Council, *Dei Filius*, 2.
3. Weinandy, 'Jesus' Filial Vision of the Father', p. 190.

heresy of distinguishing two persons in the incarnate Christ, while reducing the unity between the human and divine in Christ to merely one of will. However, quite apart from the question of how far Nestorius himself fitted the standard description of a Nestorian, identifying anyone's thought as Nestorian from the language they use is a very delicate matter. Where those indicted predate the Nestorian crisis, one risks making an anachronistic charge, and where those indicted are part of the Chalcedonian tradition, one risks mistaking a legitimate Chalcedonian shorthand for a Nestorian formula. For example, to ask in a thoroughgoing Nestorian context whether the soul of Christ has knowledge of the Word doubtless implies that this soul stands for a second person distinct from the Word. In a Chalcedonian context, however, such a question is a kind of shorthand for asking whether the Word has knowledge of himself *in his human mind*. We use a similar kind of shorthand of ourselves when we say that feet walk or eyes see or the intellect understands or the will wills – unless we have adopted an odd kind of anthropology, we do not imply that it is not *we* who walk with our legs, see through our eyes, understand through our minds or will by our wills. Likewise, when a Chalcedonian says that Christ's soul has knowledge, he means that the one person of the Word has knowledge *in his human nature*: the fact that the nature (or some aspect thereof) may be used as a grammatical subject does not make it a personal subject.[4] This is reinforced for Thomists by Aquinas's philosophical understanding of actions as pertaining to persons, meaning that, strictly speaking, *persons* act *through* their natures.[5]

However, it is not impossible that a theologian, though adhering officially to a Chalcedonian framework, may somehow slip into a Nestorian way of speaking and even thinking, and so turn the human nature into something like a second person. It is something of this sort that Weinandy seems to suspect – unfairly – of Thomism, from his contemporary Thomas Joseph White all the way back to Aquinas, because of its endorsement of Christ's beatific vision.[6] He is partly able to make his accusation by presupposing that possession of the beatific vision is by its 'definition' limited to 'someone who is not God'.[7] It is important to note that this 'definition' is in fact suspiciously Nestorianizing, as it takes too little account of the crucial Chalcedonian distinction between one person and two natures. If we were to take better account of this distinction, we might say something like possession of the beatific vision is limited to 'someone who has a created mind', where 'someone' is referred to the level of person and 'mind' to nature. We can see why

---

4. For a defence of the traditional patristic language in a Thomist context, see T. J. White, 'Dyotheletism and the Instrumental Human Consciousness of Jesus', *PE* 17 (2008): 396–422.

5. *Summa*, 3a., q. 19, a. 1 ad 3. For a contrast with the viewpoint of Duns Scotus, see C. L. Barnes, *Christ's Two Wills in Scholastic Thought: The Christology of Aquinas and Its Historical Contexts* (Toronto: PIMS, 2012), pp. 313–28.

6. 'The Beatific Vision and the Incarnate Son', pp. 605–15; 'Jesus' Filial Vision of the Father', p. 191 n.2.

7. 'Jesus' Filial Vision of the Father', p. 190.

this distinction is so significant here, when we ask whether Jesus Christ would count among those who could possess the beatific vision. On our Chalcedonian definition he would be able to possess it, because he is someone who has a created mind, a divine person who has assumed a *complete* human nature, mind included. However, on Weinandy's Nestorianizing definition, which takes too little account of the distinction between nature and person, Jesus cannot possess the beatific vision at all. This is because the man Jesus Christ is not 'someone who is not God', a non-divine person, but is the Second Person of the Blessed Trinity, God incarnate. Despite his possession of a true human mind, he just does not fit into Weinandy's class of those who can have the beatific vision, that is, the class of '*someone* who is not God'. The Christ of Chalcedon is excluded from the beatific vision, just because he is a divine person, a divine someone.[8]

The upshot is that, once Weinandy has set up his definition as he does, he is able to cast Nestorian aspersions on the whole theological project of attributing the beatific vision to Jesus – it is a Nestorian question, he says, with a Nestorian answer.[9] Though the beatific vision would be excluded from a Chalcedonian incarnation, the same would not be true of a Nestorian one. This is because, while the beatific vision could not be attributed on Weinandy's definition to the divine Word, it could be attributed to some further non-divine subject in addition to the Word. Hence, if the beatific vision were involved in an incarnation at all, it could only be where an incarnation would imply a second person, that is, where the incarnation is conceived along Nestorian lines.[10] In other words, on Weinandy's definition, the thesis of the beatific vision can only arise in the context of a Christology of two persons, from within a doctrine of the incarnation that is heretical, and thus by implication the thesis of Christ's beatific vision can itself hardly be orthodox. In an extravagant moment Weinandy even asserts that Nestorius himself would in all probability have answered the question about Jesus' beatific vision with a Yes. This beatific knowledge would have 'sanctioned' the mere union of will that existed between the two conjoined persons, the Son of God and the man Jesus.[11]

However, when we turn to the question of Christ's knowledge in the historic approach to Christology from which Nestorius emerged, namely, the theological tradition associated with Antioch, we find something quite different. There is in fact no evidence that Nestorius or any Antiochene theologian ever invoked the beatific vision to explain the union of will between the Word and the human being. A reason that may have discouraged them from doing this is the fact that the Antiochenes tended to make the object of the saints' vision Christ's humanity and not the divine Word, as can be traced in the work of Theodoret of Cyrus.[12] Were Nestorius to have applied this to Christ, he would have had the man gaze not on

8. Ibid., p. 192.
9. Ibid., p. 190.
10. Ibid., p. 192.
11. Ibid., p. 190.
12. *Interpretatio Epistolae ad Ephesios*, 2.

the Word (as Weinandy would envisage the Nestorian doctrine) but on 'himself', the man. Furthermore, an Antiochene Christology seems instinctively to have pointed its exponents towards other priorities in dealing with Christ's knowledge. Rather than attribute something so extraordinary as the beatific vision to the man, Nestorius' exegetical tradition tended to reserve to the human being what is more *ordinary*. Again this can be observed in Theodoret. Here it is ignorance, growth in wisdom and so on, rather than any extraordinary knowledge, that are attributed to the 'form of the servant' who knew at any time only what the indwelling divinity revealed to him.[13] An Antiochene Christology – and thus presumably a Nestorian one – typically attributes to the man Jesus not the beatific vision but ignorance. As a matter of fact Cyril objected that Nestorius divided Christ into two persons not because he attributed the beatific vision to 'the man', but because he attributed to him what is ordinary in human knowledge.[14]

Now it may be that the continuity that would hold between the two Nestorian subjects might have come *eventually* to be explained in terms of the beatific vision. However, though the possibility of such a theological development in Nestorianism cannot be altogether ruled out, as a matter of historical fact it is not here but in Catholic orthodoxy that the thesis arose. Certainly by medieval times, the Chalcedonian tradition has the beatific vision explain a union of knowledge that *also* presupposes a deeper union on the level of person. That such theological fruitfulness took place *here* may of course be owed to the fact that the theological tradition dependent on Chalcedon had greater opportunities than Nestorianism to develop speculative theories over the centuries. However, it may also be that the very presupposition of a hypostatic union, suggesting a more profound union between the human and divine natures than Nestorius allowed, was what *invited* a theological explanation of the continuity of the divine and human minds, something it did more powerfully than would any merely Nestorian conjunction of persons. Our question is whether such a Chalcedonian invitation was in fact answered with the beatific vision by those great figures of Christian antiquity whom Catholic tradition considers to have anticipated and applied the Council's Christology. Did these Fathers of the Church ever attribute a heavenly vision to the earthly Christ?

The Fathers certainly do not seem to have endorsed any alternative theory for explaining the impact of Christ's divine knowledge on his human mind. What has normally been alleged by opponents of Christ's earthly vision is neither that it belongs in a heretical tradition nor that the orthodox Fathers teach some alternative theory, but only that the latter never mention the idea. Galot, for example, says that they make no explicit testimony in its favour.[15] Even in the first half of

---

13. Cyril quotes him in *Apologeticus contra Theodoretum pro XII Capitibus*, 4. See also P. B. Clayton, Jr., *The Christology of Theodoret of Cyrus: Antiochene Christology from the Council of Ephesus (431) to the Council of Chalcedon (451)* (Oxford and New York: OUP, 2007), pp. 161, 173.

14. Cf. *Epistulae Paschalis*, 17.3.

15. 'Le Christ terrestre et la vision', p. 429 n.3.

the twentieth century, neoscholastics differed among themselves on the extent to which they could muster patristic support for their own theological consensus. By their own standards, any variation in the strength of patristic witness would affect the level of authority they could claim for their own position, and often the witness they felt able to produce was extremely minimal. Furthermore, if Galot is right, the Fathers' universal silence would deprive the thesis's proponents altogether of any explicit patristic argument in its favour. Moreover, should there be a case that, given the truth of Christ's beatific vision, one would reasonably expect the Fathers to have explicitly taught it, the fact of its absence would then become more powerful than a mere argument from silence. We shall argue below that the actual course of the historical development of Christological doctrine in general during the patristic period raises little expectation that any theological theory on the relationship between Christ's divine and human knowledge would have been articulated at that stage. First, however, we shall ask whether Galot is correct in charging that the doctrine makes no appearance in the patristic period at all.

What then would count as patristic endorsement of the idea that the earthly Christ possessed the beatific vision? If supporters of the thesis have sometimes been overenthusiastic in their efforts to find it in the writings of the Fathers, we should not commit the opposite error of becoming overcautious ourselves. As with Chapter 2's treatment of Scripture, we should be careful to avoid the anachronism of simply searching for the employment of the later scholastic termi-nology of the high medieval period or its detailed analyses of Christ's knowledge. We may instead find a guide in an early medieval English monk named Hwita (Wizo), who was a leading theologian in his time and the first to devote a whole treatise to our topic. Nicknamed Candidus by Alcuin, whose pupil he was, he was present in continental Europe at the very end of the eighth century, and belonged to the court of Charlemagne in 801–802.[16] His works offer us two illustrations of pre-scholastic explicit endorsements of the doctrine of Christ's beatific vision in the context of an orthodox Christology, and thus provide us with a model for what a patristic endorsement of Christ's beatific vision might look like.[17]

In his work on the passion, Candidus gave his interpretation of Christ's words on the cross to the penitent thief, 'Today you will be with me in paradise' (Lk. 23.43). According to Candidus, Jesus was saying: 'Just as my soul is always blessed with the contemplation of God … so yours will also be blessed with the same felicity through God's mercy.'[18] Though Candidus does not use a scholastic phrase such as *visio beatifica*, it is clear that the beatific vision is what is envisaged for the

16. See J. Marenbon, 'Candidus' in H. C. G. Matthew and B. H. Harrison (eds), *Oxford Dictionary of National Biography from the Earliest Times to the Year 2000* (60 vols; Oxford: OUP, 2004), vol. 9, pp. 888–9.

17. See H. de Lavalette, 'Candide, Théologien Méconnu de la Vision Béatifique du Christ', *RSR* 49 (1961): 426–9. On account of this French article, Candidus' name is often given in English as 'Candide'.

18. *Opusculum de Passione Domini*, 17.

thief's soul, which is blessed with the happiness of divine contemplation. There can be no doubt then that the thief's post-mortem happiness is identified with the happiness enjoyed in Christ's human soul while on earth, even on the cross. And as if this were not enough, the identification is made clearer still in a letter written by Candidus to answer a question conveyed to him by a friend: 'Was Christ our Lord, insofar as he was man, able to see God, while living here as a mortal among mortals?' (*Quod Christus Dominus noster, in quantum homo fuit, cum hic mortalis inter mortales viveret, Deum videre potuisset?*)[19]

The question is evidently not about Christ's divine knowledge but a vision of the Father *in his human nature*. Candidus had in mind two ways in which God might be thought to be seen through human nature: through the eyes of the body, or through the soul or spirit. He turns first to the question of physical eyes, and argues that, since God is spirit and incorporeal, all Catholic Christians agree that he cannot be seen in this way.[20] He does, however, believe that God can be seen just as he is, in his divine nature, through the human soul or spirit. Though he again does not use the term 'beatific vision', he takes it from Christ's words in the Beatitudes (Mt. 5.8) that those who shall see him will do so through pure hearts. Candidus holds it to be beyond doubt that Christ saw the Father in this way, in his human soul or spirit. Since he promised the vision of God to the pure in heart, it cannot be entertained that Christ, who willed to see the Father as far as was possible, did not see him in just the same way as will be possible for us.[21] Candidus held that Christ always had this vision, and that to think otherwise would be to hold, contrary to the Catholic faith, that Jesus was not always God – he evidently supposed that the beatific vision in some way accompanied the hypostatic union.[22]

Though Candidus contended that the earthly Jesus possessed this vision, his view is not evidence for *patristic* teaching, since he himself is not counted as a Father, having lived just after what is now usually taken to be the end of the patristic age. Catholic theology has generally come to see the mark of antiquity as essential to the identity of a Father, with the patristic period normally being thought to conclude not long before in the eighth century with John of Damascus. Nevertheless the English monk does provide us with a pre-scholastic guide for our investigation of the Fathers. He speaks specifically of a knowledge that is found in the earthly Christ's human mind, explicitly of the heavenly vision of the saints, and identifies the knowledge in Christ's mind with this blessed vision. But did any of the Fathers themselves identify a knowledge in Christ's human mind with the beatific vision, as Candidus would do? Before attempting to answer this question, it would be as well to ascertain something about how the Fathers treated the beatific vision itself before asking whether they applied such treatments to the earthly Christ.[23]

---

19. *Epistola num Christus Corporeis Oculis Deum Videre Potuerit*, 1.

20. Ibid., 2.

21. Ibid., 6.

22. Ibid., 7.

23. On the beatific vision in the Fathers, see V. Lossky, *The Vision of God* (trans. A. Moorhouse; 2nd edn; Crestwood, NY: St Vladimir's, 1983).

Already in the second century a number of themes were established that became characteristic of the doctrine in the patristic period. In response to the pagan challenge to manifest the Christian God, the apologist Theophilus ruled out the possibility that the inexpressible God could be seen with bodily eyes; instead he could be seen only with 'eyes of the soul' that have been purified of the cataracts of sin.[24] He contrasted our current perception of God with the vision of heaven, and seems to give a reply to the biblical tradition that 'no one can see God and live' by placing this vision in the context of the immortality of the resurrection.[25] According to Irenaeus, the vision of the incomprehensible God, which is not possible for human beings, is made possible by the will of God who makes himself seen through his own power and love. Irenaeus compared the vision with the fact that those who see light are in the light: those who see God are in him and receive his splendour. He speculated that, just as life is conferred through God's self-manifestation on earth, so it is the heavenly vision itself that confers immortality at the resurrection.[26] Here we have the fullness of human participation in the life of God and a full restoration of the image and likeness of God in man. Irenaeus also makes his own the teaching that the heavenly vision differs among those who are granted it, and this is linked to Christ's declaration that there are many mansions in his Father's house (Jn 14.2) and to the varying worth of their inhabitants.[27]

Such Christian themes of grace and anthropology were coming into contact with the Platonic notion of the mind's desire for and ascent to contemplation of the ineffable God, which the Fathers supposed to be indebted to the Old Testament.[28] According to Clement of Alexandria, writing in the third century, it is the Christian's goal to know God as far as is possible.[29] Knowledge of God, however, is had not through the body but through the intellect, and (according to 1 Cor. 13.11) takes place 'in a mirror' in this life and 'face to face' in the next. Since 'no one can see God and live', the final perfection of clear apprehension comes to the soul only after its separation from the body at death. Progress in holiness in this life is linked to an apophatic process of intellectual abstraction where what is known is what God is *not* rather than what he is.[30] After being purified by such knowledge, the pure in heart draw near to the Lord and are ready for the everlasting contemplation of beholding God, face to face.[31] Origen spoke of souls after death being taken through various stages of knowledge until they gaze 'face to face' on the causes of things and finally see and know God through

---

24. *Ad Autolycum*, 2.

25. Ibid., 7.

26. *Adversus Haereses*, 4.20.3. On the vision of God in Irenaeus, see R. Tremblay, *La manifestation et la vision de Dieu selon saint Irénée de Lyon* (Münsterische Beiträge zur Theologie, 41; Münster: Aschendorff, 1978).

27. Ibid., 5.36.1. Cf. Theophilus, *Ad Autolycum*, 7.

28. E.g. Clement of Alexandria, *Stromateis*, 5.14.

29. Ibid., 2.10.

30. Ibid., 5.11.

31. Ibid., 7.11.

purity of heart.[32] Though he entertains the hypothesis of souls being able to fall from heavenly divine contemplation, just as on his particular hypothesis of their 'pre-existence' they had thus fallen from contemplation prior to their union with earthly bodies, he envisages them as in fact becoming ultimately fixed in contemplation, just as Christ's pre-existent soul had been so fixed.[33] At the consummation of all things, when God is all in all and becomes all things to the blessed, he even supposes that the mind will know nothing but God, seeing him alone.[34] The idea of a continual progress of the soul in stretching out to the infinite God was given exemplary expression in the fourth century by Gregory of Nyssa and shaped his account of heaven, which is conceived along the lines of an endless exploration of the divine infinity.[35]

When we turn to Augustine of Hippo, whose writings were of immense influence for later Western theology, we find him relating the final gift of the beatific vision to the human desire for 'happiness' (*beatitudo*) or the 'blessed life' (*beata vita*), which he says consists in wisdom, that is, the vision of God.[36] This vision is not of a bodily or imaginative kind, but an intellectual gaze of the mind or heart.[37] Like other Fathers, Augustine wrote more than once against the idea that the invisible God can be seen with bodily eyes,[38] even those of Christ, and it was from Augustine that Candidus was to draw, just as Augustine himself drew on Ambrose, Athanasius, Gregory of Nazianzus and Jerome. He had at first, like Ambrose, supposed that it was possible for our minds to rise to a permanent vision of God in this life, and that this had been granted to the apostles,[39] but he then abandoned this position during a more intensive study of Paul in the period after his ordination in the early 390s. The imperfect beatitude of the present life of faith Augustine neatly contrasted with that of the future, which consists in the eternal face to face vision and enjoyment of God, the supreme good. Here (in contrast to Gregory of Nyssa's teaching), desire for God will come to *rest*.[40] Augustine continued to think, however, that the face to face vision could be

32. *De Principiis*, 2.11.7.

33. See H. Crouzel, *Origen* (trans. A. S. Worrall; Edinburgh: T&T Clark, 1989), pp. 114, 238.

34. *De Principiis*, 3.6.3.

35. *De Vita Moysis*, 2.238–9. On Gregory see M. Ludlow, 'Divine Infinity and Eschatology: The Limits and Dynamics of Human Knowledge, according to Gregory of Nyssa (*CE* II 67–170)' in L. Karfíková, S, Douglass and J. Zacchuber (eds), *Gregory of Nyssa: Contra Eunomium II: An English Version with Supporting Studies* (Supplements to Vigiliae Christianae, 82; Leiden and Boston: Brill, 2007), pp. 217–37.

36. *De Libero Arbitrio*, 2.13.35; 2.16.41.

37. See L. Ayres, *Augustine and the Trinity* (Cambridge: CUP, 2010), pp. 142–70.

38. E.g. *Epistola*, 147; *De Civitate Dei*, 22:29; *Retractationes*, 2.67.

39. *De Sermo Domini in Monte*, 12; cf. *Retractationes*, 1.18. See F. Van Fleteren, 'Per Speculum et in aenigmitate: 1 Corinthians 13:12 in the Writings of St. Augustine', *AS* 23 (1992): 69–102.

40. E.g. *De Civitate Dei*, 22.30.

had in this life but, taking into account God's words to Moses that man could not see him and live (Exod. 33.20), it could only be fleeting, where there was a kind of temporary rapture of the soul from the body towards the next life. He supposed that that was what happened to Paul, who reports a vision which took place 'whether in the body or out of the body I do not know, God knows' (2 Cor. 12.2). Likewise, following the Septuagint version of Numbers 12.8, which spoke of Moses seeing the 'glory' of the Lord, Augustine went so far as to suggest that the experience to which these particular words refer was a fleeting anticipation of the vision of God 'just as he is' promised to all God's children at the end of life.[41]

But what exactly did all these Fathers suppose was the object of this blessed vision? In Chapter 2, we saw how Scripture focused the heavenly vision of the saints on God the Father in particular, and this continued to be the case in the works of the patristic period. When writers such as Theophilus and Clement spoke of the object of this vision as 'God', they of course meant the Father, according to the normal Scriptural usage we encountered in the last chapter. Inevitably, the growing articulation of Trinitarian doctrine held this vision in a firmly Trinitarian context. For example, Irenaeus in one place conceived the pedagogical history of salvation in terms of three different but related visions of God. First, God was 'seen' by a vision of prophecy through the Spirit, which amounted only to seeing 'the likeness of the splendour of the Lord' and not to a face to face vision. Then in the incarnation we have 'adoptive vision', the climax of the Word's gradual manifestation of the Father since creation. The incarnate Son is seen, and in him the Father, since the Son is himself the manifestation of the invisible Father. Then finally, in the kingdom of heaven God will be seen 'according to Fatherhood' (*paternaliter*), where the Spirit has prepared human beings in the Son, and the Son has led them to the Father.[42] Origen said that those who come to God the Father by way of the Word would exercise their single activity of knowing God by being united as a single Son in their knowledge of the Father.[43] In other words, by their union with the Son in heaven in a single body, they will see the Father by sharing in the Son's unique knowledge of the Father.

It may perhaps be asked whether this focus on the Father was to a certain extent encouraged by tendencies among some of the earlier writers to speak of the Son as in some sense *less* than the Father and thus more suited to appearing visibly in the theophanies of the Old Testament. On this view our desire for the vision of God could then reach 'beyond' the Son to the Father himself. It is certainly true that, in view of the Arian crisis, the earlier tendency to associate theophanies exclusively with the Son underwent a severe critique from such as Augustine.[44] It is also true that Nicene teaching about the Son's consubstantial equality with the Father encouraged the possibility of reading New Testament texts about the vision of heaven as visions of the Son. Augustine maintained that in the ultimate vision

41. E.g. *Ep.*, 147.31–32.
42. *Adversus Haereses*, 4.20.5; cf. 4.6.6.
43. *Commentarii in Ioannem*, 1.16.92.
44. *De Trinitate*, 2.

the Son is seen in his equality with the Father. Nor, on account of the unity of substance or essence of all three persons, did he exclude the Spirit from this vision. Augustine said that when Christ will have handed over the kingdom to the Father, we shall contemplate God, Father, Son and Holy Spirit, that when our happiness is full we shall see the three in whose image we are made, that when we see face to face we shall see the Trinity. Not that all focus on the Father is jettisoned in his Nicene exegesis. Augustine understood Christ's handing over of the kingdom to the Father to mean that he 'leads believers to a direct contemplation of God the Father' and refers 1 Jn 3.2 to a vision of the Father, though not one in which the Father is seen to the exclusion of Son and Spirit.[45] Naturally the Nestorian controversy could focus the theology of the beatific vision to some degree on the Son – the question would be whether the saints will see in Jesus a human person or a divine person.[46] Nevertheless, the Fathers supposed continuity between our imperfect contemplation of the Trinity in this life and a direct vision in heaven that is equally Trinitarian. Where they differed among themselves was whether this was a vision of the Trinitarian God in his very essence or in his activities only.

Given the unity of the divine persons in a single οὐσία, nature, substance or essence, or however the 'form of God' might be named, it would seem to be no great leap from asserting the heavenly vision of any divine person to asserting a vision of the divine essence. For Augustine, to see God 'just as he is' is indeed to have direct knowledge of God's 'form' (*species*) or 'substance' (*substantia*).[47] It is this that Moses and Paul would have glimpsed, however fleetingly. Not, however, that Augustine thought that God's being was thereby known exhaustively or comprehended. Never, he says, does anyone 'comprehend the fullness of God' (*Dei plenitudinem … comprehendit*).[48] Thus he distinguished vision itself from complete comprehension through vision. He gives an analogy from physical vision: someone may see an object when it is perceived by sight as present in any way at all, but that does not mean it is comprehended by sight in such a way that no part of it escapes one's notice.[49] In these words lie a basis for a distinction between *seeing* the essence of God in heaven, and *comprehending* the essence of God, which remains impossible for any creature.

No such distinction was suggested, however, by those Fathers who were more directly concerned with refuting the views of the fourth-century Arian, Eunomius, who evidently claimed to have full comprehension of the Father's οὐσία even in this life. To these Fathers, the concession to creatures of any vision of God's very being was perceived as a serious threat to divine incomprehensibility. Not only then did the heresy of Eunomius spur on Fathers such as Basil to seek out a more nuanced understanding of how human ideas and words can be used of God; it led them to respond that God is known not in his inaccessible οὐσία, but

45. Ibid., 1.3.15–17; 15.6.44.
46. Cf. Lossky, *Vision of God*, p. 82.
47. *De Genesi ad Litteram*, 12.37; *Ep.*, 147.31.
48. *Ep.*, 147.20.
49. Ibid., 147.21.

only in his 'powers' (δυνάμεις), 'condescension' (συγκατάβασις) or 'activities' or 'energies' (ἐνέργειαι). It has been a matter of debate whether or not several of the Fathers, including Basil, Gregory of Nazianzus and Gregory of Nyssa, meant to apply the inaccessibility of God's οὐσία to the next life as well as to this,[50] but it is beyond doubt that John Chrysostom[51] and Theodoret did so.[52] Theodoret, whose Antiochene Christology restricted the object of the saints' heavenly vision to the man Jesus rather than the Word, also made the object of vision not the divine οὐσία but a divine glory or splendour. Quite apart from its link in this case with a Christology that had become seen as incipiently Nestorian, Pope Gregory the Great disputed the whole approach on the grounds of the *simplicity* of the divine essence: since God's splendour and his nature were thus one and the same, to see his splendour was to see his very nature.[53] Not that Gregory thought that this vision of the divine nature did away with God's incomprehensibility: according to Gregory, we shall not see God exactly as he sees himself but, because of the weight of our creaturehood, our vision is only like his and not equal to it, our rest is both like his and unlike his, and we *imitate* his eternity.[54] Thus, as in Augustine, we meet some kind of distinction between vision and comprehension. Nevertheless, following the writings attributed to Dionysius the Areopagite,[55] both Maximus the Confessor[56] and John of Damascus[57] taught the *absolute* inaccessibility of God's οὐσία to creatures. Thus we have two basic approaches to the beatific vision among the Fathers, one in which God's essence is seen but not comprehended, and another in which he is seen only in his activities and never in his essence.[58]

Having briefly summarized patristic approaches to the doctrine of the beatific vision, we are now in a position to ask whether these are anywhere applied in the period to the knowledge of Christ. Did any Father thus anticipate Candidus's identification of a vision in Christ's earthly humanity with the saints' vision of God in heaven? The results of any investigation are admittedly meagre. We search in vain for at least a surviving text where Origen speaks of Christ's soul as in possession of heavenly contemplation in the period between its union with an earthly body and the resurrection. We search again in vain for Gregory of Nyssa speaking of the earthly or even heavenly Christ enjoying an endless progress in knowledge of God's activities, or of Augustine explicitly attributing to his human mind a vision of the divine *substance*. Moreover, the few texts that were proposed

50. See, e.g. Basil, *Contra Eunomium*, 1.2; Gregory of Nazianzus, *Orationes*, 28.4; Gregory of Nyssa, *De Beatitudinibus*, 6.

51. *De Incomprehensibili Dei Natura*, 1.6; 3.3; 5.4.

52. *In Eph.*, 2.

53. *Moralia in Job*, 3.18.90.

54. Ibid., 3.18.92–93.

55. *De Divinis Nominibus*, 2.11.

56. E.g. *Centuriae de Caritate*, 1.100.

57. E.g. *Expositio Fidei*, 4.

58. For a broader perspective on these issues, see A. Lévy, *Le créé et l'incréé: Maxime le confesseur et Thomas d'Aquin* (Bibliothèque Thomiste, 59; Paris: Vrin, 2006).

by early modern scholasticism in favour of the thesis came under critical scrutiny as early as the seventeenth century, and the majority were dismissed thanks to the work of Denys Pétau.[59]

Pétau's investigations allowed but a single passage from a single Father, which he said 'seems to indicate' the teaching.[60] This was Question 65 from Augustine's *De Diversis Quaestionibus LXXXIII*, a collection that covers those years when he was revising his opinion about the possibility of certain exceptional Christians enjoying a permanent vision of God in this life. It may be argued that, if Augustine wrote this particular question when he still allowed the apostles a vision in this life, it is surely unlikely that he denied it here to Christ.[61] Though this may present an historical argument that would help us to conclude that Augustine did attribute the beatific vision to Christ in this difficult text, at the same time it would undermine the authority of the text for later theologians, because the interpretation would rest on a thesis that Augustine was certainly to reject later on, namely, that the apostles had possessed a permanent vision of God during their lifetimes. However, Augustine may well have already given up that thesis, as Question 65 gives no sign that Augustine still entertained it. Moreover, even if he had given it up, the fact that he continued to suppose that Moses and Paul had fleeting glimpses of God's being in this life should still give us historical grounds for supposing that he must surely have granted the earthly Christ such glimpses *at the very least*.

In this question Augustine was giving an allegorical interpretation of Christ's raising of Lazarus (Jn 11.1–44). During the course of his exegesis, in which the dead Lazarus signifies the soul buried by sin, Augustine explained that the cloth covering Lazarus's face indicates that we (without naming any exceptions) cannot have 'full knowledge' (*plenam cognitionem*) of God in this life.[62] At this point he makes an unmistakeable mention of the beatific vision by quoting Paul's distinction between obscure vision in a mirror and vision face to face (1 Cor. 13.12). Jesus' command to remove the cloth, now that Lazarus has come out of the tomb, means that 'after this life all veils will be taken away, so that we may see face to face', a clear reference to 1 Corinthians. Now not only is Augustine speaking of the beatific vision, but very definitely also of Christ's human nature, since he immediately calls attention to the difference between the humanity 'which the Wisdom of God assumed, through which we are freed' and the humanity of all other human beings. This difference, he says, can be understood from the fact that Lazarus, unlike Jesus, was only released *after he had come out from the tomb*. Augustine interpreted this to mean that our souls, which now have only an obscure vision in a mirror, cannot be entirely free of ignorance until after the soul

59. *De Theologicis Dogmatibus*, 6, *De Incarnatione Verbi*, 11.4.5–7.

60. Ibid., 11.4.5.

61. Cf. T. J. van Bavel, *Recherches sur la Christologie de saint Augustin: L'humain et le divin dans le Christ d'après saint Augustin* (Fribourg: Éditions Universitaires Fribourg Suisse, 1954), p. 166.

62. *De Diversis Quaestionibus LXXXIII*, 65.

is released from the body. What this implies is that in our case it is only *after death* that the veils are removed and we can possess the beatific vision, the beatific vision thus being responsible for definitively removing defects of knowledge. However, things are different with Christ, and it seems *only* with Christ, who has no such defect. In contrast to the case of Lazarus, the cloth over the face of the one who was 'not ignorant' was instead found in the tomb – unlike Lazarus, Christ did not walk out from the tomb still needing to be released (Jn 20.5–7). Given that our being freed of ignorance is associated by Augustine with our coming to the beatific vision after death, it is implied that Christ's freedom from ignorance *even before death* is associated with a pre-mortem possession of the same vision.

It is, however, an exaggeration for Galtier and Jean-Marie Salgado to say that the earthly Christ's beatific vision is taught here *explicitly*,[63] a view already attributed to Pétau,[64] who in fact never claimed anything so strong. Nevertheless, though Augustine did not explicitly identify the beatific vision as the cause of Christ's lack of ignorance, the *implication* of his exegesis is that Christ already possessed the beatific vision before death.[65] That Augustine may, however, have subsequently changed his mind on this, as he had on the earthly vision of the apostles, has been suggested to some by what he said in answer to Question 75 in the same work (assuming that the two questions come in chronological order). Augustine says here that we shall be 'coheirs with Christ' (Rom. 8.17) when our bodies become immortal at the resurrection and we are like God, seeing him just as he is. However, he wonders in what sense we can be Christ's coheirs, given that God the Father is never going to die: if he lives on for ever, how can we inherit from him? Augustine replies with the following initial speculation: the Father, though he does not really die, can be *said* to die in a certain way. Alluding to 1 Corinthians 13.12, he says that the Father's 'death' is in fact the removal of our 'imperfect vision' of him by a 'perfect vision'.[66] However, we can only be Christ's coheirs if Christ too is an heir of the Father. Referring specifically in this respect to Christ's boyhood, in which Luke says he advanced in age and wisdom (2.52), Augustine draws the conclusion that Jesus too would have been heir through this same 'death' (that is, of the Father). This means that Christ would, like us, first of all possess in his humanity Paul's 'partial vision' and then afterwards come to perfect vision. However, Augustine qualified this because he was aware that 'piety' might not allow such progress in Christ from imperfect to perfect vision, and so he passed on to other possible speculative explanations of how we can be coheirs. Augustine evidently knew that 'pious understanding' might well not permit the idea of Christ having been ignorant, even as a boy, a view he was later to endorse

---

63. Galtier, *De Incarnatione ac Redemptione*, p. 256; J.-M. Salgado, 'La science du Fils de Dieu fait homme prises de position des Pères et de la Préscolastique (IIè-XIIè siècle)', *DC* 36 (1983): 180–286 (232).

64. L. Richard, 'Une texte de saint Augustin sur la vision intuitive du Christ', *RSR* 12 (1922): 85–7 (86).

65. Cf. van Bavel, *Recherches sur la Christologie de saint Augustin*, p. 166.

66. *De Diversis Quaestionibus LXXXIII*, 75.

more explicitly himself.[67] Whether or not in Question 65 he preferred the first speculation he gave on how we are coheirs, with its suggestion that Christ made progress in knowledge, or another or any at all is not a matter on which there has been any scholarly agreement.

Whatever Augustine's final preference, there is still the problem of whether or not the first *possible* view he gave in Question 75 contradicts Question 65's earlier position on Christ's pre-mortem possession of the beatific vision. Dubarle asserted there is no reason to suppose that Christ's passing from imperfect to perfect vision in Question 75 would take place at a different time from ours.[68] Augustine has already said we shall become coheirs at our resurrection and, on Dubarle's interpretation, Christ would then have received the beatific vision at his own resurrection. However, Augustine did talk of Christ's growth in knowledge during *boyhood* rather than over the whole course of his mortal life.[69] This may mean he was thinking of Christ's reception of perfect vision taking place after a period of juvenile advancement, in which case Christ would still have possessed the beatific vision at least during his *adult* earthly life. Lebreton was surely nearer the mark when he said that Augustine had in mind Christ progressing in the vision of God during his lifetime, that is, from imperfect to perfect vision.[70] On that reading, though, it is hard to know whether the first speculation expressed in Question 75 contradicts what Augustine thought when he wrote Question 65 or not, since the latter question has nothing to say on the *precise point during his earthly lifetime* when his perfect vision arrived. Nevertheless, however we interpret Question 75, Augustine's awareness that piety shrinks from attributing ignorance to Jesus allows us to conclude that he need not have made any definite departure from his earlier implication that the earthly Christ enjoyed the beatific vision.

The Holy Office's decree of 1918 on Christ's beatific vision, to which we referred in Chapter 1, had the effect of encouraging fresh investigations of the Fathers, as a result of which further texts were brought forward. None of them, however, made explicit mention even of the beatific vision of the saints, let alone Christ's. This meant that a text's advocate had to show that the author's claim about Christ, whatever it was, needed to be explained *theologically* as involving his beatific vision. We suggested in Chapter 2 that the overall picture of Christ in Scripture requires theological interpretation of this sort. What was proposed by some scholastics was that there were *particular sayings* of the Fathers that required it. However, even what these sayings claimed in themselves about Christ was disputed: did they even speak of a blessedness or knowledge particular to *Christ's humanity*? Leontius of Byzantium, for example, certainly spoke of Christ's glory 'according to the *spirit*',[71] but was this the glory of his human soul (to be

67. *De Peccatorum Meritis et Remissione*, 29.48.

68. Dubarle, 'La connaissance humaine du Christ', p. 8.

69. Van Bavel, *Recherches sur la Christologie de saint Augustin*, pp. 172–4.

70. J. Lebreton, *History of the Dogma of the Trinity from its Origins to the Council of Nicaea*, vol. 1: *The Origins* (London: Burns, Oates & Washbourne, 1939), p. 425 n.1.

71. Leontius of Byzantium, *Contra Nestorianos et Eutychianos*, 2.

explained in terms of the beatific vision)[72] or rather the glory of his *divinity*?[73] Again Leontius spoke of Christ's 'blessedness' (μακαριότης),[74] but was this the blessedness of his human soul,[75] or rather the blessedness of his divinity?[76] For his part, Jerome had declared that 'no human being, except him who for our salvation deigned to assume flesh, had full knowledge …'[77] For some this was a knowledge in Christ's humanity that had to be interpreted theologically as the beatific vision, but Galtier would not allow it even as specific testimony to knowledge in Christ's human nature. Jerome might be taken to be saying that Christ was the only human being to possess a specifically divine knowledge. Thus, without establishing that such an endowment belonged properly to Christ's human soul, one cannot even begin to argue that it must be explained theologically in terms of his beatific vision. And even were it established that a patristic text attributed to the earthly Christ something like an extensive knowledge of creation *in his humanity*, need that necessarily mean it could only be theologically interpreted in terms of the beatific vision? As we saw in Chapter 1, scholastics also spoke of an 'infused knowledge', which could be invoked as an alternative explanation of such texts. Moreover, should Augustine's commentary on Psalm 15.10[78] indeed imply that Christ had the beatific vision, did that mean he possessed it on earth,[79] or did it strictly imply no more than that he possessed it after his resurrection?[80] Galtier concluded in 1925 that no formal patristic witness had been successfully added by any of these efforts.[81]

A further passage from Augustine was brought to scholars' attention in 1951 by T. J. van Bavel, not so long before the theological interest in supporting Christ's beatific vision collapsed.[82] It comes from towards the end of Augustine's life, and explicitly endorses Christ's earthly beatific vision. Galot paid it the compliment of disputing this text and no other in his chief attack on the doctrine.[83] The passage occurs in the *Contra Maximinum*, a written reply to a prominent Arian bishop named Maximinus with whom Augustine had had a public debate that left him too little time to reply to his own satisfaction at the

---

72. A. M. Jugie, 'La béatitude et la science parfaite de l'âme de Jésus Viateur d'après Léonce de Byzance et quelques autres théologiens byzantins', *RSPT* 10 (1921): 548–59 (554–5).

73. Galtier, 'L'enseignement des Pères sur la vision béatifique dans le Christ', *RSR* 15 (1925): 54–68 (55–7).

74. *Contra Nestorianos et Eutychianos*, 2.

75. Jugie, 'La béatitude et la science parfaite', p. 554.

76. Galtier, 'L'enseignement des Pères', pp. 57–62.

77. *Ep.*, 36.15.

78. *Ennarationes in Psalmos*, 15.10.

79. Richard, 'Une texte de saint Augustin'.

80. 'L'enseignement des Pères', pp. 64–8.

81. Ibid., p. 68.

82. Van Bavel, *Recherches sur la Christologie de saint Augustin*, pp. 166–7.

83. 'Le Christ terrestre et la vision', p. 429 n.3.

end.[84] Holding the Son not to be equal to the Father but less than the Father, who alone was invisible, Maximinus applied to them his principle that, while lesser beings are seen by greater ones, greater beings are not seen by lesser ones. This meant that, while the Son was seen by the Father, the Father was not seen by the Son except in a qualified way. The invisible Father is then seen in a strict sense by no one, a claim Maximinus wanted to ground on Scriptural passages such as John 1.18. Augustine countered this by nuancing the interpretation of John's 'no one', so that it applies only to human beings in this life, with Christ as an exception – no earthly human being has seen God except the Son. Augustine does this first through an appeal to Christ's teaching that the *angels* really do see the Father's face (Mt. 18.10), before going on to the case of Christ himself, as witnessed in John 6.46:

> But with respect to what he says – 'Not that anyone has seen the Father except him who is from God: he has seen the Father' – 'anyone' can be referred to human beings. And because he who was then speaking in the flesh was a human being, he spoke thus as if to say, 'Not that anyone among human beings has seen the Father except me.'[85]

Galot protests that this vision is divine knowledge and, as we saw in Chapter 2, this is arguably the correct interpretation of the Johannine verse. However, for Galot to assert that this was *Augustine's* interpretation of it in the *Contra Maximinum* flies in the face of what Augustine actually says there. The important point is that Augustine very definitely takes Christ to be speaking here *in the flesh*, that is, according to his humanity, and this meant more for Augustine than that Christ was using a human voice or even mind to make his point. It meant that Jesus is asserting here not that he sees God in his divine nature (though he of course does so see him) but that he sees him *in his human nature*. Furthermore, although more recent scholarship is shy of broaching the issue,[86] it is clear that Augustine took this vision to be identical with the beatific vision. Immediately after explaining John 6.46, he turned to 1 Timothy 6.16, which, he says, does not rule out the *future possibility* of humans being able to see God but refers only to our inability in this life. That they will in fact see him Augustine then proves by citing 1 John 3.2. He thus made no essential distinction between Christ's earthly vision of the Father in his humanity and the beatific vision of the saints. The vision we shall have in heaven is the vision Christ had on earth. Here we have a patristic text that, on its own terms, clearly anticipates Candidus's pre-scholastic

---

84. For an account of the dispute, see W. A. Sumruld, *Augustine and the Arians: The Bishop of Hippo's Encounters with Ulfilan Arianism* (Cranbury, NJ and London: Associated, 1994), pp. 90–119.

85. *Contra Maximinum Haereticum Arianorum Episcopum*, 2.9.

86. J. T. Ernst, *Die Lehre der Hochmittelalterlichen Theologen von der Vollkommenen Erkenntnis Christi: Ein Versuch zur Auslegung der klassischen Dreiteilung: Visio Beata, Scientia Infusa und Scientia Acquisita* (Freiburg etc: Herder, 1971), pp. 27–8, 51–2.

identification of a vision in the earthly Christ's humanity with the heavenly vision of the saints.

Far then from being a notion that arises out of the heresy of Nestorianism, Christ's earthly beatific vision may in fact be traced, however briefly, in the tradition of the orthodox Fathers. This suggests that, although it can hardly be construed as a binding 'consensus' of patristic teaching, its appearance in so pre-eminent a Father as Augustine will have *some* level of authority for a Catholic theologian. The strength of this theological authority may, however, be questioned on account of the nature or quality of the texts' exegesis. For example, the authority of what is implied by Augustine's Question 65 for Christ's knowledge has been altogether rejected by some on account of the allegorical nature of its exegesis.[87] In his study of the teachings of the Fathers on Christ's knowledge, Moloney declines even to consider the text because its allegorical method is so unfamiliar to us today.[88] As regards Augustine's more literal exegesis of John 6.46 in the *Contra Maximinum*, we have already noted that a divine rather than human interpretation of Christ's vision in this verse is arguably the correct one. Indeed Augustine himself had previously followed a divine interpretation of this verse at a time when he was arguably at the height of his theological powers.[89] It may of course be replied to these concerns that rejecting Augustine's exegesis does not necessarily cancel out the theological authority of the doctrine Augustine propounded by it. Catholic theologians routinely accept the Fathers' Nicene and Chalcedonian Christology without thereby endorsing all their diverse exegesis, not even all the particular instances of exegesis they variously make in support of the Nicene and Chalcedonian dogmas. Likewise they could accept the authority of Augustine's teaching on Christ's earthly beatific vision without thereby endorsing the particular exegesis by which he supported it. However, it might still be urged that, given how slight the quantity of patristic evidence is in this case, and the perception that such slight witness is so closely tied to particular instances of questionable exegesis, the theological authority of the texts can be nothing but minimal.

Opponents of the thesis can argue then not only from the quality of the texts but from their admittedly meagre quantity. This might well be a very strong point, if it could be reasonably expected that, given the truth of the thesis, the Fathers would definitely have borne frequent witness to it. Against this, it might be urged that the Fathers can hardly be subjected to such expectations. It is indisputable that their attentions were focused elsewhere all during the patristic period, and in Christology on questions that are evidently more basic. Before the fourth century, the general topic of Christ's knowledge was scarcely the object of any sustained

---

87. So A.-M. Dubarle, 'La science humaine du Christ selon Saint Augustin', *RSPT* 29 (1940): 244–63 (248); 'La connaissance humaine du Christ d'après Saint Augustin', *ETL* 18 (1941): 5–25 (11).

88. 'Approaches to Christ's Knowledge in the Patristic Era' in T. Finan and V. Twomey (eds), *Studies in Patristic Christology* (Dublin: Four Courts, 1998), pp. 37–66 (49–50).

89. *Tractatus in Ioannem*, 26.9.

consideration. Even once it came onto the Fathers' agenda, it generally did so as the need to oppose the thesis of Christ's ignorance as propounded by Arianism and Nestorianism, and later still by a group known as the 'Agnoetes', a task several Fathers then took up with vigour.[90] In contrast to this, any attempt at a more theoretical explanation of the communication between Christ's divine and human minds seems to have been far from the Fathers' concerns.

One reason for this may be that the articulation of the thesis itself presupposes the development and acceptance of, as well as serious reflection on, an adequate framework for understanding Christ's constitution. The Chalcedonian framework of one person in two natures, together with Leo the Great's teaching in his *Tome* (which was received at the Council) that each nature has its own distinct activity,[91] is something that was developed only over time and was not immediately accepted everywhere. Though it can hardly be claimed that its teaching was wholly unanticipated, the Council's definition was made only in the middle of the fifth century. Moreover, while its doctrine was immediately accepted in the West, it was much disputed in the East and only widely taken on board there by the end of the seventh century, and then not by everyone. In this situation one can hardly expect sustained theoretical reflection on the relationship between Christ's human and divine knowledge to be widespread. In Chapter 2 it was suggested that the thesis of Christ's beatific vision properly arises as an attempt to seek theological understanding of how his human knowing has the benefit of divine knowledge. The very articulation of this thesis therefore presupposes that developments in patristic thought had already confirmed not only the existence of extraordinary knowledge in Christ's human mind, but also the very possession of the divine mind and a human mind by the single person of Jesus Christ in the first place.

One crucial element then in these more basic developments is confirmation of the reality of Christ's human soul and mind. Without the presupposition of a genuine human mind, Christ's beatific vision can hardly be asserted at all, since this vision is, by a definition more careful than Weinandy's, knowledge inhering *in a created mind*. As we have seen, in its attribution of ignorance to the man Jesus, the Antiochene tradition carefully maintained the reality of his human psychology, though tending towards making out of it a second subject in addition to the divine Word. In contrast, the theological traditions of Alexandria concentrated more on the unity of Christ's person, but at the risk of an insufficient appreciation of his human psychology.[92] While the Alexandrian approach was complicated by disagreements between the Arians and their opponents on the divine status of Christ, there was another element shared in common by the Arians and at least some of their opponents on the constitution of Christ, which

90. See J. M. Salgado, 'La science du Fils de Dieu fait homme. Prises de position des Pères et du pré-scolastique, IIe-XIIe siècle', *DC* 36 (1983): 180–286; and Moloney, 'Approaches to Christ's Knowledge in the Patristic Era'.

91. *Tomus ad Flavianum, Lectis dilectionis tuae*, 4.

92. Cf. A. Grillmeier and T. Hainthaler, *Christ in Christian Tradition*, vol. 2/2 (trans. J. Cawte and P. Allen; London: Mowbray; Louisville, KY: WJK, 1995), p. 170.

would definitely have prevented the question of the beatific vision from being raised at all. This was the absence from Christ's humanity of any human soul or mind. On this view, the Word of God took to himself a human body, while the Word himself played the role that would ordinarily be taken by a human mind. No human mind was assumed by the Word, and without a human mind there was of course no danger of introducing a second subject into the incarnate Christ. However, without a human mind there was also no possibility of attributing the beatific vision to Christ, nor even the possibility of asking about the communication between his divine and human minds. This would remain a consistent feature of Arian theology, but came to be definitively rejected in the Nicene tradition, where the position was principally associated with Apollinarius of Laodicea, whose followers were condemned at the Council of Constantinople in 381. In support of the distinct reality of Christ's human psychology, the Fathers could appeal, for example, to Scriptural texts that spoke of Christ's knowledge in such a way that they could not be applied to divine knowledge (e.g. Mk 13.32).[93] Subsequent heretical positions, however, such as that of the anti-Nestorian Eutyches, were also to imply no true human psychology in Christ. Eutyches' Monophysite theology confused the divinity and humanity of Christ into a single nature where he was no longer consubstantial with us, and this was condemned at Chalcedon. The challenge had thus been set by these developments to appreciate the fullness of Christ's human psychology without thereby introducing into his constitution a second person. According to patristic scholarship, this was a challenge that was hardly well met.[94]

The lack of sustained reflection among the Fathers on the details of Christ's human psychology can be partly explained by their unwavering attention to the supremacy of his divine nature and person. But here again in Christ's divinity we have a necessary presupposition for asking about the access of Christ's human mind to his divine mind. One can hardly ask about the relationship between his divine and human minds unless one has confirmed his possession not only of a human mind but also of the divine one. In what sense Christ was said to be divine was the major theological dispute of the fourth century, where the Nicenes argued against anything but the full divinity of Christ, who was true God just as the Father was true God. The Arians based their contention that the Word was a creature, albeit of the highest perfection, partly on what Scripture had to say about Christ's knowledge. For example, the fact that he said of the timing of 'that day or that hour' that was to come 'no one knows, not the angels in heaven nor the Son, but only the Father' (Mk 13.32; cf. Mt. 24.36) was taken to indicate the Son's ignorance and hence creaturely status in knowledge and thus in being.[95]

93. E.g. Gregory of Nyssa, *Antirrheticus Adversus Apollinarium*, 24.

94. E.g. Grillmeier, *Christ in Christian Tradition*, 2/2, p. 521.

95. On Arian arguments, see K. Madigan, *The Passions of Christ in High-Medieval Thought: An Essay on Christological Development* (Oxford and New York: OUP, 2007), pp. 11–22.

Taking their cue from elsewhere in Scripture (e.g. Jn 10.30), the Fathers argued in response from the Son's equality in being with the Father to a fullness of knowledge that excluded ignorance of 'that day' when the last judgement would take place. The source of Christ's knowledge of the last day was thus clearly divine. As Athanasius wrote, 'As divine, being in the Father as Word and Wisdom, he knows it, and there is nothing he does not know.'[96] Arguments of this kind put forward by the Fathers might be Trinitarian – having perfect knowledge of the Father, the Son has all the knowledge of things the Father has, a knowledge he receives from the Father.[97] Other arguments were based on the Son's role in creation, alluding to the prologue of John's Gospel or to the identification of Christ as the Wisdom of God (1 Cor. 1.24), the agent of creation in the Old Testament (e.g. Wis. 9.9). Given that all things are made through him, the last day is also his creation, and like anyone else he has knowledge of what he has made.[98] The Fathers' paramount concern for Christ's divine knowledge is also manifest in how they habitually interpreted Christ's knowledge and vision of the Father in the Gospels: as we observed in the last chapter, this is divine knowledge received by the Son through his being begotten by the Father, divine knowledge that manifests his divine origin in the Father. This was, for example, the approach of Cyril.[99] Moreover, though Augustine referred Christ's vision to his humanity in the *Contra Maximinum*, as we noted above, in his work on John's Gospel he never did so – his concern was all for Christ's *divine* knowledge.[100]

The *source* of Christ's extraordinary knowledge then was his divinity, not his humanity. The Fathers did not regard an unaided human mind as having the power to know the future. Viewing the human mind of Christ in the abstract, so to speak, that is, prescinding from the union of his humanity with the Word, there was no problem in attributing ignorance to it.[101] However, given the fact of the incarnation, they did not regard Christ's human mind as unaffected by his divine knowledge. One can spot this, for example, in the way they argue from the fact that Christ shows knowledge of the events leading up to the last day to the conclusion that he must have knowledge of the last day, since the last day follows on immediately afterwards.[102] From the fact that his knowledge of

---

96. *Contra Arianos*, 3.46.

97. Basil, *Ep.*, 236; Didymus the Blind, *De Trinitate*, 3.22; John Chrysostom, *Homilia in Matthaeum*, 77.1; Cyril, *De Sancta et Consubstantiali Trinitate*, 6.

98. Basil, *Ep.*, 8.6; Cyril, *Thesaurus de Sancta et Consubstantiali Trinitate*, 22; John Chrysostom, *Homilia*, 77.1; Jerome, *Tractatus in Marci Evangelium*, 10; Ambrose, *De Fide ad Gratianum*, 2.11.94; 5.16.199.

99. E.g. *Commentarii in Ioannem*, 1.10.

100. E.g. *Tractatus in Ioannem*, 40.5. See C. Harrison, *Beauty and Revelation in the Thought of St. Augustine* (Oxford: Clarendon, 1992), pp. 212–13.

101. Cf. Gregory of Nazianzus, *Orationes*, 30.15; Maximus the Confessor, *Quaestiones et Dubia*, 66; John of Damascus, *Expositio Fidei*, 3.21.

102. Athanasius, *Contra Arianos*, 3.4; Gregory of Nazianzus: *Orationes*, 30.15; Cyril, *Thesaurus*, 22.

penultimate events is clearly in his human mind, since he is communicating this knowledge humanly to his disciples, Most has argued that the Fathers imply his knowledge of the last day to be in his human mind too.[103] Nowhere, moreover, do they explain Mark 13.32 by isolating Christ's human mind from the divine, having him know the time in his divinity but not in his humanity. Certainly they do refer such verses to the humanity of Christ rather than his divinity, as we saw above in connection with the rejection of Apollinarianism – it is as human that the Son is said not to know the day and hour. Nevertheless, they overwhelmingly react against interpreting this as meaning the total absence of this knowledge from his humanity. This is perhaps why Augustine, though he discusses it in a number of places, never himself refers Mark 13.32 to Christ speaking as man.[104] It was Gregory the Great who introduced a distinction that nicely combined the position of those who referred the verse to Christ's humanity and the position of those who preferred not to. In a letter to Eulogius, patriarch of Constantinople, written at the very end of the sixth century about the Agnoetes' ascription of ignorance of the last day to Christ, the Pope declared that Christ possessed knowledge of it *in* his human nature, but this knowledge was not *of* his human nature. According to Gregory, to deny that Christ had this knowledge in his humanity, as did the Agnoetes, was unacceptable. Though well aware of the Alexandrian origins of the Agnoetes among those who regarded Chalcedon as making too many concessions to Nestorius, Gregory perceived the anti-Nestorian Agnoetes as promoting an isolation of Christ's human and divine minds that was itself tantamount to Nestorianism, and he said so: 'You cannot be an Agnoete without being a Nestorian.'[105] Contrary to Agnoetist intentions, Gregory held that ascribing real ignorance to Christ could only end up introducing into him a second person.

In no way then can it be doubted that the Fathers took Christ's human mind to have benefit from divine knowledge. The general tendency among the Fathers was to exclude all ignorance from the human mind of Christ and regard it as endowed with knowledge of all things, the human mind benefiting from the divine knowledge of the Creator. There may be exceptions,[106] and individual cases have been subject to some debate,[107] but this holds true in general and becomes the orthodox consensus by the end of the sixth century. However, the thesis of Christ's beatific vision presupposes more than that the earthly Christ had a human mind in receipt of a divine communication; it presupposes also that this

---

103. *The Consciousness of Christ*, pp. 114–15.

104. Cf. Moloney, 'Approaches to Christ's Knowledge in the Patristic Era', p. 49.

105. *Epistula ad Eulogium, Sicut aqua frigida.*

106. E.g. Irenaeus, *Adversus Haereses*, 2.28.6 (but see 2.28.8); Ambrose, *De incarnationis Dominicae Sacramento*, 7.72, 74 (but see *De Fide ad Gratianum*, 5.18.221). See Moloney, 'Approaches to Christ's Knowledge in the Patristic Era', pp. 38, 47–8.

107. For arguments that neither text is in fact an exception, see Most, *Consciousness of Christ*, pp. 96, 116; and for a summary of differing classic positions on the development of Cyril's teaching, see p. 107.

communication took place by a human knowing in the human mind distinct from the divine knowing in the divine mind.

A quite different account, however, of the communication of Christ's divine knowledge had emerged during the sixth century among those who rejected Chalcedon's 'in two natures' and Leo's two activities as too near to Nestorianism, as dividing the natures rather than uniting them. Severus of Antioch insisted on speaking, as Cyril had done at first, of a single nature of the incarnate Word, corresponding to his single person or hypostasis. While rejecting the view of Eutyches that Christ's humanity was somehow swallowed up by his divinity and not consubstantial with us, Severus's party refused to draw the conclusion from the reality of Christ's human mind that it had its own proper knowing, different from that of the divinity. Rather, a single person and nature meant a single activity and knowledge.[108] This can be seen in the distinctive way Severans like Anthimus of Constantinople and Theodosius of Alexandria argued against the attribution of ignorance to Christ by the Agnoetes, who otherwise were also followers of Severus and Alexandrian in theological orientation. To exclude all ignorance from his rational soul, Anthimus and Theodosius argued not only from the hypostatic union but also brought forward the language of 'one nature' extended through 'one activity' to 'one wisdom' and 'one knowledge'.[109] Though Christ has a human mind, it has no human knowing of its own but had been filled from the first moment of the incarnation with divine omniscience, and thus was ignorance excluded. As Anthimus put it, Christ had 'one and the same knowledge according to his divinity and according to his humanity'.[110] To acknowledge a distinct human knowledge would, alleged Theodosius, be foolish and ungodly.[111] How the finite human mind can work with infinite divine knowledge does not seem to have been a problem for them, and the human mind does not really 'work' in a way proper to itself at all. There is then no place in this view for the beatific vision. If the beatific vision, though quite extraordinary, is proper to a creaturely mind, and if Christ's human mind has no knowledge proper to it but only the divine knowledge, Christ can have no beatific vision, even in heaven. The divine knowledge simply leaves no room for it. From a Severan perspective, to ask whether Christ had the beatific vision would indeed be a Nestorian question.

In contrast, those who remained loyal to Chalcedon and the *Tome* of Leo would in principle be committed to the position that the two natures of the one person meant two distinct activities, one human and one divine. However, without clarification of the Chalcedonian position over against that of Severus, it was difficult for the Fathers to negotiate their way through a theological account of Christ's human knowledge. This can be illustrated by the case of Fulgentius, who became bishop of Ruspe in North Africa in the first decade of the sixth

108. Severus of Antioch, *Liber Contra Impium Grammaticum*, 3.31.

109. For the Severans on Christ's knowledge, see Grillmeier, *Christ in Christian Tradition*, 2/2, pp. 362–74.

110. *Sermo ad Iustinianum*.

111. *Tomus ad Theodoram Augustam*.

century. He has in fact been suggested as teaching Christ's earthly beatific vision, but only after a confused fashion.[112] He has also sometimes been judged to hold a position on Christ's knowledge similar to that of Severus and his followers, though Pétau had thought he clearly distinguished divine and human knowledge in Christ.[113] Certainly the fact that he spoke in his writing to the Arian King of the Vandals, Thrasamund, of Christ's growth in knowledge indicates that he taught that Christ really did have human knowledge that was distinct from the divine.[114] On that score he was no Severan. However, when he considers Christ's extraordinary knowledge of his divinity in a reply to a question put by the deacon Ferrandus, he is more susceptible of being interpreted on this point in a roughly Severan fashion. It was for reasons of this kind that Galtier barred Fulgentius from consideration as a witness to Christ's beatific vision.[115] However, by the time the Severan reading of Fulgentius had been successfully challenged in the 1970s, interest in securing patristic support for Christ's vision had already waned.[116]

Fulgentius's reply is really the only truly extended treatment a Father makes about Christ's knowledge, and in that respect is more easily compared with the early medieval Candidus's treatise on whether Christ saw the Father. Fulgentius's text may have been known to Candidus, as it was certainly known to his teacher, Alcuin.[117] As with Candidus, Fulgentius was concerned with Christ's knowledge in his humanity. Fulgentius was asked a different question from Candidus, however: whether Christ had a full knowledge *of his own divinity* in his human soul, or whether, just as he did not see God with bodily eyes, so he also did not see or 'comprehend' the divine essence in his rational soul, in case something created might thereby have grasped the Creator.[118] Fulgentius was definitely aware that the distinction between Creator and creature demonstrates that the Creator is 'incomprehensible' (*incomprehensibilem*) and inexplicable to a created intellect. Nevertheless he emphasized that Christ's soul differs from all other created things in that it is one with the only-begotten Word, who is equal to the Father. He was thus wary of saying that there was some part in which Christ did not have knowledge of the whole Father and of himself and the Holy Spirit, asserting that it is alien to a healthy faith to say that Christ did not have a full knowledge of his divinity in his human soul.[119] Fulgentius backed this up by highlighting the role of the Holy Spirit. When it is said that God 'does not give the Spirit by measure' (Jn 3.34), this means that the *fullness* of the Holy Spirit is given by the Father to the Son, whereas we only receive *of* that fullness. Now Christ cannot *as God*

112. A. Michel, 'Science de Jésus-Christ', *DTC* 14 (1941), cols. 1628–65 (1635). Cf. Salgado, 'La science du Fils de Dieu fait homme', p. 250.

113. *De Theologicis Dogmatibus*, 6, *De Incarnatione Verbi*, 11.3.

114. *Ad Trasimundum Regem Vandalorum*, 1.8.

115. *De Incarnatione ac Redemptione*, pp. 256–7.

116. Ernst, *Die Lehre der Hochmittelalterlich Theologen*, pp. 35–9.

117. See Alcuin's *De Fide Sanctae Trinitatis et de Incarnatione Christi*.

118. *Epistula 14, Ad Ferrandum Diaconum de Quinque Quaestionibus*, 25.

119. Ibid., 26.

receive the Spirit, since the Spirit proceeds from him as God (Fulgentius follows Augustine on the Spirit's procession from the Father and the Son). Insofar as he is truly God then, Christ *gives* the fullness of the Spirit, but receives it insofar as he is truly *human*, and thus he is able to give the Spirit (by measure) to others.[120]

Having established that Christ received the fullness of the Spirit in his humanity, Fulgentius asks who this Spirit is. He drew his answer from the prophet Isaiah (11.1–2): he is (among other things) the Spirit of wisdom and under-standing and knowledge. Fulgentius concluded that Christ thus had a fullness of wisdom and knowledge not only in his divinity but also in his humanity. Should any of this fullness be removed from his humanity, Christ would then have received the Spirit *by measure*. So where the Spirit is *not* given by measure, that is, in the soul of Christ, 'there is full knowledge of the immeasurable divinity' (*plena sit divinitatis immensae notitia*).[121] According to Fulgentius, the fullness of truth goes hand in hand with the fullness of grace. Full knowledge of the divine nature cannot be lacking to the soul that is hypostatically united with the Word. Just as the man Jesus Christ is God in a way uniquely his, so he has a unique knowledge in his humanity of his full divinity. Were the knowledge in Christ's human soul to be a lesser knowledge of the divine nature, he would instead have not complete wisdom, but only a participation in it.[122] There is no way that Fulgentius wanted to characterize the knowledge in Christ's soul as a *participation* in Christ's divine knowledge, and here we can begin to see why Fulgentius can be interpreted as insufficiently distinguishing the human knowledge that resides in Christ's finite intellect from the infinite knowledge that belongs to the divine nature. Fulgentius was worried that, by giving Christ only a partial knowledge of his divinity, even in his created human intellect, Christ would be left on the level of a participant in Christ (that is, on our level) rather than as the Christ himself. But the true faith, he says, confesses Christ as Most High not only in his divinity, but also in his humanity.

Any suspicion that Fulgentius held the exact doctrine of Severus is dispelled by his expression of doubt that Christ knew his divinity in his soul in the same way that his divine nature has knowledge of itself. He confessed himself unsure whether to affirm that the human knowledge took place in the same way as the divine, or whether he should instead say that, while Christ knew as much in his humanity as he did in his divinity, he did not thereby know it in the same way as the divine nature knew it.[123] Fulgentius knew he had to make some such distinction between Christ's human and divine knowledge, because while the divine nature is by nature identical with its own divine knowledge (on account of divine simplicity), nothing of the sort can be said of the human soul. The knowledge in Christ's soul takes his divine nature for its object, but at the same time knowing that it itself, that is, the created soul, is not identical with the divine

120. Ibid., 27–8.
121. Ibid., 29.
122. Ibid., 30.
123. Ibid., 31.

nature. The same cannot be said, however, of Christ's divine knowledge, which instead has for its object that which it itself is, namely, the divine nature. Christ's two knowledges can be distinguished then by the fact that, though Christ has a full knowledge of the Trinity in his soul, his soul does not become one nature with the Trinity.

By the standards of later scholastic debate, which in fact took its cue from Fulgentius's text, his is hardly to be judged an adequate way to distinguish Christ's divine and human knowledge. Even Moloney's claim that for Fulgentius the knowledge in Christ's soul is not an 'exhaustive' knowledge of the Father seems to read more of later scholastic doctrine into Fulgentius's text than can strictly be found there.[124] There seems to be no sense in which Fulgentius is backing off from a knowledge in Christ's humanity that has a full comprehension of the divine essence, as later scholastics like Aquinas would do, however aware he was of the fundamental distinction between Creator and creature, to whom the Creator is incomprehensible. Nevertheless, need this inadequacy prevent one from asking whether Fulgentius taught Christ's beatific vision, even if after a relatively confused fashion? Though he does not distinguish the beatific vision from divine knowledge with the precision of a later age, it seems that he nevertheless made the distinction between Christ's divine knowledge and his extraordinary human knowledge sufficiently to ask whether he identified the latter as the beatific vision on his own terms, if not on those of later scholastic precision.

It is interesting that nowhere in the letter does Fulgentius quote those passages from John that speak of Christ's vision. This may be because, being familiar with Augustine's work on John, he knew that Augustine there always referred these to knowledge according to Christ's divinity. Nevertheless, there is no doubt that Fulgentius was happy to speak of the fullness of knowledge in Christ's soul as a 'vision'. In fact, following Augustine's contributions on the vision of God, he is happy to speak of *any* genuine knowledge of God in terms of vision – in spiritual matters, to see something is to grasp, understand or know it.[125] He concurred with Augustine that God who is Spirit cannot be seen by bodily eyes, even the bodily eyes of Jesus. God has promised the vision of himself by grace not to bodily eyes but to the rational soul. Hence, any holy soul with some knowledge of God has to the same extent received the 'grace of inner vision' (*internae visionis ... gratiam*) of him.[126] On this account, Fulgentius can hardly deny that the fullness of knowledge in Christ's soul is a vision of God – indeed, it must surely be a perfect one. Nevertheless, unlike Candidus, he did not explicitly say so.

Fulgentius did, however, bring up the beatific vision of the saints twice in his reply to Ferrandus's question. The second time was when he was arguing that we should not be afraid of confessing that Christ has knowledge of his full divinity in his humanity, just because we fear that might entail the madness of rendering

124. *The Knowledge of Christ*, p. 48.
125. *Ad Ferrandum*, 34.
126. Ibid., 31.

his human soul consubstantial with the divine nature.[127] Fulgentius seems to want to say that this knowledge will not entail Christ's soul being divine by nature, just as our beatific vision will not entail our souls being divine by nature. Recalling that Paul says that now we know in part but then we shall know as we are known, and citing 1 John 3.2, Fulgentius asserted that to the extent we shall see, to that extent shall we know. Our future knowledge he explains as the soul's vision of the divinity in which the Trinity offers itself to the just to be seen, such that for the soul 'that unceasing vision of the divinity is its unfailing fullness of beatitude' (*illa divinitatis indesinens visio, ipsa sit beatitudinis indeficiens plenitudo*). To the extent that we see, to that extent are we given the grace to be able to see. Where Fulgentius is going with this is to make the point that, even in the beatific vision, we shall not be consubstantial with the divine nature. Just as we see many different things with our bodily eyes which are not one with our flesh by nature, so when we see God, though we shall be 'like' him by imitating his righteousness, we shall not have a unity of nature with him.

Fulgentius's argument in support of the fact that Christ's fullness of knowledge does not render his soul divine by nature rests on presupposing at least a close similarity between the fullness of knowledge Christ possesses on earth and our future knowledge in heaven. The difference between his singular knowledge and ours appears to consist only in the fact that, while he possesses the fullness of grace, grace is granted to others by measure. Fulgentius had already spoken of the relationship between Christ's knowledge and ours the first time he mentioned the beatific vision in the letter, where he calls it the 'grace of vision' which will replace the 'grace of faith'.[128] At that point he was arguing that Christ had the fullness of the Spirit and others a share in his fullness. He makes it plain that this applies not only to grace in this life but also to grace in the next. Not only do those who receive the grace of faith receive not the fullness but *of* Christ's fullness, so will those who receive the grace of vision. Even in heaven we still will not have received the fullness itself, but will be filled by receiving of that fullness which always belongs only to Christ. Fulgentius thus conceived of our beatific vision as a sharing by measure in the fullness of Christ's knowledge in his humanity. There seems to be no attempt to establish a qualitative distinction between the knowledge of Christ's soul and our vision, as there was an already established distinction between faith and sight. In the absence of such a distinction, the easiest way to read Fulgentius is as implying that, on account of receiving the fullness of the Spirit in his humanity, the earthly Christ uniquely possessed in his soul the full height of the vision we shall receive from him by measure in heaven. Fulgentius's account, albeit wanting in clarity, seems explicable on its own less than perspicacious terms only by way of Christ always possessing the beatific vision.

From the case of Fulgentius we can appreciate that, without clarification on how the Chalcedonian tradition was to be distinguished on the matter of Christ's

---

127. Ibid., 33.
128. Ibid., 29.

knowledge from the Severan, a clear and unambiguous theory of his earthly vision was out of the question. Galtier viewed Eulogius and Maximus the Confessor to some degree in the same light as he viewed Fulgentius.[129] In other words, neither sufficiently established a proper distinction between Christ's human and divine knowledge on the basis of which one could claim that their teaching about Christ's knowledge should be interpreted as his beatific vision. Now it must be conceded that their refutations of Agnoetism were indeed up to a point similar to the refutations offered by the Severans. Eulogius declared: 'Christ's humanity too, which has been united to the inaccessible and essential wisdom in one hypostasis, cannot be in ignorance of anything, present or future …'[130] And on the issue of Christ's knowledge Maximus wrote that there was in the humanity a knowledge of 'all things', which came to it not by its own nature but by its union with the Word. This teaching he illustrated with an image:

> Just as iron in the fire has all the properties of fire, since it both glows and burns, yet in its nature remains iron and not fire, so too the humanity of the Lord, insofar as it was united with the Word, knew all things and displayed attributes proper to God. However, insofar as his human nature is considered as not united to the Word, it is said to be ignorant.[131]

A Severan, however, could easily have interpreted the fire in the iron as the presence of a strictly divine knowledge in the human mind. It was for reasons such as this that Galtier was doubtful about admitting such a text as witness to the beatific vision.

However, if we compare the replies to the Agnoetist position of Eulogius and Maximus with those given by the Severans, there is an undeniable difference. While all opponents of the Agnoetes appealed to the hypostatic union as the source of there being no ignorance in Christ's human mind, Eulogius and Maximus did not repeat the further Severan argument that there is only one knowledge in Christ. This is doubtless because they did not adhere to the Severan position on Christ's knowledge and activity, but instead held with Leo the Great that each of Christ's natures has its own proper activity. However, it was manifestly not the intention of Eulogius to speculate on exactly *how* Christ's human mind, with its own proper activity, had the benefit of divine knowledge, but merely to refute the Agnoetes. Maximus's Chalcedonian commitment surely means that the fiery quality of the iron is rightly interpreted as the human mind benefiting from the divine mind through the presence of a distinct human knowledge. However, it is true that neither Maximus nor John of Damascus after him pursued speculation on the exact character of the impact of Christ's divine knowledge on his human mind, what John called an 'enrichment' of Christ's humanity,[132] despite their

129. *De Incarnatione ac Redemptione*, p. 257 n.2.
130. Eulogius is quoted in Photius, *Bibliotheca*, 230.
131. *Quaestiones et Dubia*, 66.
132. *Expositio Fidei*, 3.21.

commitment to Leo's principle.[133] That opponents of Monoenergism saw the two activities as involving two distinct activities of knowledge is beyond doubt,[134] but perhaps they were wary of opening up a new speculative debate about the details of Christ's humanity that did not press itself upon them. Certainly, in the period between Eulogius and Maximus, the wider controversy about Christ's activities had become focused on whether or not he had one *will* or two, with Maximus the champion of the latter position, rather than directly on Christ's *knowledge* as such.

In the light of this wider, complex picture of development, which encompassed confirmation of the reality of Christ's divine knowledge, his human mind and his human knowledge, it can hardly be surprising that patristic witness to Christ's distinct vision of the Father in his human nature was so slight. Hence, any objection to the thesis on the grounds that its patristic support is meagre loses any weight it might have had in defeating the thesis. What we find in the Tradition of the Fathers more generally is of a piece with the Chalcedonian reading of Scripture we followed in the last chapter: Christ's distinct human and divine knowing do not exist in isolation from one another but rather the human enjoys the benefit of the divine. The appearance, however brief, in the writings of the Fathers of Christ's earthly vision of the Father in his human mind only serves to confirm the possibility, which we suggested in Chapter 2, that such a vision can help us make theological sense of the continuity between Christ's human and divine minds. Should the Fathers, or at least even one or two of them, have thrown their weight behind an alternative theory, that would surely have counted for something significant in favour of the alternative theory and against Christ's beatific vision. However, though the Fathers are almost entirely silent about this vision, they were certainly not in the business of actively advocating an alternative account of the impact of his divine knowledge on his human mind. Thus, if the Fathers can be supposed to offer support to any theory at all, it can only be to the earthly Christ's beatific vision.

133. See D. Bathrellos, *The Byzantine Christ: Person, Nature, and Will in the Christology of Saint Maximus the Confessor* (Oxford and New York: OUP, 2004), pp. 176–89.

134. John of Damascus, *Expositio Fidei*, pp. 315–18.

Chapter 4

'IT'S NOT GOOD THEOLOGY!'

We concluded in Chapter 2 that the overall biblical presentation of Christ the Teacher calls for some kind of theological explanation of how his human mind benefits from divine knowledge, a point with which a Chalcedonian opponent of Christ's beatific vision can easily agree.[1] However, following those hints from the Fathers examined in Chapter 3, we ourselves intend to explore the possibility of such an account being provided by the attribution of heavenly knowledge to the earthly Christ. This amounts to saying that, while the thesis of Christ's beatific vision on earth may not be contained in Scripture in any very obvious way, it does have a solid support there, a foundation on which a speculative theory of his beatific vision can be built.[2] This is consistent with the fact that the neoscholastics did not generally reckon the earthly Christ's vision *de fide*.[3] The majority held that, short of a magisterial pronouncement comparable to Nicaea's ὁμοούσιον, a Catholic theologian could not be so confident as to say that God has revealed such a thing to faith. It is certainly the case that some older theologians had thought it *de fide* or, being personally convinced that the Church had progressed to a point where a definition was ready to be made, had reckoned the thesis 'proximate to faith'.[4] Again, it is certainly true that some of those who have more recently reacted against the rejection of Christ's beatific vision have likewise dubbed it proximate to faith.[5] Nevertheless, Billot, Galtier, Garrigou and the majority of neoscholastics were content to count it a matter of theology – of the understanding of faith – rather than of faith itself.

Opponents of the thesis, however, are convinced not only that it makes no bold appearance in Scripture and Tradition: they also take the view that as a theological theory it has 'no support' there, as Galot puts it.[6] This implies more

---

1. E.g. Galot, 'Le Christ terrestre et la vision', pp. 446–8.
2. Lagrange, *Saint Jean*, p. 28.
3. D. Ols, 'A propos de la vision béatifique du Christ viateur', *DC* 36 (1983): 395–405 (403).
4. For a survey, see Leeming, 'The Human Knowledge of Christ', p. 235.
5. Ols, 'La vision béatifique du Christ viateur', pp. 403–4; M. Corvez, 'Le Christ voyait-il l'essence de Dieu pendant sa vie mortelle?', *DC* 36 (1983): 406–11 (408).
6. Galot, 'Le Christ terrestre et la vision', p. 429.

than that the idea of the earthly Christ's beatific vision is just unmentioned by Bible and Fathers; it implies the idea is bad speculative theology too, and unable to make convincing sense of the contents of Scripture and Tradition. While we have argued in Chapter 3 that the Fathers in fact provide more evidence for Christ's vision than opponents often allow, albeit evidence that is admittedly slight, Chapter 2 established that there are certain things in Scripture concerning Christ's knowledge that require *some kind of theological explanation*. Opponents of the earthly Christ's beatific vision routinely hold that there is some better explanation of the data than that theory, for example, one rooted in Rahner's self-consciousness theory, or whatever it might be. In this chapter we shall begin our response by sketching out a positive case for the plausibility of the earthly Christ's beatific vision. We shall show how the theory is consistent with the intimate knowledge of the Father attributed to Christ in the New Testament, and that it is not only theologically sound but also fruitful, especially insofar as it illuminates the impact of divine knowledge in Christ's human mind, such that he could be a human communicator of divine truth. First, however, we shall clarify why we are following this theory on the relationship between Christ's united yet distinct minds, when contemporary philosophical theology is proposing quite different approaches.

Contemporary philosophical theology tries to illuminate a relationship of 'accessing relations' between Christ's human and divine minds by the use of analogies drawn from such places as computer technology and human psychology. The latter includes the relationship between the conscious and subconscious, brain hemisphere commissurotomy, multiple personality, hypnosis and visual agnosia.[7] From the psychology of religion comes the analogy of a Hindu mystic who sometimes enters into a deeper consciousness of unity with Brahman,[8] and from science fiction that of a superintelligent alien invader of earth who enters the mind of a human person.[9] While it may be a quite legitimate theological procedure to try out such analogies, they seem at least at first glance less illuminating in this case than analogies of such kinds often do elsewhere. It may even be that the application of some of them, such as a Freudian 'divided mind', tends to encourage us to think of Christ's human and divine minds as isolated from each other rather than capture the impact of divine knowledge on the human mind taught by the Fathers. Sometimes this is even the intention.[10]

7. For recent discussion, see T. V. Morris, *The Logic of God Incarnate* (Ithaca and London: Cornell, 1986), pp. 102–7; E. Stump, *Aquinas* (London and New York: Routledge, 2003), pp. 410–26; R. Cross, 'Incarnation' in T. P. Flint and M. C. Rea (eds), *The Oxford Handbook of Philosophical Theology* (Oxford: OUP, 2009), pp. 452–75; J. Jedwab, 'The Incarnation and Unity of Consciousness' in A. Marmodoro and J. Hill (eds), *The Metaphysics of the Incarnation* (Oxford: OUP, 2011), pp. 168–85; A. Loke, 'The Incarnation and Jesus' Apparent Limitation in Knowledge', *NB* 94 (2013): 583–602.

8. Hanson, 'Two consciousnesses', p. 474, attributes this to Hugo Meynell.

9. Stump, *Aquinas*, pp. 420–2.

10. E.g. R. Swinburne, *The Christian God* (Oxford: Clarendon, 1994), pp. 199–212.

I am suggesting that, in contrast to the foregoing approach, it is worthwhile to pursue another option in the quest for theological understanding, which is to search for an explanation *within* Scripture and Tradition, in the realm of the Christian *super*natural, turning to what Catholic theological methodology calls 'the analogy of faith'. This means that, in contrast to the attempt to understand the relationship between Christ's human and divine minds in the light of computer technology and so on, we should look to gain understanding of the impact of Christ's divine knowledge on his human mind by viewing it in the light of another aspect of Christian belief. This technique was used to significant effect in twentieth-century scholasticism by Rahner who, by way of the analogy of faith, successfully shifted the whole nub of the Catholic theology of grace from the created modification of the human soul in justification to the uncreated special presence and self-communication of the divine persons themselves. This he did through a refocusing of the neoscholastic theology of grace in the light of the Thomist theology of God's Trinitarian self-communication to the mind in the beatific vision.[11] In the present case then, we have not only begun our theological enquiry out of the reading of Scripture, but we also continue it by looking *within* the Scriptures themselves for the source of our theological solution, and view Christ's admittedly mortal life in the light of the immortal life of the saints in heaven.

It might be thought that, since Christ lived an earthly life, it would be entirely illegitimate – bad theology – to consider his knowledge in an eschatological perspective.[12] However, quite apart from the hints in the Fathers we looked at in the last chapter, there are good reasons to suppose that a theological understanding of the life of the blessed will be a particularly fruitful resource for reflecting on Christ's life on earth. One reason is on the part of the saints and another is on the part of Christ. The former reason is that beatific knowledge involves some kind of access of the human mind to the God who knows, which is the very thing we want to illuminate in the case of the earthly Christ. The latter reason can be appreciated by considering more broadly the tenor of Christ's teaching and his entire ministry, recalling that his saving mission was essentially *eschatological* in character. Christ's ministry and teaching responded to Jewish hope for a fresh presence of God in their history. In his teaching Jesus proclaimed that the kingdom of heaven was at hand (e.g. Mk 1.15). The Gospels present him as making present this future heavenly kingdom in a variety of saving ways throughout his earthly life and beyond, in his teaching, exorcisms, miracles, transfiguration, death and resurrection, in the fulfilment of his prophecies and his Second Coming. We may say that in all these ways he somehow brings heaven to earth (cf. Lk. 11.20). Given this general eschatological orientation of Christ's earthly life, our purpose is to attempt an understanding of his knowledge as man and its access to the divine in the light

11. Rahner, 'Some Implications of the Scholastic Concept of Uncreated Grace' in *Theological Investigations*, vol. 1, pp. 319–46.

12. E.g. R. M. Allen, *The Christ's Faith: A Dogmatic Account* (London and New York: T&T Clark, 2009), pp. 50, 59, 66.

of the eschatological knowledge of God and access to the divine enjoyed by the human inhabitants of heaven.

Theological consideration of the beatific vision and its application to the earthly Christ has been common since the rise of scholasticism in the twelfth century, once the ambiguity in Fulgentius's exposition, which we observed in the previous chapter, had reappeared and been overcome.[13] The ambiguity was eventually resolved in favour of knowledge in Christ's created human mind distinct from his divine knowledge, and a strictly Severan position thus successfully avoided. Debate then became focused on exactly how Christ's human knowledge differed from his divine knowledge, whether in extent or merely intensity of power. The first scholastic interpretation of the knowledge in his soul as the beatific vision came, if not from Peter Abelard himself, then from his school, which spoke of the created soul's most perfect vision of God, yet one short of divine knowledge itself.[14] Peter Lombard, whose *Sentences* became the standard textbook of theology second only to the Bible, spoke of Christ assuming in his humanity not only defects that pertained to our state of sin in this life, but also the 'perfect contemplation of God' that pertains to the state of our heavenly homeland.[15] By the thirteenth century, the theory of Christ's earthly beatific vision was commonplace among scholastics, who now commented on the *Sentences* as a matter of course.

In our own application of the beatific vision to the earthly Christ, we shall draw – in a way that is both selective and constructive[16] – on the theological explanation of the biblical and patristic doctrine of the beatific vision given by the theological tradition stemming from *Aquinas*.[17] We shall do this for a number of reasons. First, it was Aquinas's doctrine that was both used and then displaced in the last century, as we saw in Chapter 1. Secondly, Aquinas's account introduced important new elements into theological discussion of this doctrine, and advanced it beyond the theories of his contemporaries.[18] For example, his Dominican teacher, Albert the Great, had been unable to justify the distinction between vision of the divine essence and comprehension, which we saw emerging among some of the Church Fathers in Chapter 3. Albert had concluded that, since the divine essence could never be totally comprehended, neither could it ever be seen or known as such.[19] As we shall see below, Aquinas was able to move

13. On more or less successful resolutions in the early medieval period, see M. Colish, *Peter Lombard* (2 vols; Leiden: Brill, 1994), vol. 1, pp. 438–43.

14. Abelard, *Sententie*, 196.

15. *Sententiae in IV Libris Distinctae*, 3.16.

16. Cf. M. Levering, *Jesus and the Demise of Death: Resurrection, Afterlife, and the Fate of the Christian* (Waco, TX: Baylor, 2012), p. 132 n.5.

17. For Aquinas on the beatific vision, see Torrell, *Recherches thomasiennes*, pp. 177–97.

18. On the originality of Aquinas's theology of the beatific vision in its historical context, see Trottmann, *La Vision Béatifique*, pp. 309–17; and Maillard, *La Vision de Dieu chez Thomas d'Aquin*, pp. 188–221.

19. See Trottmann, *La Vision Béatifique*, pp. 191–4.

the discussion beyond this impasse. Thirdly, in its details Aquinas's account has stood well against challenges from later scholastics of a different hue, such as the Franciscan Duns Scotus and the Jesuit Francisco Suárez.[20] Scotus's theory, for example, may be taken to preserve human freedom in the beatific vision in a way that Aquinas does not, since Scotus's account allows that (were it not for divine providence) the beatified will could choose to withdraw its act of adhesion to God, something Aquinas would not allow. However, it can be replied that Aquinas in fact has the more profound understanding of freedom, where the latter is brought to its eschatological perfection by a higher participation in the freedom of God, whose own perfection means he can never withdraw from the happiness of his own knowledge of himself. To depart from the beatific vision would be a defect in true freedom, not an instance of it. These are issues I have dealt with elsewhere.[21] As for Suárez's account of the beatific vision, he differs from Aquinas, for example, by insisting on the production of a finite concept in the beatific act of knowing, something he saw as indistinguishable from every act of human cognition.[22] However, as we shall see below, Aquinas has good reason for rejecting the production of such a concept in this case, while also employing a key role for the production of such concepts in acts that are closely related to the beatific vision.

Aquinas's approach to the beatific vision is then not entirely uncontroversial among Catholic theologians. Some might even consider it to be bad speculative theology to apply his theology of the beatific vision to the earthly Christ, just because his account of the beatific vision is somehow bad theology. John McDermott finds in it 'inconveniences' and 'ambivalences'.[23] Some of his criticisms are related to the broader range of Aquinas's theology,[24] making it impossible for us to give adequate consideration to them here: his ultimate goal is not simply to set aside Aquinas's account of the beatific vision but to advance 'the abandonment of the scholastic natural–supernatural distinction'.[25] It is possible, though, that in abandoning Aquinas on the beatific vision, McDermott must also abandon the very teaching of Scripture itself on the reality of this eschatological *vision*, which we examined in Chapter 2. McDermott's central problem with Aquinas here is that he allows for the finite to *know* the infinite, for the intellectual creature to know – by grace – God just as he is.[26] Aquinas, broadly speaking, does not

20. For some reflections on Scotus's approach and its application to the earthly Christ, see T. Pomplun, 'Impassibility in St. Hilary of Poitiers's *De Trinitate*', in J. F. Keating and T. J. White (eds), *Divine Impassibility and the Mystery of Human Suffering* (Grand Rapids, MI and Cambridge: Eerdmans, 2009), pp. 187–213 (209–13).

21. See S. F. Gaine, *Will there be Free Will in Heaven?: Freedom, Impeccability and Beatitude* (London and New York: T&T Clark, 2003).

22. *De divina substantia et ejusque attributis*, 2.11.

23. J. M. McDermott, 'How Did Jesus Know He Was God? The Ontological Psychology of Mark 10:17–22', *ITQ* 74 (2009): 272–97 (283, 291).

24. Ibid., pp. 291–4.

25. Ibid., p. 297.

26. Ibid., pp. 289–91.

understand the finite and infinite in such a way that they inhabit a single 'universe', which means that he allows for the infinite and finite in their radical difference to come truly close to one another, so to speak, rather than be somehow kept by their difference at a 'distance' from one another. God is not another member of the universe alongside creatures but its *Creator*, and this is what allows for the infinite God to be not only divine but also to assume finite humanity in the incarnation.[27] Likewise, divine causality in creation does not compete with creaturely causation: an effect can be both caused in its totality by its finite creaturely cause *and* in its totality by the infinite cause of all creation. McDermott is sympathetic to this account of divine transcendence up to a point,[28] but denies that the infinite is free to be known by the finite, as Aquinas believes takes place in the beatific vision. Picturing the infinite and finite more spatially than does Aquinas, McDermott objects that what is finite can never measure up to the infinite in the order of knowledge. We shall see how Aquinas deals with this issue below.

All this leads McDermott to reject both a beatific vision in Jesus and a beatific vision in the saints, strictly speaking. In the case of Christ, prior to the intellect and will of his human nature, there is the divine person who knows and loves: McDermott can thus replace any 'beatific vision' in Christ's humanity with the personal knowledge and love pertaining to his divinity.[29] But then he also generalizes this account of the incarnation into an anthropology, where every human person has a transcendental personhood prior to the intellect and will of their nature.[30] While in our case, this 'spiritual–material-center' is human, in the case of the Word incarnate, in a way that seems to verge on a kind of Apollinarianism, the 'spiritual–material center' is divine. So, while the beatific vision for the divine person of Christ is reinterpreted as divine knowledge, for human persons it takes place as a personal 'union' prior to intellect and will, affecting the knowledge of the intellect in a way that does not seem to be radically different from the way the intellect can know God in this life.[31] There can be no beatific vision as such in the intellect, because the distance between the finite and infinite can, on McDermott's view, only be bridged by love and never by knowledge or 'sight'.

While McDermott's more wide-ranging rejection of the scholastic tradition may give us prudent pause for thought before accepting his critique of Aquinas on the beatific vision, his very critique of Aquinas on the beatific vision should make us wary of accepting a position that seems to evacuate an account of human beatitude of the *vision* of God to which Scripture attests. We shall then continue to work with Aquinas's account of the beatific vision, not only for the reasons given above, but because, unlike some of his critics, Aquinas truly does try to give a theological account of the teaching of Scripture in such verses as 1 John 3.2: we shall *see* him just as he is. Our purpose in the remainder of this chapter is both to

27. Cf. H. McCabe, *God Matters* (London: Chapman, 1987), pp. 57–8.
28. 'How Did Jesus Know He Was God?', p. 282.
29. Ibid., p. 294.
30. Ibid., pp. 280–1.
31. Ibid., p. 296.

display the advantages of a Thomist theology of the beatific vision, and to begin to explore whether the application of this theology has the potential to make at least partial sense of the general picture that emerges from the Gospels of our Saviour. As we saw in Chapter 2, this is a Saviour who reveals his Father to human beings and teaches them about heavenly things, one who not only has divine knowledge but is gifted with the ability to communicate it through his human mind, one who even in his humanity surely enjoys a powerful and intimate knowledge of the Father.[32] We need then to give an outline of this Thomist account of the beatific vision and, guided by Aquinas's acceptance of the axiom that something is always received in a recipient according to the particular mode of the recipient,[33] to ask how this vision might be received in particular in the mind of the earthly Christ.[34] We shall begin by placing Aquinas's account of the beatific vision in the context of his wider account of human beatitude, before passing on to the primary object of the vision, the means by which it takes place, the secondary objects seen in the vision and finally the expressibility and communicability of the contents of the vision.

The happiness or beatitude of the human creature plays a central role in the structure of Aquinas's theology.[35] Together with the natural flourishing of this life that is proportioned to human nature itself, Aquinas identifies a more perfect final end for human beings, which lies above their nature and in the next life, a beatitude by which they share in a higher way in the very beatitude of God the Holy Trinity, participating in the divine nature. While their perfect or complete beatitude will extend to the human animal in its entirety, body as well as soul, sense as well as intellect, the very core of this beatitude formally consists in a 'vision' graciously granted to the human intellect. It is this glorious act of intellect in which beatitude formally consists because it is by this graced act that the supreme good is somehow *attained*, such that even the separated soul may pass without its body from the life of earth to the life of heaven, prior to the resurrection.[36] What is envisioned in the case of the earthly Christ is that he is blessed not with heavenly beatitude to its full extent, that is, with a completely glorified body and soul, but with at least this essential core of ultimate human flourishing in the intellect, by which a rational creature is brought to fulfilment. In this way Christ can be said to have lived a human life on earth that was both earthly and heavenly, an earthly life from a bodily point of view and a heavenly life in the

---

32. For Aquinas on Christ as Teacher, see P. Klimczak, *Christus Magister: Le Christ Maître dans les commentaires évangeliques de saint Thomas d'Aquin* (Fribourg: Academic, 2013).

33. E.g. *Summa*, 1a., q. 79, a. 6.

34. For another account of Aquinas on the beatific vision and his application of it to Christ, see Allen, *Christ's Faith*, pp. 41–54.

35. On Aquinas's theology of ultimate beatitude, see C. Leget, *Living with God: Thomas Aquinas on the Relation between Life on Earth and 'Life' after Death* (Leuven: Peeters, 1997), pp. 207–53; Levering, *Jesus and the Demise of Death*, pp. 109–25.

36. *Summa*, 1a.2ae., q. 3, a. 8; q. 4, a. 5.

mind, inaugurating the kingdom of heaven on earth. Like his contemporaries, Aquinas spoke of the earthly Christ as both '*comprehensor*', that is, one who has already 'attained' to beatitude in this essential respect, and as 'pilgrim'(*viator*), one who was still on the way to beatitude in all its completeness.[37]

Though Aquinas held that there is much more that is seen in this beatific vision, there is no doubt that he teaches that it is God himself who is attained as its primary object, and we shall treat of this primary object first. Aquinas learns from the Bible that God has revealed that we shall see him just as he is, and he interprets this to mean an intellectual vision of the divine substance or essence and the three divine persons. He could not avoid knowing, however, that it had been a matter of controversy whether or not the divine essence itself is or even can be seen by a created intellect. As we saw in Chapter 3, the Fathers had been divided on the question. Some early thirteenth-century theologians, including some of Aquinas's fellow Dominicans, had, like the ninth-century theologian Eriugena, followed those Fathers who thought that not even heaven could involve access to the divine essence. This opinion was later to be officially endorsed by the Eastern Orthodox Churches, in the fourteenth century. However, it had already been censured in the 1240s by the bishop of Paris, William of Auvergne, before Aquinas had begun his theological studies there.[38] Aquinas had then to deal with the fact that the vision of the divine essence itself could not easily be construed as supported by a patristic consensus, where he might merely adjudicate among different theological arguments proposed in support of a common position. Instead, he faced divergent conclusions among the Fathers themselves, all of whom he wished to treat as revered authorities, including Chrysostom and Dionysius, whom he quotes with great frequency. What was required of him was a more nuanced and critical, as well as respectful, retrieval of his patristic authorities.

How he seems to have dealt with this challenge was to concern himself not so much with the *conclusions* of those Fathers who denied the vision of the divine essence as with their *arguments*. Arguments from the limitations of creaturely knowledge he takes to be good not for the conclusion that the divine essence cannot be *seen* by creatures, but instead for the conclusion that the divine essence cannot be *comprehended* by them, where comprehension meant not merely attainment of the divine essence (a broader meaning of the word 'comprehend') but *exhaustive* knowledge of it (a more precise meaning).[39] The fact that he concerned himself thus with his authorities' arguments meant he did not feel the need to reject the authorities outright, but took them to be proving only what all the Fathers could in fact be taken to agree on, namely, that the divine essence cannot be *totally comprehended* by any creature. He did this by developing the distinction made by Fathers who granted vision of the divine essence, that is, the distinction between knowing or seeing something and exhaustive comprehension

37. Ibid., 3a., q. 15, a. 10.

38. On the thirteenth-century debate, see Trottmann, *La Vision Béatifique*, pp. 115–86; and on Eriugena, ibid., pp. 76–83.

39. *Summa*, 1a, q. 12, a. 1 ad 1.

of it.[40] It is sometimes mistakenly supposed that Christ's possession of the beatific vision, as traditionally conceived, meant that he had 'a comprehensive vision of the divine essence'.[41] However, since Aquinas distinguishes vision and comprehension, once his theology of the beatific vision is then applied to the human mind of Christ, it means that by it he too would have seen the divine essence but not comprehended it. This is one way in which Aquinas and his contemporaries dealt with the question over the distinction between the knowledges in Christ's human and divine minds – while he comprehended God in his divine mind, he merely saw him in his human mind. While we shall explore Aquinas's account of the distinction between vision and comprehension later in the chapter, we shall now pass on to our examination of Aquinas's theory of the vision of the divine essence, and its application to the earthly Christ.

There is no question for Aquinas that the vision of the blessed described in 1 John 3.2, which we wish to apply to the earthly Christ, must include knowledge of God's essence. A remote basis for this lies in Aquinas's doctrine of God. While a material creature can be distinguished from the essence it instantiates – an individual human being is not identical with human nature, and an individual dog is not identical with canine nature – God who is pure form and entirely simple cannot be so distinguished, except in our limited way of thinking. In reality, God is absolutely identical with his own divine essence.[42] Since God is entirely simple, to see him just as he is must be to see his essence, and Aquinas normally speaks of the beatific vision in terms of God's essence. Nevertheless, we should note that the argument from simplicity must also hold for anything that is identical with God. So, for example, the beatific vision is also for Aquinas a vision of divine truth and goodness, justice and mercy.[43] But if this is the case, why did he come to prefer to speak so much in this connection of the divine essence?

An answer can be found in the fact that, for Aquinas, although all these and other such terms, including essence, refer to the same divine substance, they are not synonyms. Instead they signify God under different descriptions, in differing ways. They do this because they are drawn from a language suited in the first place to the created world of creaturely complexity, where the perfections signified by these terms really do exist distinctly from one another. The various terms are then stretched beyond their ordinary use to refer to the simple God.[44] Aquinas could thus speak of the object of vision at times under the description of divine truth and at times under the description of divine goodness, and so on, depending on context.[45] Aquinas very often spoke of the vision of God under the description of

40. Ibid., 1a., q. 12, a. 7.

41. Weinandy, 'Jesus' Filial Vision of the Father', p. 198.

42. *Summa*, 1a., q. 3, a. 3.

43. E.g. ibid., 2a.2ae., q. 1, a. 2 ad 3.

44. Ibid., 1a., q. 13, a. 4. See G. P. Rocca, *Speaking the Incomprehensible God: Thomas Aquinas on the Interplay of Positive and Negative Theology* (Washington, DC: CUA, 2004), pp. 77–195.

45. E.g. ibid., 2a.2ae., q. 1, a. 2 ad 3.

his essence because he envisages the beatific vision as a gracious fulfilment that meets the natural human desire to know *what* God is, that is, to know his quiddity or essence. While the beatific vision had been linked with the human desire for beatitude since patristic times, to link it with the natural desire to see God's *essence* as such was an original element in Aquinas's approach.[46]

On Aquinas's account, human happiness lies essentially in the exercise of the mind, which is the highest activity of human nature, meaning that the core of beatitude is a matter of the intellect or reason.[47] Following Augustine, he distinguished between higher reason and lower reason, meaning by these two 'parts' of reason not that they are two distinct faculties or separated compartments in the mind or intellect, but that the single human reason was able to know realities higher than itself as well as lower realities.[48] Higher reason is reason insofar as it takes eternal realities for its object, and lower reason is reason insofar as it takes temporal realities for its object. These objects are closely related in our human mode of discovering reality and acquiring knowledge, since we come to knowledge of the eternal by way of knowing what is temporal. As a result of knowing God's created effects, the desire is aroused to want to know their cause, and a most important part of knowing anything is to know *what* it is, its essence.[49] In the case of God this is fulfilled not by any knowledge of God appropriate to this life, which is more knowledge of what God is *not* rather than of what he is, but only by the heavenly vision of the divine essence itself in the higher reason.[50] This vision of what God is brings the desire to know God, which was elicited by lower reason's knowledge of his effects, to rest.[51] While this fulfilment trumps any rival account of ultimate human happiness,[52] it does not rule out further desire in accordance with the state of the blessed for what is beyond the essence of happiness itself. While having reached their own beatitude in heaven, souls separated from their bodies continue to desire in their separated state to be reunited with their bodies and that their bodies share in beatitude, to desire that they may know the heavenly fellowship of all the elect and to desire that all creation be renewed.[53] The point is that, while they continue to desire that God's will be done and his goodness be further manifested, they have no further desire for God himself who is the very core of their happiness, in the sense that their desire for him is now fulfilled by their eternal knowing of him.

46. Trottmann, *La Vision Béatifique*, pp. 309–12.

47. On Aquinas's use of the terms mind, intellect and reason, see J. P. O'Callaghan, 'Imago Dei: A Test Case for St. Thomas's Augustinianism' in M. Dauphinais, B. David and M. Levering (eds), *Aquinas the Augustinian* (Washington, DC: CUA, 2001), pp. 100–44.

48. *Summa*, 1a., q. 79, a. 9. The interpretation given by M. Levering, *Christ's Fulfillment of Torah and Temple*, pp. 62–63, conflates the distinction between higher and lower reason with that between speculative and practical intellect.

49. *Summa contra Gentiles*, 3.50.1–4; *Summa*, 1a., q. 12, a. 1; 1.2ae., q. 3, a. 8.

50. Ibid., 3.38–40; *Summa*, 1a, q. 12, a. 2.

51. *Summa*, 1a.2ae., q. 3, a. 8.

52. *Contra Gentiles*, 3.63; *Summa*, 1a.2ae., q. 3, a. 8.

53. E.g. *Summa*, 1a.2ae., q. 4, aa. 5–8; cf. 2a.2ae., q. 83, a. 4 ad 2.

So if we apply this Thomist theology of the heavenly vision to Christ in his earthly state, we should expect him to have been not one who in his humanity was seeking after God, aflame with *desire* for God, but one whose desire for God was already brought to perfect rest through knowledge of him. Of course we may expect to find him, in accordance with his earthly state, still desiring the further manifestation of God's goodness, aflame for the extension of his kingdom. He may desire, for example, the glorification of his body and the redemption of the world.[54] And indeed what we find in the Gospels is consonant with this application of knowledge of God's essence to Christ's human mind. Jesus says, for example, that his food is to do the will of his Father (Jn. 4.34), implying desire that the Father's will be done (cf. Mt. 26.39; Mk 14.36; Lk. 22.42). However, there is nothing in what he says about his relationship with the Father that necessarily implies that he had the need or desire to come closer to God in his personal knowledge of him – he never says, for example, that he is seeking the Father's face. Jesus appears in the Gospels as no searcher after God, but as one who, out of his remaining and rest in deep knowledge and love of the Father, actively seeks to do his will. Though his life was at that time on earth, while the life of the saints is in heaven, this general picture of rest and desire in Christ is consistent with the theory of his possessing the heavenly knowledge enjoyed by the blessed.

Mention of Jesus' relationship with his Father turns our attention to the fact that, according to Aquinas, the beatific vision also has the divine persons for its primary object. It would seem especially pertinent for us to dwell on how the Trinitarian character of a Thomist theory of the beatific vision can be drawn out, in view of the general revival of Trinitarian theology during the last century,[55] including the rise of neoscholastic interest in the proper relationships to each of the divine persons given to the justified by the life of faith and grace,[56] and the current interest in the contribution made by Aquinas's own Trinitarian theology.[57] Again, it follows from divine simplicity that there can be no vision of the divine essence just as it is without knowledge of the divine persons. According to Aquinas, each divine person, though really distinct by way of relation from the other two persons, is identical with the single divine essence.[58] To see the essence therefore is to see each divine person, and by the same act of vision 'we enjoy the three persons'.[59] While it is true that, in our limited knowledge of God in this life, which is not knowledge of the divine essence as such, we can think of God's essence, goodness and so on without thinking of the divine persons, this cannot

54. Cf. ibid., 3a., q. 7, a. 4.

55. E.g. Rahner, *The Trinity* (London: Burns & Oates, 1970).

56. E.g. W. Hill, *Proper Relations to the Indwelling Divine Persons* (Washington, DC: Thomist, 1955).

57. For a masterly account of Aquinas's Trinitarian theology, see G. Emery, *The Trinitarian Theology of St Thomas Aquinas* (Oxford and New York: OUP, 2007).

58. *Summa*, 1a., q.39, a.1.

59. *Scriptum super Sententiis magistri Petri Lombardi*, 1.1.2.1.

hold for the face to face vision of God just as he is.[60] There were certainly debates not long after Aquinas's time as to whether God might hypothetically grant a vision of the divine essence without a vision of the divine persons, but Aquinas had no time for such fancies.[61]

Not only does vision of the essence mean vision of the persons but, according to Aquinas, no individual person can be seen without the other two. We can appreciate why this must be from his treatment of the distinctions between the divine persons. He holds that, even in this life, one cannot have proper knowledge of a divine person except through knowledge of how he is distinguished from the other two persons, and the persons are distinguished among themselves by their relations.[62] These relations of origin Aquinas takes as known only on the basis of divine revelation: the Father, who proceeds from no one, begetting the Son, and the Holy Spirit proceeding from Father and Son.[63] The Father is thus distinguished by the relation of fatherhood, the Son by sonship and the Holy Spirit by procession. This means that one cannot have proper knowledge of a divine person without knowledge of the other two, because by their very nature these relations are included in each other and knowing one relation properly will mean knowing them all.[64]

For example, to see the Father must also be to see the Son. Aquinas took the name 'Father' to signify the distinctive relation that constitutes his very personhood, and so the person himself.[65] According to Aquinas, it is on account of this personal property of fatherhood that the Father eternally begets the Son – it is of his very person, so to speak, to engender his only Son, communicating to him his whole divinity, everything but the fact that he is Father of the Son.[66] Hence, we are unable to gain distinctive knowledge of the first person of the Trinity as such, even in this life, without identifying him as the *Father of the Son*. Thus, to see the Father just as he is will be to see that he is the Father of the Son, and thus to see the Son also. And likewise with our knowledge of the Son, whom Aquinas, following John's Gospel, prefers to consider first under the proper name of 'Word'. In his search for theological understanding of the second person of the Trinity, Aquinas employed an analogy from the theory of human knowledge he developed during his career, drawing in particular on Augustine. When we make an act of knowledge, Aquinas came to hold, we produce a concept, a kind of 'mental word' in which we express our knowledge, the fruit of our act of knowing, as it were, which is intrinsically relative to one who forms the word.[67] By analogy, Aquinas envisions the Father as eternally speaking or conceiving his Word, expressing

---

60. *Summa*, 2a.2ae., q. 2, a. 8 ad 3.
61. See Trottmann, *La Vision Béatifique*, pp. 364–5.
62. Cf. *Summa*, 1a., q. 40, a. 3.
63. Ibid., 1a., q. 27.
64. *Super Sent.*, 1.1.2.1. Cf. *Summa*, 1a., q. 42, a. 5.
65. *Summa*, 1a., 33, a. 2 ad 1.
66. Ibid., 1a., q. 40, a. 4.
67. *Contra Gentiles*, 1.53; 4.11.

in that Word his entire knowledge of himself, of the whole Trinity and of all creation.[68] Thus, for us to have a proper knowledge of the Word as such, even in this life, is to know him as the Word *of the Father*, and so to have knowledge of the Father too. Those who see the Word in heaven must therefore see the Father also whom the Word perfectly articulates. Moreover, proper knowledge of these two divine persons must include knowledge of the Holy Spirit, whom Aquinas thought of as proceeding by way of love, on analogy with the love that follows our own conceiving of a mental word.[69] Hence not even the Father's begetting of the Son can be properly understood in this life if the Word is not understood as the 'Word breathing Love', where the Father, in begetting the Son, communicates to his Son the breathing forth of the Spirit, of him who is thus the Love of both Father and Son.[70] The upshot is that, just as already takes place in its own lesser way in the earthly life of faith and grace, so in the future life of vision all three persons will be enjoyed, each in his personal property and order of relations with the others.

Our proper relations with all three divine persons allow us to single out any divine person as the object of the beatific vision, according to context. For example, since the beatific vision is an act of knowledge, and on Aquinas's theology the Word proceeds by way of knowledge, a connection is easily made such that we can speak here of knowledge of the Word.[71] In the case of Christ, who is the Word incarnate, the fittingness of speaking of a vision of the Word will be the more pronounced.[72] Nevertheless, knowledge of the Word is inevitably fully Trinitarian, since the Father expresses his knowledge of the whole Trinity in the Word.[73] In an explanation of Paul's doctrine of a future vision 'face to face' and not 'in a riddle', Aquinas focuses in particular on the relation of Father and Son, and on the Son as manifesting the *Father*. He does so in the context of commenting on Christ's promise at the Last Supper that he will 'speak plainly of the Father and not in figures' (Jn 16.25), which Aquinas allows may possibly be referred to the beatific vision. We learn from this interpretation that in Paul's face to face vision, 'the Father will be proclaimed to us plainly, and not in figures', a clear manifestation of the Father by his divine Son.[74] Although the Father's Word gives expression to the whole Trinity, it is the manifestation of the *Father* that Aquinas picks up from Jesus' words in John. This should recall the fact that, as we saw in the last two chapters, Scripture and the Fathers tend to speak primarily of the Father as the object of the beatific vision, even if not to the exclusion of Son and Spirit. And if we ask how a Thomist account of the beatific vision can make sense of this primary focus on the Father among the three divine persons and

68. *Summa*, 1a., q. 34.
69. Ibid., 1a., q. 37, a. 1.
70. Ibid., 1a., q. 43, a. 5 ad 2.
71. E.g. ibid., 1a., q. 58, a. 7.
72. E.g. ibid., 3a., q. 10, a. 1.
73. Ibid., 1a., q. 34, a. 1 ad 3.
74. *Super Ioannem*, 16.7.2150.

their relations, an answer lies in the Trinitarian structure of creation and biblical salvation history, which Aquinas conceived as a kind of circular movement.[75] Just as the processions of Son and Spirit from the Father, the ultimate principle without principle, cause the procession of creatures from God, so the missions of the Son and Spirit are responsible for returning creatures to that ultimate principle which is the Father. In line with patristic doctrine, it is by way of these missions that we make our return to the ultimate principle from which we originally came forth by creation, and from which Son and Spirit themselves both proceed. As the source of the Son and the Spirit, the Father is the one to whom we are conveyed by the missions of Son and Spirit, and this helps us make sense of why the Father is so easily spoken of in particular as the person we shall see in the beatific vision, the one who is the ultimate goal in our sights.

Hence, we must suppose that, if Christ possessed this beatific vision while on earth, he saw the three persons as well as the divine essence. The vision in his human mind must equally be Trinitarian, informed by the three divine persons in their mutually ordered relations. How, though, does this relate to the fact that this Jesus *is* the divine Son, eternally constituted by the relation of sonship, the perfect expression of the Father, one who with the Father breathes forth the Holy Spirit, one sent to us by the Father to return us to himself? Given Aquinas's principle that whatever is received is received according to the mode of the receiver, it seems especially pertinent to dwell on how the Trinitarian vision would be received into a human mind united to the divine *Son*. Might there be any distinction to be made between the beatific vision received into the mind of the incarnate Son and a beatific vision received into the mind of an incarnate Father, for example? Rahner argued that it would be impossible for any divine person but the Son, the one who reveals the Father, to become incarnate.[76] Aquinas, however, thought it only 'most fitting' that the Son rather than another person take flesh for our salvation.[77] He argued that since the divine power, which includes the power to become incarnate, is shared equally by all three persons, any person could in theory assume human nature.[78] The fact then that it was the Son who took flesh should not only prompt us to consider why that should be so fitting, but encourage an exploration of how the Trinitarian vision would be received in an incarnation of *this* particular divine person rather than any other, that is, whether it might be received in a filial mode.

As we conceded in Chapter 2, on a Chalcedonian reading it is less controversial to take much of what Scripture has to say about Jesus' extraordinary knowledge as evidence of knowledge in his divine nature. On this reading, we find that Scripture points us to a certain focus of the Son's divine knowledge on the Father who begets him. Indeed there is a definite preference for speaking of the mutual knowledge of Father and Son, where the Father's knowing is focused on his Son and vice versa. The fact that the Son is the Father's *only* begotten, while the Spirit

---

75. *In Sent.*, 1.14.2.2.
76. Karl Rahner, *The Trinity* (London: Burns & Oates, 1970).
77. *Summa*, 3a., q. 3, a. 8.
78. Ibid., 3a., q. 3, a. 5.

proceeds in contrast from *both* Father and Son, enables in the former case the revelation of a one-to-one personal relationship of mutual knowledge. We find this, for example, in the words of Jesus: 'All things have been delivered to me by my Father; and no one knows the Son except the Father, and no one knows the Father except the Son …' (Mt. 11.25–26; cf. Lk. 10.21–22). Again, in the discourse on the Good Shepherd in John's Gospel, Jesus makes mention of the fact that 'the Father knows me and I know the Father' (10.15). Furthermore, we have seen how John's prologue states that, 'No one has ever seen God; the only-begotten God who is in the bosom (εἰς τὸν κόλπόν) of the Father, he has made him known'(1.18). Some exegetes take the Word's being εἰς τὸν κόλπόν to indicate that the one who here sees God is ever turned towards the Father, as though to the Father's breast or chest.[79] Without concluding that the Son is thereby deprived of knowledge of himself and the Holy Spirit, this surely suggests that the Son's eternal knowing has, by way of his eternal filial relationship, a certain focus on the Father.

Now, on Aquinas's theology, each divine person is constituted by a relationship that implies divine knowledge of all three persons, and the Son is no exception. How then can we explain the particular foci of knowledge attested in Scripture? Now there is an order among the persons themselves and their relationships in their possession of the divine essence, the Son for example receiving the divine essence from the Father precisely as his Son – each person possesses the single divine essence precisely *as* the person he is, in his own mode, so to speak. We may surely suppose that this is reflected in a certain order in the persons' possession of the single divine knowledge, which, by way of divine simplicity, is identical with the divine essence. Thus each divine person will possess the divine knowledge in such a way that his mode of knowing of the entire Trinity brings with it a certain order. In the case of the Son, he receives being and knowledge from the Father as his only begotten. Proceeding from the Father as the Word that perfectly expresses the Father's perfect knowledge of himself, the Son also knows the Father perfectly. We may suppose that, as the Father's only Son, the Son receives divine knowledge from the Father in such a way that, in the order of knowledge of the entire Trinity, he has a certain orientation towards the Father who begot him. Likewise the Father, in perfectly expressing his perfect knowledge in his only-begotten Word, may be said to be orientated in order of knowledge on the Son. These relationships of fatherhood and sonship thus underlie the fact that, while each person knows himself and the other two divine persons exhaustively, there is nevertheless a certain order to the three persons' knowledge of themselves.

Should the Son then become incarnate, that must mean the taking flesh of the very one who eternally receives the divine essence and thus divine knowledge from the Father as his only Son, whose personhood is constituted by this unique relation of sonship and his eternal knowledge of the Father. In the case of such an incarnation, we may surely expect any impression of divine knowledge in his human mind to imitate the order of knowing present in the Son's divine

79. Cf. F. J. Moloney, *The Gospel of John* (Sacra Pagina, 4; Collegeville, MN: Liturgical, 1998), p. 44.

knowledge. Any beatific knowledge received in the Son's human mind will thus share in the orientation of the order of his divine knowledge, being received in a filial mode. Just as his eternal knowing has a certain focus on the Father, so his human knowledge, as a participation in his divine knowledge, will likewise be focused on the Father. Such an orientation is indeed what we find in the earthly Christ in the Gospels, not only in those sayings that may be argued to refer specifically to divine knowledge, but also in those where Jesus may be taken with less difficulty to be giving expression to a knowledge in his humanity, such as John 8.14 and 8.55. The focus on the Father in these verses is exactly what we would expect of a beatific vision received in a filial mode in the human mind of the divine Son. Even if no verse can be tied down absolutely to knowledge in Christ's human mind, we can hardly expect the impression of divine knowledge in his human mind to be ordered in a radically different way from his divine knowledge.

It is here that a Thomist theory of Christ's earthly beatific vision differs in one significant way from Rahner's alternative theory of a direct but non-beatific vision. Since the latter vision is explained by *self*-consciousness, this explanation more narrowly renders the person of the *Word* and not the entire Trinity the object of Christ's vision as such.[80] The Son certainly has self-consciousness of his own person, the Son, but he cannot likewise have *self*-consciousness of the other two persons. Thus the Father and the Holy Spirit are not directly seen by this act of 'vision', precisely because it is an act of self-consciousness on the part of a different person. This introduces a certain mismatch between the structure of Christ's 'vision', which is focused on the Word, and what appears in the Gospels, which one would suppose on Rahner's theory to be a thematization of Christ's unthematized vision, but where the focus turns out to be on the Father.[81] In contrast, the beatific theory has the single act of beatifying knowledge take in the entire Trinity, each person being identical with the divine essence and mutually related in such a way that one person cannot be seen in this way without the others. While Rahner's theory is thus more narrowly filial, the filial character of Christ's *beatific* vision does not exclude the other two persons from being directly known by the very same act of knowledge. Moreover, the very filial character of this act of beatific vision also means a focus on the Father within the order of this Trinitarian knowledge, while Rahner's theory has its focus exclusively on the Word. This mismatch of Rahner's theory with the general Scriptural orientation of Christ's knowledge towards the Father is highlighted by the fact that, for the period during which Balthasar adopted the theory (he eventually seems to have dropped it),[82] he felt the need to seek a solution to this problem by emphasizing the Son's 'mission-consciousness', his consciousness of himself as *sent by the*

---

80. Cf. 'Knowledge and Self-Consciousness of Christ', pp. 211, 213.

81. Riedlinger, *Geschichtlichkeit und Vollendung des Wissens Christi*, p. 153; W. Kasper, *Jesus the Christ* (London: Burns & Oates; New York: Paulist, 1976), p. 271 n.60.

82. *Theo-Drama: Theological Dramatic Theory*, vol. V: *The Final Act* (trans. G. Harrison; San Francisco: Ignatius, 1998), pp. 124–5.

Father.[83] However, to interpret Christ's vision as beatific with its focus on the Father, rather than in terms of self-consciousness with its narrower focus on the Word, has the advantage of not introducing any such problem to be solved.

Not only does the beatific theory of Christ's vision of the Father not encounter this difficulty; it also has a number of theological advantages of its own. For example, it provides us with a particular reason for understanding why it is most fitting that it is the *Son* who becomes incarnate as our Saviour. If we are to be returned to the Father, our ultimate principle, by being enabled to know him, then the incarnation of his only Son, whose knowledge has a certain direction towards the Father, seems most appropriate. If the incarnate Son were to have like knowledge of the Father in the human mind he assumes in his mission, then it can have a saving role in bringing the saints to knowledge of the Father through their union with their Saviour. This illumines the causal link that scholastic theology maintains between Christ's beatific knowledge and that of the blessed. The common orientation towards the Father in Christ's knowledge and that of the blessed also enables us to retrieve and integrate the insight of Origen to which we referred in Chapter 3: United to Christ in heaven, the saints gaze on the Father as one Son. It is as though Christ's Mystical Body in heaven were the 'place' one needs to be in order to see the Father, the 'viewpoint' from which the Father can be clearly and directly seen. Here lies the beginning of part of an answer to Rahner's complaint that standard scholastic eschatology in his time gave no proper consideration to the continuing significance of Christ's humanity in heaven.[84] So, just as Aquinas holds the grace of the members of the Body of Christ on earth to be derived from the pre-eminent grace of Christ the Body's Head, a 'capital' grace which is present in his humanity and identical with his own habit of grace,[85] we may likewise suppose that the members of Christ's Body in heaven enjoy the beatific vision by way of sharing derivatively in Christ's own vision of the Father, which is again present in his humanity. It is as though the saints were to see the Father with Christ's own eyes through their union with him. Though Rahner rejects the beatific character of Christ's earthly vision, he still wants to make a causal link between his earthly vision and that of the saints.[86] This is better secured, however, where not only is the vision of the saints beatific, but so is that enjoyed by the earthly Christ, the latter beatific vision being the cause of the former.

Having established what is the primary object of the beatific vision, we need to ask how this vision takes place: how can any human mind, including that of

83. Ibid., III, pp. 172–3. For a general critique of developments in Balthasar's theory of Christ's immediate vision, see Pitstick, *Light in Darkness*, pp. 166–71.

84. 'The Eternal Significance of the Humanity of Jesus for our Relationship with God', in *Theological Investigations*, vol. 3: *The Theology of the Spiritual Life* (trans. K.-H. and B. Kruger; London: Darton, Longman & Todd; Baltimore: Helicon, 1967), pp. 35–46 (37–8).

85. *Summa*, 3a., q. 7, aa. 1, 5.

86. *Foundations of Christian Faith: An Introduction to the Idea of Christianity* (London: Darton, Longman & Todd, 1978), p. 200.

Christ, exercise this beatifying knowledge of God the Holy Trinity?[87] It certainly cannot be obtained via the means that knowledge is normally realized in us under the light of human reason, so long as our account of human knowing recognizes the infinity of God, the finite power of the human mind and the finitude of its ordinary means of knowledge.[88] The limitation then is not on the side of God but on the side of ordinary human knowing. According to Aquinas, God is in himself supremely intelligible, and it is the intrinsic weakness of our intellect that prevents us from knowing him, like bats blinded by the light of the sun.[89] Aquinas's approach to the beatific vision in respect of the finitude of the natural human means of knowledge, drawn from Aristotle, is another of his original contributions to the whole question.[90] He holds the normal means of human knowledge to be a kind of created modification of the mind, which forms the basis of our act of knowing. On his account, the intellect abstracts the form of the object known through the senses from its material conditions. In this way, a representation of the object is impressed on the mind, and this impression Aquinas calls an 'intelligible *species*'. This similitude is a modification of the intellect and thus the means *by which* we come to knowledge of the object in question. This *species* is distinct from the mental word, a further similitude *in which* we then express our knowledge, which we have seen Aquinas use as an analogy for the begetting of the divine Word.[91] Later Thomist terminology distinguished these two similitudes in human knowledge as the *species impressa*, that impression on the mind *by* which we know, and the *species expressa*, that *in* which we subsequently express or mentally verbalize our knowledge.

Even were the incarnate Son to assume and live out this natural human process of acquiring knowledge by means of intelligible *species*, it must even in this case remain inadequate for any coming to a vision of God in his human mind. Among the reasons for this is that no created similitude or likeness can ever act as a means of coming to know God's essence, which is uncircumscribed, infinite being, because every created *species* is as such finite and limited in scope. According to Aquinas, if we were to work from the assumption that God were seen by means of some necessarily inadequate likeness of him, we would end up concluding that he would not be seen as he really is at all, which would contradict

---

87. For an account of the medieval debate on the means of beatific knowledge, see Trottmann, *La Vision Béatifique*, pp. 209–410.

88. There have been some theories of knowledge proposed by Catholic philosophers that allow for an infinite means of knowing in all human knowledge. The neothomists rejected this as a confusion of the natural and supernatural orders. See G. A. McCool, *Nineteenth-Century Scholasticism: The Search for a Unitary Method* (New York: Fordham, 1989), pp. 113–28.

89. *Contra Gentiles*, 3.54.8; *Summa*, 1a., q. 12, a. 1.

90. Trottmann, *La Vision Béatifique*, pp. 312–17.

91. *Super Ioannem*, 1.1.25. For Aquinas's epistemology in relation to contemporary concerns, see J. P. O'Callaghan, *Thomist Realism and the Linguistic Turn: Toward a More Perfect Form of Existence* (Notre Dame, IN: University of Notre Dame Press, 2003).

Scripture.[92] However, given that we shall see him just as he is, we must conclude that God is seen in heaven in some way other than by a created *species*, one that in fact lies beyond the natural human means of knowledge and comes by way of a divine gift of supernatural grace.[93]

Aquinas explains how this comes about by drawing on his account of how *God* knows God. He identifies God's own *means* of knowledge, that by which he knows, as the divine essence, which is possessed by all three divine persons. While he thinks of the begetting of the Word as that *in which* the Father expresses his knowledge, on the analogy of us expressing our knowledge in a 'mental word', he does not think of the procession of the Word as God's *means* of knowledge, that *by which* he knows. There is no suggestion that an otherwise ignorant Father comes to knowledge by begetting the Word. Rather, the divine essence is identified as God's means of knowledge, on analogy with our own *species impressa*. This is the single means of knowledge enjoyed by all three divine persons. Here the knower, the known and the means of knowledge are all identical by way of divine simplicity in an unlimited intimate unity of knowledge – God knows himself through himself: he is his own intelligible *species*, so to speak.[94]

Aquinas draws on this understanding of divine knowledge to explain how human beings can be granted the vision of God's essence. God, who is supremely intelligible in himself, makes himself known by making his essence not only the object but also the *means* of the saints' knowledge. Indeed it would not be possible for him to be the object of knowledge *just as he is* without being also the means of that knowledge. Replacing the *species* of natural knowledge *with himself*, God gives to the inhabitants of heaven that same means of knowing by which he knows himself.[95] Aquinas writes, 'When a created intellect sees God through his essence, that essence is the "intelligible form" of the intellect.'[96] Our minds will be flooded by the self-gift of God's own essence, and we shall then know God just as God knows God. No more perfect means of knowing the triune God could in fact be given to the saints, no greater access to the divine mind, because there can be no more perfect means of knowing the divine essence than the divine essence itself. And, should Christ then be granted this vision while on earth, what would be bestowed on his human mind would be the divine means of knowledge than which there is no greater, because he would see the Father through nothing less than the Father's very own essence, that essence with which the person of the Father is identical by way of divine simplicity, and not through any mere finite representation.[97] This is at least consonant with the portrayal of Christ's unique earthly knowledge of God in the Gospels, even if we have to refer many individual texts to his divine knowledge alone, since the Gospels hardly give the impression

---

92. *Summa*, 1a., q. 12, a. 2.
93. Ibid., 1a., q. 12, a. 4; *Contra Gentiles*, 3.49.
94. Ibid., 1a., q. 14, a. 2.
95. *Contra Gentiles*, 3.51.2; *Summa*, 1a., q. 12, a. 9.
96. *Summa*, 1a., q. 12, a. 5.
97. Cf. *Super Ioannem*, 6.5.947.

that his knowledge of the Father was in any way lacking appropriate perfection or could have been significantly greater.

Not only though would Christ's means of knowledge of the Father have this note of particular perfection, it would also imply a certain profound unity and intimacy between his divinity and humanity in the order of knowledge. In addition to their hypostatic union in the order of being, Christ's divine and human minds would be united by a common means of knowledge. While Christ's human mind would naturally possess its own proper finite means of knowing, it would also share by grace in the infinite divine means of knowing, uniting Christ's human and divine minds in this single means. This sharing of the divine essence as that by which God is known would thus give rise to a union in the order of knowledge between Christ in his humanity and the triune God as the object of his intimate knowledge. While Aquinas certainly treats all knowledge as unitive – when we ordinarily come to know some object that remains apart from us, we are nevertheless *united* with the object through its form coming to exist in our minds after a mental or intentional fashion in the *species intelligibilis*[98] – this unitive aspect is even more pronounced in the beatific vision, since God's essence, which is absolutely identical with God's existence, *itself* comes to exist in the mind and no mere representation of it. According to Aquinas, God graciously *unites* himself to the created intellect as an intelligible form.[99] Sometimes the vision of God is treated by theologians as an inadequate theory of eternal life on the ground that the idea of looking at an object does not include such a unitive element, despite the fact that Aquinas's account of this vision evidently does.[100] The beatific vision is thus hardly knowledge of something that is held 'over against' us, as Weinandy supposes,[101] but is rather a profoundly intimate point of access for the saint to the knowledge of the divine mind. And so the beatific vision gives us a plausible way of making sense of the intimate union of knowledge with the Father that surely belonged in Christ's humanity.

The fact that the saints' means of knowledge is the divine essence rather than an individual divine person, such as the Word, does not mean that a Thomist theology of the beatific vision is not at this point Trinitarian, as was made clear in the scholasticism of the twentieth century.[102] In the case of the object of the beatific vision, proper relations to each of the divine persons did not prevent us from speaking of any individual divine person as the object of this vision, depending on context. In a similar way, what in fact belongs to the divine essence, that is, to all three persons in their unity, can be assigned to a particular person by way

---

98. E.g. *Contra Gentiles*, 1.65.9.

99. Ibid., 3.51.4; *Summa*, 1a., q. 12, a. 4.

100. Balthasar, *Theo-Drama* V, p. 425. Pitstick, *Light in Darkness*, p. 172, takes him to task.

101. Weinandy, 'Jesus' Filial Vision of the Father', pp. 190, 200.

102. E.g. J.-B. Terrien, *La grâce et la gloire ou la filiation adoptive des enfants de Dieu étudiée dans sa réalité, ses principes, son perfectionnement et son couronnement final* (Paris: Lethielleux, new edn, 1901), vol. 2, pp. 171–2.

of what theologians call appropriation. This is a procedure that can be observed, from Aquinas's point of view, in both biblical and patristic writings. Aquinas himself came to appreciate traditional instances of appropriation not merely as matters of pious convention, but as ways of further manifesting Trinitarian faith.[103] Thus a link can be made between what is proper to a divine person and something that is akin to that divine characteristic. For example, while divine wisdom and knowledge are identical with the divine essence, it is proper to the Word to proceed by way of intellect. Hence whatever touches on intellect can be appropriated to the Son, and so Paul manifests the Son's personhood more clearly by calling him the Wisdom of God (1 Cor. 1.24), and Aquinas speaks of all created knowledge as a participation in the Word.[104] Likewise, Aquinas makes sense of the appropriation of gifts of grace to the Spirit through his understanding that it is proper to the Spirit to be the Gift common to Father and Son, since, proceeding from both, the Spirit is eternally apt to be given.[105] Both these appropriations, knowledge and gift, are relevant to the beatitude of heaven. Aquinas argues that, since the divine essence is beyond natural human power to obtain, it can only be given to the blessed as a gift of divine grace.[106] Hence the divine self-donation to the saints that takes place in the beatific vision can be fittingly appropriated to the Spirit, just as the gracious self-communication of God to the justified on earth is appropriated to the Spirit who is Gift. And since the divine essence is given in heaven precisely to be the saints' means of knowledge, it can from that perspective be appropriated to the Word.

These appropriations apply not only to the uncreated gift of God himself in the beatific vision, but to the further gift it introduces into the intellect to dispose the intellect to receive the uncreated gift. The metaphysics of this uncreated gift and the created gift that accompanies it was the subject of much speculation in twentieth-century scholasticism.[107] Aquinas had called the latter gift the 'light of glory'(*lumen gloriae*), a theological term already in use among Aquinas's contemporaries for a heavenly light, which Aquinas unequivocally referred to the created modification of the intellect rather than to an uncreated gift.[108] The necessity of the light of glory was later proclaimed in 1312 by the Council of Vienne to counter any claim that God could be seen without it.[109] Aquinas argued that our natural light of reason, even when elevated by supernatural faith, works in proportion to finite *species*, and is thus inadequate to such a means of knowledge as the divine essence. Hence, to receive the divine essence as means of knowledge, the minds of the blessed must be elevated by a new supernatural

103. *Summa*, 1a., q. 39, a. 7. See Emery, *Trinitarian Theology of St Thomas Aquinas*, pp. 312–37.

104. *Super Ioannem*, 1.3.

105. *Summa*, 1a., q. 38.

106. *Contra Gentiles*, 3.52; *Summa*, 1a., q. 12, a. 5.

107. E.g. Rahner, 'Some Implications of the Scholastic Concept of Uncreated Grace'.

108. Trottmann, *La Vision Béatifique*, pp. 321–5.

109. *Ad Nostrum Qui*, 5.

light, the light of glory.[110] So while the *species* is that *by which* we ordinarily know and the light of reason that *under which* we ordinarily know, in the act of beatific knowledge the divine essence is that *by which* we know and the (created) light of glory that *under which* we know. Aquinas used the light of glory to explain the special likeness of the saints to God (cf. 1 Jn 3.2) and to interpret those passages of Scripture that speak of heaven in terms of light (e.g. Rev. 21.23). As with the divine essence being the saints' means of knowledge, we have here a gift of divine grace, indeed the consummation of grace in glory, which can thus be appropriated to the Holy Spirit, who is Gift, but also to the Word insofar as it is an intellectual participation in him. Thus we may say that the Spirit gives himself intimately in a consummate way to the blessed, making of their minds a new creation, so that by means of the Word dwelling within them they may gaze for all eternity on the Father.

Applying these Trinitarian appropriations and gifts of grace to the human mind of Christ, we are able to manifest our Trinitarian faith once again by thinking of how his intimate knowledge of the Father was rooted in a consummate gift of the grace of the Holy Spirit. In his humanity he received not only the gift of the Holy Spirit himself, but the gift of the light of glory, which as the consummation of all grace we receive in this life elevated Christ's mind to a fittingly perfect knowledge of the Father. The bestowal of the Spirit himself and of this gift is consonant with the Gospels' portrayal of Christ's life as shaped by the Spirit in various ways. While his conception takes place through the Holy Spirit (Mt. 1.20), the Spirit descends on him at his baptism (Mt. 3.16), after which he is described as 'full of the Spirit' (Lk. 4.1); he is driven by the Spirit into the desert (Mk 1.12), returns to Galilee 'in the power of the Spirit' (Lk. 4.14), and so on. To him the Spirit is given 'without measure' (Jn 3.34). The influence of the Spirit has definite created effects in Christ's life, and we may suppose that these included created gifts, which are distinct from the uncreated Spirit himself but which we may appropriate, as gifts, to the Spirit. Insofar as the grace of the light of glory is not the uncreated Spirit himself, but a certain recreation or modification of Christ's mind, we may likewise appropriate it, like all gifts of grace, to the Spirit. Thus, it was through the Spirit's grace that the humanity united by him in person to the divine Word was also intimately united to the Word in a further way, in a union of knowledge. Thus the Word does not remain in any way alien in the order of knowledge to his own humanity, but for the sake of our salvation indwells in knowledge that humanity which is his by the hypostatic union. His unity in being is graciously followed by a unity in means of knowing between his humanity and his divinity, which is the result of the divine essence, the divine means of knowledge appropriated to the Word, being communicated into his human mind. Just as Christ as God possesses knowledge by way of the divine essence, so he as human possesses knowledge through exactly the same means as a gift of the Spirit's grace. Thus the

110. *Summa*, 1a., q. 12, a. 5. McDermott, 'How Did Jesus Know He Was God?', p. 291, argues unconvincingly that Aquinas is unclear whether the light of glory is strictly supernatural or natural.

application of a Thomist theology of the beatific vision to the earthly Christ is consistent with what we find in the Gospels of Christ as a man uniquely blessed by God's Holy Spirit.

Aquinas's account of the means of vision also has important implications for how he nuances the patristic distinction between vision and comprehension, and this too has a particular application in the case of Christ. As we have already noted, Aquinas accepted the traditional terminology of calling those who have arrived at the beatific vision *comprehensores* and those who are on the way in this life 'pilgrims', because the former have attained to the essential goal of the journey so as to 'attain to' or 'comprehend' God. However, he distinguished their 'comprehension' or attainment of beatitude from the more precise use of the term 'comprehension', which indicates exhaustive knowledge.[111] Thus he can distinguish between knowing what something is and the exhaustive knowledge of it that is properly called comprehension, a knowledge where something is known as fully as it can be known. His example is knowledge of the fact that the angles of a triangle add up to two right angles. Someone may only be said to know this to the full extent it can be known, that is, comprehend it, when he has a mathematical understanding of *why* the angles add up this way.[112] However, although someone may be able to gain exhaustive knowledge of a finite truth of geometry, no creaturely act can attain to a comparable knowledge of the Holy Trinity. Despite the fact that the blessed have in the divine essence an infinite means of knowing, it never delivers them full comprehension of the infinite God. This inescapability of God's absolute incomprehensibility to the blessed is an important theme Rahner draws from Aquinas – God is present to them precisely as an unfathomable mystery, his very incomprehensibility being positive content for their vision rather than something to be regretted.[113]

On a Thomist account, the inability of the saints to comprehend God is again not because of a limitation in God's intelligibility, but because of a quite proper limitation in creatures, namely, the finitude of the saints' inevitably creaturely *act* of knowledge, and the finitude of the created light of glory that elevates it to the divine essence. Though the means of knowledge is infinite, the finite act of knowledge that takes place under the finite light of glory is as such unable to take full advantage, so to speak, of the divine essence's infinity. Only the infinite God has in his divine nature an act of knowledge of infinite power, which is identical with the infinite divine essence. Hence only God as God can take full advantage of his infinite means of knowledge and know himself with absolute perfection, as fully as he can be known. Only divine knowledge can comprehend God.[114] In contrast, though the saints have the same infinite means of knowledge, their

111. Ibid., 1a., q. 12, a. 7 ad 1.

112. Ibid., 1a., q. 12, a. 7.

113. Rahner, 'An Investigation of the Incomprehensibility of God in St Thomas Aquinas' in *Theological Investigations*, vol. 16: *Experience of the Spirit: Source of Theology* (trans. D. Morland; London: Darton, Longman & Todd), pp. 244–54.

114. *Summa*, 1a., q. 14, a. 3.

acts of knowing through this essence remain finite creaturely acts. Hence, no creaturely act, though it sees God's essence by means of God's essence, can know that essence exhaustively, knowing it to the extent that it can in itself be known. Hence for Aquinas, Christ will never comprehend God in his creaturely humanity, but only in his divinity.[115]

Given that the saints' knowledge cannot be exhaustive, how does Aquinas interpret the character of this non-comprehensiveness? It cannot be explained by a lack of mathematical knowledge, as with triangles. He also cannot deny that their vision extends to the whole divine essence, as in the case of objects of physical vision one can see part of something but not the whole, as though God's essence could somehow be divided up into parts, with one part seen but another out of view. Nor can it be because one saint has a better means of understanding than another, as though we were concerned with variable finite *species* and not the divine essence. Rather his explanation draws on different levels of perfection of vision, which also helps him explain the traditional teaching of differing levels of heavenly glory among the saints, to which we referred in Chapter 3. As where two people can see the same extent of a physical object, but the one with keener sight will see it more perfectly, so the saints will all see God and all of God, but some more perfectly than others. Since the human mind has no power of itself to see God, this variation in the perfection of beatific acts is explained by varying levels of participation in the light of glory. The blessed will see God more or less perfectly, based on varying levels of participation in the light of glory, which are proportioned to different degrees of holiness from their earthly lives.[116] But what of Christ's vision in his humanity? He too cannot make a comprehensive act of knowledge, since his act of knowledge is finite and limited by the finitude of his light of glory. Moreover, since this light is finite, one can always conceive the possibility of a higher degree of it, and so Aquinas admitted that Christ could never be gifted with a 'highest' degree of it, absolutely speaking.[117] What is in fact fitting to Christ's humanity, as the humanity of the divine Word, is that it be gifted with the highest degree of vision in the actual order of things God has created.[118] Moreover, because this vision of God is to be the salvific cause of ours, it must be greater than ours, since, according to Aquinas, the cause is always greater than its effect.[119] Christ was granted the most perfect beatific vision in the order of things God has actually made.

Not that the object of beatific knowledge, according to Aquinas, is limited to God the Holy Trinity. It extends also to creatures, and we shall now examine Aquinas's account of the secondary objects of the beatific vision, in order to ask how it too can be applied to Christ. Aquinas grounds his account of the saints' beatific knowledge of creatures in his account of God's own divine knowledge, in

115. Ibid., 3a., q. 10, a. 1.
116. Ibid., 1a., q. 12, a. 6.
117. Ibid., 3a., q. 10, a. 4 ad 3.
118. Ibid., 3a., q. 10, a. 4. Cf. 3a., q. 7, a. 12.
119. Ibid., 3a., q. 9, a. 2.

which the beatific vision is of course a participation. Since God knows himself comprehensively as the primary object of his knowledge, his knowledge of his essence includes absolutely perfect knowledge of his power, which is identical with his essence by way of simplicity. Thus, in his knowledge of his essence he has knowledge secondarily of all that is in his power to do, the infinity of possible worlds he could create, which Aquinas calls his 'simple understanding', as well as of the things of which he is actually the cause, which Aquinas calls his 'knowledge of vision'.[120] All this is of a piece with the fact that nothing external can inform God about God or anything else; there is in him no potential for knowing to be actualized, either about himself or about creatures, as there is in us. God knows all creatures not by receiving information from them themselves, but by his own essence. He does not know his creatures through any *species* derived from without, as we ordinarily know creatures, but only through *himself*, that is, through his essence.[121] Aquinas distinguished between knowing something in itself through its own *species* and knowing it in another through an image of it, as when for example we perceive something by seeing it in a mirror rather than seeing the thing itself. It is not entirely dissimilar for God, because he sees things not in themselves but in *himself*, seeing things as they pre-exist in him as their cause, knowing them in knowing himself as the primary object of his own knowledge and thus knowing them perfectly. Since his act of knowledge is identical with his essence by way of divine simplicity, he necessarily knows everything of which he is the cause by one and the same act, and not by several acts in succession. It is in this way that Aquinas provides a theological explanation of divine omniscience, an attribute he of course finds revealed in Scripture (e.g. Heb. 4.13).[122] God knows all things in a single, eternal exhaustive grasp of his own essence, a single knowledge common to all three persons of the Trinity. It is through nothing other than his essence that God knows both the entire Trinity *and all creatures*, including the human nature he knows to be hypostatically united to the Word. Thus, when we come to the beatific vision, we are coming to know God in just the same way that he knows *us*. This is how Aquinas interprets Paul's 'I shall know *just as* I am also known' – the saints know God by the very same means that he knows *them*, that is, through the divine essence.[123]

Not only though will the saints know God as he knows them, but they will also know his creatures as he knows his creatures, that is, by the same means. Since God shares with the blessed his own means of knowledge, which is a means of knowing creatures as well as himself, Aquinas envisions him granting to the blessed a knowledge of creatures in their knowledge of the primary object of vision.[124] This is what Aquinas means when he speaks by appropriation of those enjoying the beatific vision as having knowledge not only of the Word but 'in the

---

120. Ibid., 1a., q. 14, a. 5; q. 14, a. 9.
121. Ibid., 1a., q. 14, a. 2.
122. Ibid., 1a., q. 14, a. 5.
123. Ibid., 1a., q. 12, a. 6 ad 1.
124. Ibid., 1a., q. 12, a. 8.

Word'.[125] He sees the saints' manner of knowing things in God as dependent on how they are present in God, that is, as effects in their cause. Thus he relates the primary and secondary objects of the beatific vision as cause and effect, just as they are related in God's own divine act of knowledge. In knowing the cause of creatures, the blessed also have knowledge of his effects. All this knowledge takes place, according to Aquinas, not successively in many acts as though through many *species*, but in a single act through God's one essence, a kind of participated eternity, which imitates the eternity of God's great single act of knowing himself and all things.[126] In this one act of beatific vision, the inhabitants of heaven know both God and what they know in God.

However, it is important to note that the range of knowledge had through created finite acts in the divine essence can hardly be the same as comes through God's infinite act of knowledge. Just as no finite act of knowledge, even with the divine essence as its means, can comprehend God, so no such act can take in all that God can do. No saint's act of beatific knowledge can match God's infinite act of 'simple understanding'. Aquinas considered each saint to know more or less in God, according as they know their cause more or less perfectly. In the case of purely creaturely causes, the more intelligent grasp the cause better than the less intelligent, and so have a greater grasp of that cause's effects. Likewise, the more perfectly God is known, the more of his effects are known in knowledge of him.[127] Aquinas surmises that each of the blessed will have a range of knowledge in God that is properly suited to that individual.[128] This range, however, will always include knowledge of Christ's humanity as its principal component, since it is through this humanity that the blessed have been saved and brought to heaven so as to see God just as he is. Thus Aquinas could speak of beatific knowledge as related to two main truths: 'the divinity of the Blessed Trinity and the humanity of Christ'.[129] This is how he interpreted Christ's words to the Father in Jn 17.3: 'This is eternal life: that they may know you, the only true God, and Jesus Christ whom you have sent.' These are the two principal truths of faith in this life and of the vision of heaven. Moreover, as well as an appropriate knowledge of salvation, this knowledge will always include a general scientific account of creation, such as will satisfy the intellect.[130]

How then would this apply to Christ? This brings another element to Aquinas's response to the question of how Christ's knowledge in his humanity differs from the knowledge in his divinity. While by his divine knowledge he knows the infinity of worlds that God could make, the knowledge in his humanity cannot be thus comprehensive so as to match God's 'simple understanding'. But what exactly

125. Ibid., 1a., q. 12, a. 10.

126. Ibid., 1a., q. 12, a. 10.

127. Ibid., 1a., q. 12, a. 8.

128. Ibid., 3a., q. 10. a. 2.

129. *Compendium Theologiae seu brevis compilatio theologiae ad fratrem Raynaldum*, 1.2.

130. *Summa*, 1a., q. 12, a. 8 ad 4.

would Christ see in God, if not all of what God could do? As is the case with all the blessed, Aquinas envisions Christ's supremely perfect vision in the actual order of things as giving him a range of knowledge *suited to himself*. Knowing the essence of God in his human mind, he would know in that vision all that it is fitting for the Saviour to know, his human mind being equipped with an access to the divine mind that would enable him humanly to carry out his saving mission. The Saviour will know his humanity as the means of salvation, like all the blessed, but in this case will of course know it to be his own, the humanity of the divine Saviour. When the nature of Christ's knowledge of his identity emerged as a topic of debate among neoscholastics in the twentieth century, whatever role they would or would not assign here to Christ's consciousness, his beatific vision almost always remained crucial to explaining how he knew who he was, until Rahner advanced his particular theory.[131] Moreover, since all things have a bearing on the Saviour who is, for example, the judge of all (Jn 5.27), Aquinas took him to know in the Word 'everything that exists throughout time, including the thoughts of men', because *everything* pertains to his mission.[132] In other words, though he does not have the 'simple understanding' of divine knowledge in his humanity, he shares the scope of its 'knowledge of vision'. This helps Aquinas make sense of the extraordinary knowledge of human hearts found in the Gospels, which he can thus assign to Christ's humanity as well as to his divinity. Finally, like all the blessed, he too would have a satisfying general scientific knowledge of creation.

Thus far we have seen how, by way of a participation in divine knowledge, Christ's mind could have access to the divine. However, can this theory of Christ's beatific vision also illuminate the passing on of the content of his vision to others? In order to see how the beatific knowledge in Christ's humanity could become the basis of his human teaching, we first need to ask how it could be humanly expressed. Could the content of the beatific vision have been humanly verbalized, whether interiorly in the mind or externally in the spoken word? As we have seen, in the ordinary human act of knowledge, Aquinas distinguished the *species* by which we know, the light of reason under which we know and the mental word in which we express our knowledge. If, in the beatific vision, the *species* is replaced by the essence of God and the mind elevated by the light of glory, what role can there be for a mental word *in which* the saints know the divine essence and all the knowledge it contains? Whether there is a *species expressa* that mentally verbalizes knowledge of the divine essence has been debated among Thomists since the fourteenth century.[133] Can the saints articulate their knowledge of the divine essence by thinking or saying what God is, in such a way that it could be humanly communicated?

Clearly, on Aquinas's account, there can be no place for expressing any definition of God whatsoever. According to Aquinas, when we ordinarily express the essence of something we come to know, we do so by defining it, by giving its

131. E.g. Galtier, 'La conscience humaine du Christ', *Gregorianum* 35 (1954): 225–46.
132. *Summa*, 3a., q. 10, a. 2.
133. Trottmann, *La Vision Béatifique*, pp. 383–4.

place in a wider class or genus, together with whatever differentiates it from other kinds within this same wider class. Man is thus defined as a rational animal.[134] But in the case of God, we have an object of knowledge that cannot be so defined. This is not because our minds are too weak to discover or express his definition, even when elevated by the light of glory, but because the absolutely simple God just has no definition to be grasped.[135] He is not a member of some wider class, as though he were a member of the universe rather than its Creator. Thus it is not that we are unable to tell each other what God is and define him here on earth, but will be able to do so in heaven. Even the blessed who see God's essence by way of God's essence cannot define what that essence is, and the same would be the case of Christ, even though he be granted the beatific vision. This does not mean that he or the blessed do not know God's essence, but that they cannot express that essence in a definition, just because God's essence is indefinable.

However, given that God's essence cannot be expressed by a definition, can it be properly expressed by the blessed in some other non-defining way? On Aquinas's principles, it cannot. The same reasons that exclude a *species impressa* adequate to knowledge of God's essence also exclude such a *species expressa* – no created, finite word of the mind could be equal to the infinite God. This inexpressibility extends not only to the saints' knowledge of God but also to what they see in God. On Aquinas's account, creatures are not known through the beatific vision by way of successive acts, with the blessed using each time a different *species impressa* proper to each thing known. Rather they are known not in themselves, where they could be expressed, but are known in their cause, in the inexpressible divine essence, by a single act of ineffable vision. The only 'word' that can adequately express the infinite God and thus all things in God is one who is truly God, the divine Word eternally spoken by the Father to whom he is equal. No human language can ever adequately express what God is, no matter what the heavenly circumstances, but only the comprehensive divine language of the Word. This infinite Word can never be the product of a finite human act of knowledge, however elevated by grace, but only of the Father's own infinite act of comprehensive knowledge. The saints are thus gifted with a beatific knowledge they cannot adequately express, and we cannot suppose that even the formulations of Trinitarian and other Christian doctrine made by faith in this life, however well articulated, could ever add up to a mental expression adequate to the saints' vision.

Were Christ then to possess the beatific vision, he too would be unable to produce an adequate mental verbalization of what God is and of what he knows in God by the 'knowledge of vision'. Even the one who *is* the Word of God, the Word made flesh, is gifted with a knowledge in his humanity that he cannot adequately express in word or thought. The beatific vision exceeds the normal workings of human knowledge, even in the case of Christ.[136] The inexpressibility of his beatific knowledge thus became of considerable importance among

---

134. *Summa*, 1a., q. 13, a. 1.
135. Ibid., 1a., q. 3, a. 5.
136. Cf. ibid., 3a., q. 11, a. 5 ad 1.

twentieth-century theologians.[137] That knowledge might be inexpressible is not of course something entirely unfamiliar to us. We can often struggle or even find it practically impossible to express to our satisfaction what we are sure we know, including in matters of faith and religious experience. Lonergan proposed the analogy of the light of the human intellect, a light on account of which we know so much but an understanding of which even philosophers have difficulty in expressing.[138] Jacques Maritain compared the situation of the blessed to the inability of someone with only a thousand dollar note and no change to buy a cup of orange juice from a dispensing machine: without a moneychanger, he could die of thirst![139] The inexpressibility of this knowledge thus sharpens the question of how Christ can teach us his knowledge of God and so on in a humanly expressible way. The beatific vision certainly gives Christ's human mind a share in divine knowledge, but how can this knowledge be communicated in *human* teaching if it is inexpressible? Lonergan compared the earthly Christ to a scientist seeking understanding and a philosopher seeking truth that they do not yet possess, while each nevertheless already has a sort of knowledge of what they are looking for, such that they can recognize it when they find it. Christ, in contrast, already enjoyed the end of knowing God, but from there used his human powers and capacities to render the ineffable what Lonergan termed *effabilis*, that is, speakable or 'effable'.[140] Maritain and others have given their own views on the question of what played the role of 'moneychanger' for Christ, and we shall touch on some of these in Chapter 6. For now we are going to enquire how *Aquinas*'s account of the heavenly life enjoyed by the blessed can help us.

Aquinas did not suppose that the beatific vision is the only act, or indeed the only intellectual act, that the saints make in heaven. In addition to the single, ongoing act of vision, he assigns the blessed a succession of further acts, including acts of the intellect.[141] In a similar way, the earthly Christ, while enjoying the inexpressible beatific vision, would have been able to make a succession of acts, intellectual and otherwise, but in his historical, earthly context, exactly as we find him doing in the Gospels. Among the successive acts that the saints make are those where the knowledge contained in the beatific vision is somehow 'translated' into a mode proportionate to the light of the human mind and thus made humanly communicable. In no way is this 'translation' truly possible for the primary object of the vision, God himself, whose essence is infinite and can never be adequately represented by a finite likeness. However, as we have noted, there are also the secondary objects that are known in the beatific vision, and these are in themselves finite. As such they will be open to appropriate finite expression.

137. E.g. A. Durand, 'La science du Christ', *NRT* 71 (1949): 497–503 (499–501).

138. Lonergan, *De Verbo Incarnato* (Rome: Gregorian, 3rd edn, 1964), p. 406.

139. J. Maritain, *On the Grace and Humanity of Jesus* (trans. J. W. Evans; New York: Herder, 1969), pp. 72–3.

140. *De Verbo Incarnato*, p. 407.

141. *Super Sent.*, 1.1.4.2 ad 2; *Quaestiones Disputatae de Anima*, 20 ad 13. Cf. *Contra Gentiles*, 2.101.3; 4.95.6.

Sometimes commentators neglect to recall the fact that Aquinas held that any of the blessed 'can from his vision of the divine essence form in himself the likenesses of things which are seen in the divine essence' (*ex ipsa visione essentiae divinae potest formare in se similitudines rerum quae in essentia divina videntur*).[142] Such an act of forming such a finite likeness or similitude would of course be an intellectual act distinct from the act of beatific knowledge itself, though it would necessarily presuppose that act of vision. Aquinas compared this new act to the process by which the imagination can from its images of gold and of a mountain form a new image of a 'golden mountain', and similar processes in the intellect by which already existing ideas are brought together to form new ideas. The ability of the saints to form such similitudes in the first place is presumably to be attributed to their light of glory, since the light of reason has no power to give the mind access to the vision of God. But if the light of glory can elevate the mind even to the vision of God, there would seem to be no reason why it could not also enable acts of forming similitudes from this vision, so that the saint can somehow 'translate' from the beatific vision what is in itself translatable, not the essence of God itself, but what is seen in God. In principle this could include not only knowledge of creatures, but of how knowledge of creatures can be fittingly applied to God. We have already noted that our human language, since it cannot express God adequately, always turns to concepts appropriate to creatures, which it stretches to refer to God. It is quite possible then that the beatific vision could be the source of such suitable notions. Were the earthly Christ also to have been blessed with the light of the glory and the beatific vision, he too would have been able to perform such acts of 'translation', just like any of the saints. As Aquinas puts it, Christ's blessed soul was able 'to form likenesses of the things which it sees' (*formare similitudines eorum quae videt*).[143] This ability would have equipped him with a message that was at once rooted in divine knowledge and humanly communicable.

Since Aquinas followed Augustine in taking Paul's experience of being caught up to the third heaven to involve a fleeting glimpse of the divine essence, he took the apostle's hearing of 'unspeakable words (ἄρρητα ῥήματα) which it is not lawful (ἐξὸν) for man to utter' (2 Cor. 12.4) to be an example of forming intelligible likenesses from what is seen in the divine essence,[144] the language of 'hearing' neatly expressing the reception of such 'words' from God. Aquinas held that, after the vision ceased, Paul continued to retain a habit of *species* from his vision, by which he was able to recall in a human, finite way some of those finite realities he saw in his vision of God. Presumably then, if the earthly Christ were granted a continual vision of God, he too would have been able to draw from it and retain

---

142. *Summa*, 1a., q. 12, a. 9 ad 2. A. Patfoort, 'Vision béatifique et théologie de l'âme du Christ: Á propos d'un ouvrage récent', *RT* 93 (1993): 635–9 (36), remarks on this omission in the case of C. Sarrasin, *Plein de grâce et de verité: Théologie de l'âme du Christ selon Thomas d'Aquin* (Vénasque: Carmel, 1992).

143. *De Veritate*, q. 20, a. 3 ad 4.

144. *Summa*, 1a., q. 12, a. 9 ad 2; 2a.2ae., q. 175, a. 3.

such a habit of *species* or, in more Pauline language, to have heard some kind of heavenly words (cf. Jn 17.8). However, Aquinas also took Paul to be saying in this verse that he had some difficulty in thinking over and expressing his purely intellectual knowledge and expressing it in words, which Aquinas seems to have attributed to the fact that Paul was at the time of this experience withdrawn from the senses and so from the sense images that normally accompany human knowledge (cf. v. 2).[145] In Christ's case, however, we may suppose that there could have been no such difficulty of expression. Christ's soul, after all, unlike Paul's, was not withdrawn from the body and its senses during his earthly possession of the beatific vision. As we shall see in Chapter 6, Lonergan held that, while an ecstasy of the soul from the body may be appropriate to one being caught up from ordinary knowledge into a glimpse of the divine essence, that would not be the case for one whose ordinary knowing in the body had itself developed against the wider horizon of possession of the beatific vision.

It is worth noting, however, that Paul himself may have meant no more than that he was simply *forbidden* to speak the 'unspeakable words' he 'heard', rather than that he found them difficult to express.[146] We can grasp the possible significance of him being so forbidden when we recall that Paul was including this experience in an account of his 'weaknesses', as he sought to give a defence of himself in the face of unfavourable comparisons that were being made of him with his 'stronger' rivals. It is in itself a puzzle for exegetes that Paul included in a narrative of his weaknesses what was on the face of it a strength, namely, being caught up to heaven. I suggest that the weakness in this case consists not so much in the nature of the experience itself as in Paul's inability to communicate the 'words' he had heard. Perhaps his 'stronger' rivals, claiming to have experienced admission to heaven, had impressed the Corinthians by communicating what they had allegedly heard. The weak Paul, in contrast, had nothing impressive to say, because he was forbidden by God to speak what he had heard. Now let us suppose that, in the case of Christ, it was indeed *his* mission, unlike Paul's, to speak the words *he* had heard from his Father, to communicate what he had seen through use of the likenesses he had formed out of the beatific vision. This then is how the theory of Christ's vision can illuminate what he said to the apostles in John 15.15: 'Everything that I have heard from my Father I made known to you.' And likewise John 17:8: 'I have given them the words [ῥήματα] which you gave me.'[147]

We can conclude then that the theory of the earthly Christ's beatific vision is a plausible one, because it can help us in this way to illuminate the picture of Christ we find in the Gospels, that is, of one who teaches us humanly of divine things. Were Christ's mind to have been elevated by the light of glory on earth, he would have possessed not only the vision of the inexpressible God and of things in God, which would have provided a divine source for his teaching, but also the

145. Ibid., 2a.2ae., q. 175, a. 4 ad 3.
146. Cf. Rowland, *The Open Heaven*, p. 383.
147. For Aquinas's own interpretation of these verses, see *Super Ioannem*, 15.3.2017; 17.2.2201.

ability to form from this vision, by an historical succession of temporal acts, a communicable knowledge of creatures and of creaturely concepts appropriate to apply to God. In that way he would have been a true teacher of divine things, his divine knowledge being received in an appropriate way into his human mind by way of the beatific vision, which would then have been a source from which he could draw knowledge of a sort that could be humanly taught and communicated to his disciples. He would thus be endowed with a unique ability from his most perfect and intimate knowledge of the Father to proclaim the Father's kingdom with authority.

Despite the foregoing argument, the problem will remain for many critics that this theory, however plausible it may be in some respects, yields an earthly Christ whose knowledge is *too* perfect, *too* intimate, for the purpose of our salvation. Those who reject this theory as a possible theological explanation of the contents of Scripture and Tradition often do so because they hold that the beatific theory is based on too narrow a reading of Scripture, ignoring the fuller picture of the Saviour that the Gospels provide. This fuller picture would reveal a Christ who has many features on earth for which the theory of his beatific vision allegedly cannot account, and which in fact exclude this vision from his mind. Should this charge prove correct, the theory of Christ's beatific vision could have no true foundation in Scripture and Tradition after all; it would lose all plausibility, and we should be forced to look elsewhere for an explanation of Christ the Teacher. In Part Two we shall examine these features one by one, and test the theory of Christ's beatific vision against them.

Part II

Chapter 5

'BUT JESUS HAD FAITH!'

We noted in Chapter 1 how in 2006 the Congregation for the Doctrine of the Faith took issue with Jon Sobrino's understanding of Jesus as a man of *faith*. Sobrino himself had already acknowledged as long ago as 1976 that it was a 'polemical formulation' to speak of 'Jesus' faith'.[1] This was partly because it struck out against what he called a more 'abstract' treatment of Christ's humanity, which he plainly associated with scholasticism. Though the thesis already had a history outside Catholic circles, to attribute faith to Jesus was still a relative novelty among Catholics.[2] Sobrino's characterization of scholasticism's approach as 'mythical thinking about Jesus' recalled Rahner's observation that statements about Christ's beatific vision now sounded 'mythological'.[3] Sobrino wrote that the polemical nature of his own formulation was clear enough from the fact that Aquinas himself excluded faith from Jesus on the ground that he possessed the beatific vision.[4] He does not question Aquinas's principle that faith and sight of the same object are mutually exclusive. Later on he says, 'Faith does not signify possession of God and his kingdom but rather an ongoing search for them.'[5] We saw in the last chapter how Aquinas's theory did not exclude from Jesus or any of the blessed the desire to do God's will and extend his kingdom, but did exclude from them any further search for God himself. Sobrino doubtless agreed that vision excludes

---

1. *Christology at the Crossroads* (trans. J. Drury; London: SCM, 1978), p. 80.
2. E.g. W. Thüsing, 'New Testament Approaches to a Transcendental Christology' in K. Rahner and Thüsing, *A New Christology* (London: Burns & Oates, 1980), pp. 44–211 (143–54). For a brief summary of the idea of Christ's faith in recent Catholic theology, see Allen, *Christ's Faith*, pp. 21–3; and M. W. Elliott, 'Πίστις Χριστοῦ in the Church Fathers and Beyond' in M. F. Bird and P. M. Sprinkle (eds), *The Faith of Jesus Christ: Exegetical, Biblical, and Theological Studies* (Milton Keynes: Paternoster; Colorado Springs and Hyderabad: Hendrickson, 2009), pp. 277–89 (286–9). Allen's *Christ's Faith* argues the case from the perspective of Reformed theology, in conscious opposition to Aquinas's position on the earthly Christ's beatific vision.
3. Rahner, 'Dogmatic Reflections on the Knowledge and Self-Consciousness of Christ', pp. 194–5.
4. See *Summa*, 3a., q. 7, a. 3.
5. *Christology at the Crossroads*, pp. 95–6.

an ongoing search for God, and this search he assigns to faith, and to the faith of Jesus. As Aquinas himself recognized, faith does not bring desire for God to rest, but sets it aflame.[6] Sobrino's Christ is thus a rather different Saviour from the one who would see the Father and reveal him. Sobrino declared that Jesus did not reveal the Father, strictly speaking, but instead revealed the Son. He did not reveal the 'absolute mystery' but how one may respond to that absolute mystery.[7] In other words, he revealed faith. An argument may thus be constructed: Christ had faith while on earth; faith and vision are mutually exclusive; so the earthly Christ could not have enjoyed the beatific vision. In the course of this chapter we shall argue that Christ did not in fact possess the theological virtue of faith, that faith and vision are indeed mutually exclusive, meaning that the only viable alternative is a Christ who truly saw his Father while on earth.

If we are to investigate whether or not Christ had faith, we must start in the same place we began our investigation of his beatific vision, in Scripture. In this case there is no danger of searching anachronistically for the formula of a later age, as there was in the case of the *visio beatifica*. As Dulles puts it, 'The word "faith" might be described as *the* Christian word.'[8] Both the noun πίστις and the verb 'to believe' (πιστεύω) are very much part of the normal vocabulary of the Bible. It is said, for example, in the Old Testament that Abraham 'believed' (LXX: ἐπίστευσεν) the Lord (Gen. 15.6). The verb is regularly used for a positive response to Jesus in the New Testament (e.g. Jn 2.11), where the noun is also often applied to people in the same category (e.g. Lk. 6.20) and to the holy men and women of the Old Covenant (Heb. 11.1–39). That the noun and the verb share the same range of meaning is suggested by the fact that in Romans 4.9 Paul substituted the noun for the verb when making reference to Genesis 15.6. A survey of Scripture easily demonstrates that the biblical notion of faith and believing has a number of elements to its overall range of meaning. These are normally taken to include fidelity or faithfulness, trust or confidence, assent or belief, endurance, and possibly obedience.[9] Context sometimes focuses the particular meaning on one of these elements. As Dulles notes, overall usage in the Old Testament tends to emphasize trust or confidence, with faith tested by obedience and fidelity, and with belief or assent present by implication. This latter cognitive element becomes more pronounced in the New Testament, partly because of the necessity of believing *that* Christ was risen from the dead and had fulfilled Jewish hopes, although the element of confidence or trust certainly continues to be central.[10] The cognitive element was also of particular concern to the Fathers and to the analyses

---

6. *Contra Gentiles*, 3.40.5.

7. *Christology at the Crossroads*, pp. 105–6.

8. A. Dulles, *The Assurance of the Things Hoped For: A Theology of Christian Faith* (New York and Oxford: OUP, 1994), p. 3.

9. On doubts about the element of obedience, see D. Hunn, 'Debating the Faithfulness of Jesus Christ in Twentieth-Century Scholarship' in Bird and Sprinkle, *The Faith of Jesus Christ: Exegetical, Biblical, and Theological Studies*, pp. 15–31 (17–18).

10. Ibid., p. 17.

undertaken within medieval scholasticism.[11] Whether or not the highlighting of a particular element in any particular case in Scripture ever excludes the presence of others altogether has been debated, but it may well be that, though not emphasized, the other elements are always present to some degree.[12] Given then how much 'faith' is *the* Christian and indeed biblical word, could anything have been more straightforward for the authors of the New Testament than to say that Jesus 'believed' or lived by 'faith'?

An examination of the New Testament shows that it is never there said that Jesus 'believed', nor is it ever clearly said that he had 'faith'. Nevertheless, Sobrino asserts that it is said 'explicitly' in Mark 9.23 that Jesus believed. He is citing Jesus' words to a father who has asked him, if he were able, to exorcize his son: 'If you are able! All things are possible to him who believes (πιστεύοντι).' However, it is not explicit in this reply whether or not believing is required on the part of Jesus or on the part of the father. When we look at other healings in Mark's Gospel, however, we do find that believing or faith is a crucial element on the part of those who benefit from Christ's miracles. For example, he tells the woman healed from a flow of blood: 'Daughter, your faith has saved you' (5.34). And when we turn back to the father's response to Jesus, we find him saying, 'I believe (Πιστεύω); help my unbelief!' (9.24). So, once again, we find that it is believing on the part of the beneficiaries of Jesus' mighty works that is at issue, and not any faith on the part of Jesus himself.

While nothing is explicitly said in Scripture about Jesus' believing, there are some instances where the noun πίστις has been read as applying to a quality in Jesus rather than in someone else, and Sobrino took this position in his work.[13] Certainly the meaning of the genitive case in the Pauline phrase πίστις Χριστοῦ (Rom. 3.22, 26; Gal. 2.16, 20; 3.22; Eph. 3.12; Phil. 3.9) has been much debated among exegetes in recent years.[14] Paul is convinced that justification does not come by observing the Jewish law but by πίστις Χριστοῦ, a faith that is referred to Christ by the genitive case. But how does this use of the genitive case relate the 'faith' (πίστις) through which comes our justification to 'Christ' (Χριστοῦ)? If πίστις Χριστοῦ were read as a subjective genitive, it would mean 'Christ's faith', while if it is read as an objective genitive, it would mean others' 'faith *in* Christ'. On the former reading, God would justify us by means of Christ's *own* faith, while on the latter he would justify us through the gift of our having faith *in* Christ.[15] Prescinding from the wider context of Scripture and Tradition, either reading

11. For Aquinas on faith, see *Summa*, 2a.2ae. qq. 1–7.

12. Cf. R. B. Hays, 'ΠΙΣΤΙΣ ΧΡΙΣΤΟΥ and Pauline Christology', in E. E. Johnson and D. M. Hay, *Pauline Theology*, vol. 4: *Looking Back, Pressing On* (Atlanta: Scholars, 1997), pp. 35–60 (58–9).

13. *Jesus the Liberator*, p. 156.

14. For some recent contributions to the 'πίστις Χριστοῦ debate', see Bird and Sprinkle, *The Faith of Jesus Christ*.

15. For a short history and summary of the debate, see Hunn, 'Debating the Faithfulness of Jesus Christ in Twentieth-Century Scholarship'.

seems in itself possible. Proponents of a subjective genitive have certainly made arguments against an exegesis based on an objective genitive, but there has not been one argument that has not had its reply from the other side. For example, it has been claimed that an objective genitive would introduce 'redundancies and tautologies' into verses where uses of πίστις Χριστοῦ occur, such as Galatians 2.16, which would read: 'knowing that a man is not justified by works of the law but through faith in Jesus Christ (διὰ πίστεως Ἰησοῦ Χριστοῦ), even we who have believed in Christ Jesus (εἰς Χριστὸν Ἰησοῦν ἐπιστεύσαμεν), in order that we may be justified by faith in Christ (ἐκ πίστεως Χριστοῦ) and not by works of the law, because no flesh will be justified by works of the law'.[16] On this reading, the use of the objective genitive would make its meaning come close to the use of the verb and preposition in the middle part of the quotation, such that the whole could be accused of needless repetition on the level of ideas expressed. One response is that the threefold repetition of 'by works of the law' and 'justified' may even require such a threefold repetition of the idea of 'faith in Christ'. As R. Barry Matlock notes, debate over similar texts 'has shown that one person's "redundancy" might be another's "emphasis"'.[17]

Proponents of the subjective genitive have sometimes focused in on the argument that the objective genitive is at least unlikely on purely linguistic grounds. According to Matlock, they have generally done this by taking fidelity as the normal meaning of πίστις, and the normal use of the genitive with πίστις in Hellenistic Jewish literature to be subjective.[18] Having made these assumptions, it is argued that Paul would have been unlikely to depart from such linguistic conventions. However, as we have already indicated, the primary connotation of πίστις in the New Testament is arguably not fidelity at all but trust and belief. Nevertheless, it seems there is certainly plenty of evidence of the use of a subjective genitive with πίστις in several Hellenistic Jewish writers, as well as of a certain preference for indicating faith *in* an object by the use of a preposition, which also occurs in Paul.[19] However, it has also been pointed out that there is also evidence for the use of the objective genitive.[20] For example, Matlock reports that the Greek historian Plutarch, who was a younger contemporary of Paul, used πίστις with an objective genitive some thirteen times in his *Lives*. Since he indicated the object of πίστις only once with the preposition περί and five times with πρός, his preferred method of indicating the object of faith turns out to be the objective genitive.[21] This suggests that, in using the same genitive, Paul would

16. G. Howard, 'Faith of Christ' in Freedman et al., *Anchor Bible Dictionary*, vol. 2, pp. 758–60 (758).

17. R. B. Matlock, '"Even the Demons Believe": Paul and πίστις Χριστοῦ', *CBQ* 64 (2002): 300–18 (307).

18. Ibid., p. 303.

19. Howard, 'Faith of Christ', p. 758.

20. Harrisville, 'Before ΠΙΣΤΙΣ ΧΡΙΣΤΟΥ: The Objective Genitive as Good Greek', *NT* 48 (2006): 353–8.

21. Matlock, 'Even the Demons Believe', p. 304.

indeed not have been departing from Greek linguistic convention, a linguistic convention that perfectly well allowed him to mean by πίστις Χριστοῦ 'faith *in* Christ', as well as to allow him parallel expressions by means of prepositions to indicate faith's object.[22]

It is hard not to regard the whole πίστις Χριστοῦ debate as standing at something of a stalemate. The texts, however, and indeed the whole debate over them, may be viewed in the light of a wider reading of Scripture and Tradition. Looking only within the Pauline corpus, we find πιστεύω occurring more than 50 times and πίστις over 140 times. In all cases of the verb, it is never once predicated of Christ, and in all but the handful of cases of πίστις Χριστοῦ we have been considering, the noun is *definitely* attributed to others, and to others who believe in Christ, and not to Christ himself. Given these facts, we may draw the conclusion that Paul would be unlikely to apply πίστις to Christ without making his meaning plain. Indeed it may even seem unlikely from this that Paul's πίστις Χριστοῦ was attributing faith to Christ at all. That others in the first century understood Paul to have meant the faith enjoyed by Christians rather than one enjoyed by Christ is suggested when we look outside the Pauline corpus to the Letter of James, where faith is also a prominent theme.[23] James appears to be responding to a misunderstanding of Paul's teaching that justification comes by faith and not by works of the law. This misunderstanding seems to have involved the idea that one could be justified by a faith present in oneself in such a way that it need not be active in good works. James says to the contrary that people are justified by works and not by faith alone (2.24). To his opponents he responds, 'What is the benefit, my brothers, if someone says he has faith but does not have works? Is his faith able to save him?' (2.14). A presupposition shared by both James and his opponents is that the faith in question is the Christian's faith. James does not counter them with any idea that it is Christ's own faith by which we are justified, but rather accepts that the justified are justified by a faith that is present in them themselves. Thus can James also be understood to use an objective genitive to exhort his brethren 'to have faith in our Lord Jesus Christ of glory (πίστιν τοῦ κυρίου ἡμῶν Ἰησοῦ Χριστοῦ τῆς δόξης) without partiality' (2.1). However, all this is not only historical evidence for the fact that at least some people interpreted the πίστις Χριστοῦ of the Pauline doctrine of justification to be faith *in* Christ. Since James' letter has the authority of Holy Scripture, the Catholic principle that one part of Scripture is to be interpreted in terms of another means that Catholic theologians may have here an authoritative interpretation of Paul's πίστις Χριστοῦ as faith in Jesus Christ and not as any faith of Christ's own.[24]

When we look beyond Scripture itself to the traditional interpretation of Scripture, we find that a survey of the Fathers shows that not one of them ever

22. On the linguistic arguments, see S. E. Porter and A. W. Pitts, 'Πίστις with a Preposition and Genitive Modifier: Lexical, Semantic, and Syntactic Considerations in the πίστις Χριστοῦ Discussion' in Bird and Sprinkle, *The Faith of Jesus Christ*, pp. 33–53.

23. Matlock, 'Evens the Demons Believe', pp. 306–7.

24. Cf. *Dei Verbum*, 12.

explained πίστις Χριστοῦ as a subjective genitive.[25] Indeed Augustine categorically rejected this interpretation. Commenting on Romans 3.22, he said that it does not mean a faith 'by which Christ believes' (*non qua credit Christus*).[26] When writers of the patristic period took the trouble to spell out the meaning of πίστις Χριστοῦ, rather than simply quote or repeat the phrase as they more often did, they always did so by taking it as an objective genitive.[27] Augustine does this very thing in the same passage as was quoted above: the phrase means 'the faith by which one believes in Christ (*fidem qua creditur in Christum*)'. Later in the same work he does the same for Galatians 2.16.[28] Writers of the period who were Greek speakers provide a special linguistic witness to the objective interpretation,[29] and not even the Arians seem to have latched on to a subjective interpretation of πίστις Χριστοῦ as an argument against Christ's true divinity.[30] One example of a Greek speaker taking the objective interpretation is Chrysostom. Commenting on Philippians 3.9, he said that Paul tells us the kind of faith he means: a faith by which one knows Christ and the power of his resurrection and a participation in his sufferings (cf. v. 10).[31] This is obviously not a faith belonging personally to Christ but to those who believe in him. Now while Chrysostom's status as a native Greek speaker makes his reading to be particularly valued as a historical witness from a linguistic point of view,[32] as a Father of the Church he also gives Catholic theologians an authoritative guide on how to interpret the phrase. The fact that the Fathers only ever explicitly read this genitive in an objective sense, and never explicitly in a subjective sense, suggests that they always understood it in an objective sense, even when merely quoting it. We may then have here an authoritative patristic consensus as to how the phrase should be understood, that is, as the gift of *our* faith *in* Christ. Given the principle of patristic authority for interpreting Scripture that we mentioned in Chapter 3, this would mean that a Catholic theologian could not read the Pauline texts in such a way as excluded the Fathers' interpretation.

However, a comparable wider context is also not far from the more recent increase in support among exegetes for a subjective genitive.[33] Partly this may be explained by the relation of much of Pauline studies to the legacy of the Protestant Reformation, and in particular of Martin Luther. Much recent exegesis of Paul has

25. Roy A. Harrisville III, 'ΠΙΣΤΙΣ ΧΡΙΣΤΟΥ: Witness of the Fathers', *NT* 36 (1994): 233–41 (236–7). A different line on the idea of Christ's faith in the Fathers is taken by I. G. Wallis, *The Faith of Jesus Christ in Early Christian Tradition* (Cambridge: CUP, 1995), pp. 190–212, but for a refutation of his interpretations see Elliott, 'Πίστις Χριστοῦ in the Church Fathers and Beyond' in Bird and Sprinkle, *The Faith of Jesus Christ*, pp. 278–82.

26. *De Spiritu et Littera*, 9.15.

27. Harrisville, 'ΠΙΣΤΙΣ ΧΡΙΣΤΟΥ', pp. 237–40.

28. *De Spiritu et Littera*, 32.56.

29. E.g. Origen, *Commentarii ad Romanos*, 3.26.

30. See Athanasius, *Contra Arianos*, 2.6, 9.

31. *De Incomprehensibili Dei Natura*, 2.

32. M. Silva, *Philippians* (Chicago: Moody, 1988), p. 29.

33. See the critique of this in Matlock, 'Even the Demons Believe', pp. 311–18.

been concerned to liberate his texts from the 'individualistic' reading established by Luther in his reaction against late medieval Catholic theology. Part of Luther's continuity with Catholic Tradition, however, was to read πίστις Χριστοῦ as an objective genitive, inscribing this interpretation into his German Bible. It may be that it is part of a reaction against Luther's general reading of the text to abandon his objective genitive, which favours the faith given to the individual Christian, in favour of the subjective genitive, the faith belonging to the Saviour.[34] Paradoxically, this move also favours an identifiably 'Lutheran' concern to de-emphasize yet further any role human beings might have in their justification, even that of being recipients of the gift of believing, by shifting the focus away from a faith given to the justified themselves to a saving faith exercised by Jesus. On a subjective genitive reading, one is justified not by a faith of one's own, so to speak, but by the faith of Jesus Christ. Hence, for many the debate may be weighted in favour of the subjective genitive by a dogmatic desire to minimize any role for human beings in their justification, which leads to an exegesis more Lutheran than Luther's.[35] Now while I am not in principle against exegetes reading Scripture in the light of a doctrinal tradition – far from it – I will simply note that this particular doctrinal tradition is not that of Catholic theologians, for whom the role of a graced free will in justification should pose no problem.[36] Hence Catholic theologians should have no such grounds for favouring a subjective genitive. Rather, their own doctrinal tradition will encourage them to read πίστις Χριστοῦ, along with the Fathers (and Luther), as faith in Christ. So, for Catholics, the occurrences of πίστις Χριστοῦ in Paul will provide no argument in favour of Christ having faith.

Sobrino also cites Hebrews 12.2, which, he says, explicitly witnesses to Christ having faith.[37] However, as with Paul's πίστις Χριστοῦ, the text can in itself be taken in different ways. The question is again whether 'faith' refers here to a faith of Jesus' own or to the faith of others. The writer, who has identified himself and his readers as 'not of shrinking back for destruction, but of faith for security of life' (10.39), is exhorting his audience to look to Jesus, whom he describes as the ἀρχηγόν and τελειωτήν of faith'. By τελειωτής, a term which is making its first literary appearance, is meant 'perfecter' – Jesus brings faith to perfection. The question is whether it is just the faith of others that he brings to perfection or also his own. The writer certainly believes that Christ himself is perfected by God through suffering (2.10), but does he now mean that Christ brings a *faith of his own* to perfection? At the centre of the debate is the term with which 'perfecter' is paired: ἀρχηγός. This word had already appeared in 2.10, where Jesus, the one who is perfected by suffering, was said to be the ἀρχηγός of the salvation of the sons God is bringing to glory. The term can mean a chief or

---

34. Cf. Howard, 'Faith of Christ', p. 759; Hays, 'ΠΙΣΤΙΣ ΧΡΙΣΤΟΥ and Pauline Christology', p. 36 n.4; Matlock, 'Even the Demons Believe', p. 312 n.67.

35. E.g. Hays, 'ΠΙΣΤΙΣ ΧΡΙΣΤΟΥ and Pauline Christology', p. 56; M. Hooker, 'ΠΙΣΤΙΣ ΧΡΙΣΤΟΥ', *NTS* 35 (1989): 321–42 (322, 341).

36. E.g. Council of Trent, *Decretum de iustificatione*, 5.

37. *Christology at the Crossroads*, pp. 89–91.

leader, an originator or founder, and is applied to someone who is first in time or rank. Its pairing in this case with τελειωτής suggests that Christ is at least the source of faith, as well as the one who perfects it. Since the writer established the 'pre-existence' of the Son at the beginning of his letter (1.2–4), it is easy to understand Christ as initiating the faith not only of Christians but of men and women who lived before his human birth, and indeed the writer has only just spoken of these at some length before he named Christ the 'founder and perfecter of faith'. What is at issue, however, is whether Christ is not also the source of the faith present in others precisely through living by faith himself, by 'pioneering it', so to speak – 'the pioneer and perfecter of faith'. On this reading, Christ would be not only first in rank, but first to go ahead of Christians and live by faith, although it would be more difficult to see how he could be the pioneer of faith in this temporal sense for the saints of the Old Covenant, who had predeceased him.

In whatever way ἀρχηγός may be understood in relation to faith in this verse, it is evident that the verse does not unambiguously attribute faith to Christ. This is perhaps significant in view of the fact that in the preceding chapter, πίστις had been explicitly indicated as a quality of Abel, Enoch, Noah, Abraham, Sarah, Isaac, Jacob, Moses, the Israelites at the Red Sea, Rahab, Gideon, Barak, Samson, Jephthah, David, Samuel and the prophets, and many other unnamed men and women (11.2–39). They are presented to the letter's audience as examples of people who lived by faith, but when the author comes to tell them to look to Jesus, who endured the cross and is seated at God's right hand, he fails to state in the same explicit way that Christ did what he did by faith. There is no doubt that Christ is to be 'looked to' as a leader, and is presented as an example to follow, but it is not clear that it is any *faith* on the part of the leader that is meant to be followed, because faith is just not clearly attributed to him by the writer. Instead the writer identifies Christ as faith's founder and perfecter. Not only should this immediate context make us wary of supposing that the author wanted to ascribe faith itself to Christ, but so should the fact that he, like the other authors of the New Testament, never once clearly attributes faith or believing to Christ. Moreover, when we examine how 12.2 has been traditionally understood, we find that it was never interpreted in patristic times as meaning that Christ had faith. The Latin Bibles produced in the early Church translated ἀρχηγός as 'leader' (*princeps*) or 'source' (*auctor*), hardly implying that Christ himself necessarily 'pioneered' faith. As for the Greek Fathers, Chrysostom took the passage to mean that Christ is responsible for the faith within us.[38]

But if Christ is never said in the New Testament to have believed or even to have had faith, he is more than once said to be 'faithful' (πιστός), the adjective connected with πιστεύω and πίστις. Thus it might be deduced from the use of the adjective that he had the quality of faith or believing after all. However, we should be careful of drawing the conclusion from the fact that someone is πιστός that they may equally well be said to exercise faith or believe. Although God is described in the Scriptures

---

38. *Homiliae in Epistolam ad Hebraeos*, 28.4.

as πιστός, he is never clearly said to 'believe' or live by 'faith'.[39] An examination of the occurrences in Scripture of πιστός suggests that its actual range of meaning is narrower than πιστεύω, πίστις or even the adjective's negation, ἄπιστος. Πιστός always means either faithful, in the sense of exercising fidelity, or also, by implication, trustworthy or reliable, since one who is faithful is thereby trustworthy. Thus, when Moses declares to the people in Deuteronomy 7.9 that the Lord is God, he identifies him as a πιστός God who keeps covenant and steadfast love with those who love him and keep his commandments. The meaning of πιστός is obviously that God is 'faithful' to his covenant with Israel. With the verb to believe, however, we have a word with a wider number of different elements and emphases, as we have seen, not all of which are easily associated with God. In the Old Testament, 'to believe' is not only to be faithful, to exercise fidelity, but also to trust, possibly to be obedient, and so on. It would surely have been difficult for God's people to have rightly made sense of the idea that God would be obedient to creatures or would need to assent on trust to something that was not open to his sight. The fact that *all* the elements associated with 'believing' and 'faith' cannot be attributed to God may be what precludes the use of these words of God. However, with the adjective πιστός we have a narrower range of meaning – fidelity and trustworthiness – which can happily be predicated of God. Thus, we cannot assume from the fact that someone is said to be πιστός that he can rightly be said to believe or have faith.

Likewise, when we come to Christ being described by πιστός, we find a narrower range of meaning. Early in Hebrews, Jesus is described as a 'faithful (πιστός) high priest in the things of God' (2.17). Here we are concerned with Christ's fidelity in making expiation for sins. A few verses later, the author says that Jesus, the high priest, was 'faithful to the one who appointed him, just as was Moses in [all] his house' (3.2). Moses is compared with Christ as one who was faithful in all God's house as a servant to one who was faithful in his house as Son, but in each case we are concerned with fidelity in discharging one's office. And when we come to the Apocalypse, Christ is early on described as the 'trustworthy (πιστός) witness' (1.5; 3.14). Bearing witness, and fundamentally that of Jesus himself unto death, is central to the book. Here Christ's credentials are set out – his testimony is faithful and thus reliable, and so can be trusted. However, though he is described as 'faithful', he is never described as having 'faith' or as 'believing', with their wider range of meaning. And again, a saying presented in 2 Timothy 2.13 contrasts our own infidelity with the fidelity of Christ by using the verb for us but only the adjective for Christ: though we may 'be unfaithful' (ἀπιστοῦμεν), he is always 'faithful' (πιστός).

That Scripture as a whole never ascribes faith to Christ seems already to have been realized in patristic times, as we can see from Augustine.[40] Athanasius too

---

39. However, Howard, 'Faith of Christ', p. 759, does suggest retranslating some passages, such as Jesus' words in Mk 11.22, 'have faith in God' (Ἔχετε πίστιν θεοῦ) as 'hold on to the assurance of God'. P. Foster, 'Πίστις Χριστοῦ Terminology in Philippians and Ephesians' in Bird and Sprinkle, *The Faith of Jesus Christ: Exegetical, Biblical, and Theological Studies*, pp. 91–109 (94), calls such readings 'both forced and foreign to the context'.

40. *Contra Maximinum*, 2.23.7.

noted the fact that, as with God, Scripture's description of Christ as πιστός did not imply that he believed or had faith.[41] But what is it among the elements of the Scriptural meaning of πίστις that makes it unsuited to Christ who is nonetheless rightly described as πιστός? It cannot be obedience, as we suggested was the case with God when we considered Deuteronomy 7.9, since Christ is said in Scripture to be 'obedient unto death' (Phil. 2.80). While Christ may not be obedient as God, strictly speaking, on a Chalcedonian interpretation, he is certainly obedient to the Father in his humanity. In fact, nearly all the elements of the meaning of faith, endurance and so on, can be definitely verified in Christ in Scripture, leaving only the possibility that the element which makes 'faith' as a whole inappropriate to attribute to him is that of cognitive assent to what is not manifest, to what remains unseen.

We can conclude then that a faith of Jesus' own makes no bold appearance in the Bible. It will of course be impossible to argue that the beatific vision is excluded from Christ by his faith if he did not have faith after all. However, the fact that Scripture is silent about any faith Christ might have had cannot be taken as showing without further ado that he did not have faith. We should recall that we ourselves have already argued in Chapter 2 that Christ's possession of the beatific vision was perfectly compatible with the fact of Scripture saying nothing explicit about it. Perhaps the same might be said of faith. Before returning to this important point below, we shall first examine the next part of the argument against Christ's vision from faith, namely, that faith and the beatific vision are always mutually exclusive. For, if this premise were to prove false, one could hardly argue from it either that Christ's faith excluded vision, or that his vision excluded faith.

To claim in this way that faith and vision are mutually exclusive is not to assert that someone cannot believe one object and see another. Thomas the apostle, for example, saw Jesus risen from the dead, and so believed something distinct, namely, that he was his Lord and God (Jn 20.29). The principle under investigation is that simultaneous faith and vision of precisely the same object are mutually exclusive, meaning that one cannot both see God and believe in him at the same time, so to speak – either one sees him or one believes in him. Whether we were to conclude that Jesus did not have faith because he had vision, or that he did not have vision because he had faith, we would in both cases be presupposing that they are mutually exclusive. Thus both sides of the debate – Aquinas and Sobrino – can appeal to the very same principle, though the arguments of neither side would work if it could be shown that the principle were false. We shall begin our examination of the principle by looking to see whether it plays any role in Scripture.

Crucial to the debate is what comes nearest in Scripture to a 'definition' of faith by bearing the literary marks of a definition from Greek philosophy:[42] 'Faith

---

41. *Orationes contra Arianos*, 2.6, 9.

42. H.W. Attridge, *The Epistle to the Hebrews: A Commentary on the Epistle to the Hebrews* (Hermeneia – A Critical and Historical Commentary on the Bible; Philadelphia: Fortress, 1989), pp. 307–8.

is the substance of what is hoped for, the proof of things (πραγμάτων) not seen (ὀυ βλεπομένων)' (Heb. 11.1).[43] This verse comes immediately after the writer of Hebrews has placed himself and his audience among those who are 'of faith' and before his account of the faith lived by Abraham and the rest. From the details of this account we know that faith definitely includes the element of belief as well as trust, fidelity and so on (e.g. 11.3). That all these people believed in what was at least at the time of belief *unseen*, those under the New Covenant as well as the Old, is plainly part of the meaning of 'faith'. Not that the author's language is entirely consistent. He speaks of those who, seeking a promised heavenly homeland, 'died in faith, not having received what was promised, but having seen (ἰδόντες) and greeted it from far off, and having confessed that they were strangers and sojourners on the earth' (v. 13). Those who believe are thus said to 'see' what is unseen *in a qualified sense*, 'from far off', just as 1 Corinthians 13.12 speaks of seeing in a mirror, in a riddle, rather than face to face.

But in what sense does the author of Hebrews take the object of faith to be 'unseen'? Is it merely that such things cannot be perceived through the physical sense of sight? Certainly, many things that are believed in are physically perceptible future realities that are just not yet so perceived by those who for the moment believe in them, such as their heavenly homeland and any events 'not yet seen' (cf. v. 7). Presumably the 'definition' implies that people no longer believe in such things when they have physically seen them. But there are also other things included in the object of faith that are not in themselves physically perceptible at all (though their effects may be), such as divine power (v. 19), divine faithfulness (v. 11), the creation of the world by God (v. 3) and his very existence (v. 6). The author speaks of God's invisibility, when he explains Moses' faith in leaving Egypt by his enduring 'as though seeing him who is unseen' (v. 27). As far as physical sight is concerned, all these realities must always remain unseen, and if physical sight were all that were meant in the definition, they would continue to be the object of faith in heaven, even on the part of Christ's humanity. But, as we noted in Chapter 2, there was already in the Old Testament as well as the New a wider notion of 'seeing' that encompassed seeing by the mind or knowledge, a use with which our author was certainly familiar (cf. 4.13), which was continued in the Fathers, and it is not difficult to conclude that we have such a meaning in 11.1. But if we have here this wider notion of 'seeing', then even the invisible realities, when 'seen', would no longer be the object of faith. Though Hebrews speaks of a future seeing the Lord at his Second Coming (9.28; 12.14), the letter nowhere refers to the beatific vision. However, if we interpret 11.1 together with the doctrine of the beatific vision we find elsewhere in Scripture (e.g. 1 Jn 3.2), then we will be able to conclude that *what will be seen* by the latter vision can no longer be the object of faith.

One much debated passage on the relationship between faith and vision is 1 Corinthians 13.13. Following his statement that we see through a mirror but then

43. Alternatively, πραγμάτων may be taken with 'hoped for', giving the translation, 'Faith is the substance of things hoped for, the proof of what is not seen.' The essential meaning of the 'definition', however, would remain unchanged.

face to face, and that now he knows in part but then shall know just as he is also known, Paul goes on: 'And *now* remain faith, hope and charity, these three; but the greatest of these is charity.' What is the meaning of Paul's 'now' (νυνὶ)? Should it be temporal, it would mean that Paul was saying only that faith endures in the present life, for now. But if it were logical, indicating the conclusion of his argument about charity and spiritual gifts, it would permit the possibility that Paul was saying that faith would endure for eternity, which would mean it must be compatible with face to face vision. However, we should note that a logical now would not necessarily imply anything about faith's continuation into the next life, and 'remain' could also be taken logically, indicating that the three 'remain' only in the sense that they 'remain on the table' in the argument over against the spiritual gifts Paul has already dealt with.[44] Moreover, once one takes into account the fact that the argument put by Paul to the Corinthians is about the surpassing value of charity in the Church *in the present life*, even a logical now would lead to a conclusion that was only about the here and now.[45] Nevertheless those who hold faith to have a continuing role in heaven understandably adopt the logical meaning of νυνὶ.

One point in their support is that Paul has just used ἄρτι in its normal sense as a temporal now – 'now we see through a mirror'. Why change to the more ambiguous νυνὶ if his meaning is again to be temporal?[46] One answer is that Paul has just twice compared present and future with ἄρτι and τότε – '*now* we see through a mirror in a riddle, but *then* face to face; *now* I know in part, *then* I shall know just as I am also known' – and, since he is no longer making such comparisons, for purely rhetorical reasons switches his temporal now from ἄρτι to νυνὶ.[47] Since Paul uses νυνὶ elsewhere in a temporal sense, as is clear from the context of Romans 3.21,[48] the same use is hardly implausible in this case. This reading can be supported from the Fathers of the Church: although Irenaeus interpreted the verse to mean that faith would endure for eternity,[49] there settled among the Fathers a consensus that it would not so endure. Despite efforts to argue for a more fluid picture in Augustine,[50] there is no doubt that he too thought faith passed away into sight.[51]

---

44. A. C. Thistleton, *The First Epistle to the Corinthians: A Commentary on the Greek Text* (Grand Rapids, MI and Cambridge: Eerdmans, 2000), p. 1071.

45. G. D. Fee, *The First Epistle to the Corinthians* (Grand Rapids, MI: Eerdmans, 1987), p. 650.

46. Balthasar, '"Fides Christi: An Essay on the Consciousness of Christ"' in *Explorations in Theology*, vol. 2: *Spouse of the Word* (San Francisco: Ignatius, 1991), pp. 43–79 (71).

47. Collins, *First Corinthians*, p. 487.

48. Cf. Conzelmann, *1 Corinthians*, p. 230.

49. Irenaeus, *Adversus Haereses*, 2.28.3.

50. M. Hanby, 'These Three Abide: Augustine and the Eschatological Non-Obsolescence of Faith', *PE* 13 (2005): 340–60 (351–52); Allen, *Christ's Faith*, pp. 74–8. Augustine's reference to faith in *De Civitate Dei*, 32.29, would in fact seem to pertain to this life, not the next.

51. E.g. *De Doctrina Christiana*, 1.39.43.

That Paul certainly thought faith and vision incompatible can also be supported from a wider reading of his own letters. In his second letter to the same Church, Paul says that Christians 'walk by faith, not by vision' (2 Cor. 5.7). Of course in itself this does not rule out the possibility that those in heaven may walk by both faith and vision, but it does at least leave the hint that one day they might walk by vision rather than by faith. And in his letter to the Romans, he says that 'hope that is seen is not hope, for who hopes for what he sees?' (8.24). Thus, for him, hope and vision are incompatible, and so *mutatis mutandis* the same may be said for faith and vision: faith that is seen would not be faith, for who would merely believe in what he actually sees? Paul could thus have easily endorsed Hebrews' definition: 'Faith is the assurance of things *hoped for*, the proof of things *not seen*'.

That faith and sight are mutually exclusive is thus not without support in Scripture and Tradition, and further reflection can help us make sense of why the two cannot co-exist. One certainly cannot deny the fact that *either* one sees God as he really is *or* one does not. A middle way between the two is surely impossible. *Either* one sees God clearly, face to face, *or* one does not; *either* the essence of God is evident to one *or* it is not. Not that this means that everyone who lacks the beatific vision must necessarily possess faith as a way of knowing God, as though it were not a gift of grace. Someone to whom the essence of God is not evident may be altogether lacking explicit knowledge of God, with at best a set of opinions about which they cannot be certain.[52] Again, someone to whom the essence of God is not evident may in principle have a purely natural knowledge of God of which they can be certain through philosophical arguments.[53] Aquinas allows that human reason, by its own natural powers, can reach certain truths about the Creator from its knowledge of the creatures he has made, but cannot reach other truths about God, such as what he is essentially and the fact that he is a Trinity.[54] Thus, someone who lacks vision need not necessarily have faith but may be in a position of having at best a philosophical knowledge of God, and likewise someone who lacks faith need not necessarily have vision, but only at best a philosophical knowledge of God. But if the latter knowledge has its limitations, knowledge of the divine that lies beyond the power of human reason to obtain can only come by way of a supernatural elevation of the human mind. If knowledge does not come by natural means, then it must come by supernatural.[55]

The beatific vision is itself an example of such supernatural knowledge, where the divine essence itself is gifted to the human mind as a means without which God cannot be clearly seen, as we saw in Chapter 4. One question is how someone can possibly enjoy certain supernatural knowledge of God, of what is nonetheless *not* made evident to him by way of this heavenly communication of the divine essence to the mind. The answer can only be that, if one does not see for oneself, then one relies for certainty on the witness given on the basis of some other

52. *Summa*, 2a.2ae., q. 1, a. 4.
53. Ibid., 2a.2ae., q. 1, a. 5.
54. Ibid., 1a., q. 32, a. 1.
55. Ibid., 2a.2ae., q. 2, a. 3.

knowledge that *is* in fact based on vision. If I have not seen some earthly object for myself, I can justifiably be certain about it through the testimony of a reliable witness who *has* seen it. Thus a higher knowledge of God is made available to us by divine revelation, which makes use of lesser, more obscure means of knowledge than the beatific vision, such that a believer wills to accept on divine authority what he has not seen clearly for himself.[56] God, who on account of his perfection cannot lie, is able to make this revelation because of his perfect vision of himself, and through the gift of supernatural faith he enables believers to derive from his authority certainty of what in itself remains unclear and obscure to them. Aquinas holds that, through the gift of faith, God causes 'the intellect to assent to things not seen' (*non apparentibus*).[57] Without either faith or vision, it is impossible for human beings to have certain knowledge of what is so transcendent, such as that God is Father, Son and Holy Spirit. For such knowledge they need one or the other, faith or vision.

It is here that we meet the mutual exclusion of faith and vision. Not only do rational creatures need one or the other for such knowledge of what is so transcendent, but it must be *either* one or the other. Once human beings see for themselves in heaven, their certainty can no longer be derived from the authority of divine witness, because what was formerly unseen by them is now plainly open to their sight.[58] Now it might be urged against this position that its mutual exclusion of faith and vision depends on a narrow understanding of faith that defines it only in intellectual terms.[59] In response one can say that this mutual exclusion depends necessarily not on the theory of faith being narrowly intellectualist, but on the cognitive element being recognized as a key constituent feature of faith's total reality. Hence, even where faith is broadly understood in terms of all its Scriptural elements, the recognition of this essential element of assent to what is unseen means that the act of faith as a whole and vision of the same object will be mutually exclusive.

Balthasar recalls that some medieval theologians allowed that the gift or habit of faith *did* continue into heaven, but that in the state of vision it never passed into act.[60] This theory would have the merit of being able to cope up to a point with an exegesis of 1 Corinthians 13.13 that had faith remain for eternity, should that exegesis have proved unavoidable – the gift of faith would endure for ever but always be inactive. Aquinas, however, was among those who thought that even the habit, which was of its very nature suited to a situation where God was still unseen, passed away or rather passed into vision. The fact that faith no longer remains hardly lessens its importance for Aquinas but reinforces the close relationship that obtains for him between faith and vision. Intending to recast the

56. For a discussion of the certitude and obscurity of faith in Catholic theology, see Dulles, *The Assurance of Things Hoped For*, pp. 229–36.

57. *Summa*, 2a.2ae., q. 4, a. 1.

58. Ibid., 2a.2ae., q. 2, a. 4.

59. Cf. Allen, *Christ's Faith*, pp. 69, 78–82.

60. 'Fides Christi', pp. 68, 70.

'definition' of Hebrews 11.1 in a scholastic idiom, he spoke of faith as 'that habit of mind whereby eternal life begins in us, causing the intellect to assent to things not seen'.[61] Faith, by which we believe God so as to make our way to our heavenly beatitude, is itself the 'beginning' of that eternal life in us. If we value faith so highly as to think of it as the very 'seed' of the beatific vision, we can appreciate that, just as for a seed to germinate fully means that there is no longer a seed, so where faith comes to maturity, there is no longer any faith.

These principles cannot but apply to the earthly Christ. In Chapter 2, we argued that the portrayal of Christ in the Gospels shows him possessed of an extraordinary, that is, supernatural knowledge of God in his human mind. He does not appear there devoid of explicit knowledge of God, at best giving out a set of opinions of which he is not certain, nor is he a figure making purely philosophical arguments for the existence of God and the place of religion by an appeal to reason alone, relying on a merely human knowledge for his grasp of the Jewish Scriptures and so on. But if we cannot explain Christ's human knowledge as a whole in only natural terms, we must explain it partly in supernatural terms: Christ's knowledge of the Father in the Gospels is surely one that surpasses the power of human reason to obtain. Thus we must conclude of Christ's human mind what must be concluded of any created mind elevated by supernatural knowledge. Either Christ has such knowledge of God by seeing the divine essence for himself in his human mind, or he has knowledge of what he does not see there by accepting it on the authority of divine knowledge. However one conceives the broader picture of Christ's human knowledge, it must therefore include within it *either* the vision of the blessed *or* the knowledge that arises from the habit of faith. Without either one or the other of these it must be reduced in respect of knowledge of God to the purely natural level. But, whichever of these he *does* have, it must exclude the other.

Attempts to find a supernatural 'middle way' between faith and vision thus founder. Some opponents of Christ's earthly beatific vision grasp this and make no attempt to deny that Christ must have possessed the virtue of faith. For example, working from the fact that the New Testament declares Christ to be a prophet, Torrell drew on Aquinas's account of prophecy rather than the beatific vision to explain his extraordinary knowledge.[62] Aquinas himself explained Christ's ability to prophesy by what he saw under the light of glory, from which he was able to form similitudes through which to convey to people what was in itself remote from the ordinary knowledge of those among whom he was living.[63] While Christ was thus a prophet in an unusual sense, prophets in general prophesied by way of a light that, while surpassing the power of human reason, lacked the perfection of the light of glory. Like the natural light of the human mind in its own sphere, the light of glory perfected the intellect chiefly by being the means under which knowledge was given of the principle of the things manifested by the light in

61. *Summa*, 2a.2ae., q. 4, a.1.
62. 'S. Thomas d'Aquin et la science du Christ', pp. 404–8.
63. *Super Ioannem*, 4.6.667, 6.2.867–68; *Summa*, 3a., q. 7, a. 8.

question. So, as the natural light of the intellect gives knowledge of the first principles of natural reason, so the light of glory gives knowledge of the divine essence. The 'prophetic light', however, gave no such knowledge of God as its basic principle, and was thus an imperfect light. A further way this imperfect 'prophetic light' differed from the perfect light of glory was that it was not thereby habitual. The perfect light of glory is given to Christ and the blessed in an abiding way so that they make a single act of knowing that participates in God's eternity, though it can also be given in a passing way, as Aquinas holds it was given to Paul (and Moses). The imperfect prophetic light, however, is only ever granted transiently, according to Aquinas, and never habitually, or else the prophets in Scripture would have been able to prophesy at any time, which is not what Aquinas reads there (e.g. 2 Kgs 4.27). Thus, while the perfect light of glory has been given in both an abiding way and a transient way, the imperfect prophetic light is only given in a passing fashion.[64]

Torrell, however, explains Christ's prophecy by postulating in him an *abiding* light, which is neither the light of glory nor a transient prophetic light. To distinguish this unique abiding light especially from a merely prophetic light, Torrell calls it a 'Christic light' (*lumière christique*).[65] It does not deliver knowledge of the essence of God, but an extraordinary knowledge that still surpasses the power of human reason, more powerful in intensity and extent than the transient prophetic light. Another way in which it differs from Aquinas's understanding of prophecy is that it is shorn of infused *species* and images, visions in the mind, imagination or the physical sense of sight. For Aquinas, the *sine qua non* of prophecy is undoubtedly the prophetic light itself, through which the prophet is able to make judgements that surpass natural human ability. Others can receive a divine presentation of images or whatever it may be, but not the prophetic light through which to interpret them. Hence, Nebuchadnezzar can have dreams sent by God but is unable to interpret them. Daniel does not have the dream himself, which is reported to him without any supernatural means, but has the light to discern the meaning of the dream (Dan. 4.1–27). On Aquinas's principles, it is not Nebuchadnezzar but Daniel who is the prophet, because Daniel is the one with the prophetic light, even if not the dream. Nevertheless, Aquinas does reckon the prophet *greater* who has not only the prophetic light, but also either extraordinary forms presented through the senses (for example, the writing on the wall in Dan. 5.25), forms infused by God into the imagination or somehow specially arranged there by God out of what had come in an ordinary way through the senses (for example, the vision of a boiling pot facing from the north in Jer. 1.13), or by the impression of intelligible *species* onto the mind (where Aquinas is thinking of the wisdom of Solomon or the apostles).[66] Torrell, however, though committed to a special infusion of light, is inclined to dispense with the infusion of images and *species*, which he thinks interferes with Aquinas's general Aristotelian preference

---

64. *Summa*, 2a.2ae., q. 171, a. 2.

65. 'S. Thomas d'Aquin et la science du Christ', p. 408.

66. *Summa*, 2a.2ae., q. 173, a. 2.

to have knowledge begin in the senses.[67] The role of Torrell's 'Christic light' then is simply to enable Jesus to extract the divine meaning of what comes to him through his senses.

The important point to note in all this is that in no way are the divine realities Jesus may discern in his prophetic knowledge of the world something he is thereby seeing directly. Rather, we have in this case an indirect knowledge of God that comes through perceiving God's created effects, not a vision of God by way of receiving God's own essence into the mind.[68] Torrell acknowledges that, if Jesus, who is full of grace and virtue, did not directly see the essence of God, he must have had the virtue of faith. Torrell never asserts that his account, nor indeed any non-beatific account of Jesus' knowledge in terms of prophecy or infused knowledge or mysticism or anything of the sort, can dispense with belief on the part of Jesus. When the word of God comes through a prophetic light, whether or not it involves the infusion of finite *species* or images, the recipient still needs faith in order to *believe* the judgement he makes, because he does not actually see for himself the divine reality to which it refers. Thus, were a non-beatific Jesus to have the most powerful prophetic knowledge, he would still need the gift of faith in order to give firm assent to what he discerned by prophecy. Prophetic knowledge simply does not substitute for faith in someone who lacks vision. Likewise, just as prophecy here presupposes the gift of faith, so does mysticism. Torrell rightly observes that the experiential knowledge of God attributed to mystics by Catholic theology does not remove from them the necessity of believing, since it is the highest perfection within the life of faith itself and not a step beyond it. In short, there can be no 'third way' between an account of Jesus' supernatural knowledge that includes his beatific vision and an account that includes him having faith.

Galot, however, was forced to search out such a 'third way' because his starting-point was the denial of both faith and vision to Jesus, neither of which he thought supported by Scripture. Denying both of these, Galot needed an account of Christ's human knowledge that did justice to its extraordinary nature but which did not appeal to either gift. He attempted to find this by explaining Christ's human knowledge of himself, of the Father and of his mission by analogy with mystical experience and in terms of an 'infused knowledge' (*connaissance infuse*).[69] He speaks of Christ having 'certain pieces of infused information' that equip him for his mission.[70] Here again we have at bottom a reworking of Aquinas's theory of prophetic knowledge, though in this case one that more retains the infusion of some *species* and images as Christ's means of knowledge. Galot envisages these as infused at different times during Jesus' life so as to enable the ongoing development of his self-knowledge and so on. However, he struggled to distinguish all this knowledge adequately from faith and vision. At first, though denying that Christ's human knowledge involved vision, he nevertheless spoke of it as 'evident' and Christ's

67. 'S. Thomas d'Aquin et la science du Christ', pp. 406–7.
68. White, 'The Earthly Christ and the Beatific Vision', p. 517.
69. *Who is Christ?*, pp. 339–43; 'Le Christ terrestre et la vision', p. 446.
70. Ibid., p. 362.

certitude as 'intuitive'. This drew the criticism from Daniel Ols that he was involving himself in self-contradiction by asserting both that such things were evident to Christ and that they were not evident to him.[71] Galot's response seems to have been to avoid more scrupulously any suggestion that the object of this knowledge was manifest to Jesus, and to concentrate simply on his certitude. He stressed that Jesus, in his humanity, 'possessed certitude of his identity' and a knowledge of the Father of 'absolute certitude', without this amounting to a vision.[72] But since certitude is also attributed to faith, it is left unclear how any of this knowledge removed Christ from the realm of faith. Should he not know the truth of all these things because they are evident to him, he will still be in the position of believing them. Ultimately, Galot's rejection of Christ's beatific vision can only lead him to subscribe to one of the very things he does not want to admit, that Christ had faith.

O'Collins, while wanting to admit more generally that Christ had faith, will not admit that he had faith in such things as his identity and saving mission. These he *knew* rather than *believed*.[73] O'Collins relies for an account of such knowledge on Galot.[74] But if Galot's theory does not in fact manage to dispense with the necessity of faith, a theory that does so still remains to be sought out. Might it be that a solution can be found in Rahner's theory of a direct vision of the Word by way of Christ's self-consciousness? Could one, while acknowledging the mutual exclusion of faith and vision, hold that Christ had this direct vision and not faith, while at the same time refusing to identify this vision with the beatific vision? One problem with this approach would be whether Christ's self-consciousness can be properly construed as a 'vision'. In his contribution to the neoscholastic debate on Christ's consciousness, Lonergan argued persuasively that self-consciousness should always be conceived as *subjective experience* rather than along the lines of perception or knowledge of self as an *object*.[75] Rahner, however, like many Catholic theologians of the period, did in fact assimilate his notion of subjective self-consciousness to perception or knowledge of an object.[76] It was this that enabled him to characterize Christ's self-consciousness as a direct or immediate *vision*, a seeing of the Word as its object, while denying that it was knowledge of an object.[77] And once self-consciousness was thus misconstrued, it was an attractive possibility for Rahner to propose it as an alternative to Christ's beatific vision of the triune God. But if we acknowledge that Christ's subjective, unthematic

71. 'La vision beatifique du Christ viateur: notes de lecture', pp. 401–2.

72. 'Le Christ terrestre et la vision', pp. 439, 447.

73. *Christology: A Biblical, Historical, and Systematic Study of Jesus* (2nd edn, Oxford: OUP, 2009), p. 275.

74. Ibid., pp. 274–75.

75. Cf. Lonergan, *The Ontological and Psychological Constitution of Christ* (Ontario and London: University of Toronto, 2002), pp. 156–69.

76. For a critique of this understanding of consciousness, see Moloney, 'The Mind of Christ in Transcendental Theology: Rahner, Lonergan and Crowe', *HJ* 25 (1984): 288–300.

77. 'Knowledge and Self-Consciousness of Christ', p. 209.

self-consciousness is not to be mistaken for a vision, then its ability *qua* vision to exclude faith loses all plausibility. In fact, self-consciousness, not being another kind of knowledge of an object, is something compatible with both the knowledge of faith and the knowledge of vision, and is not an alternative to either of them. Self-consciousness is not another kind of knowledge that will deliver certainty about its object either through the latter being manifest or in some other way, but a subjective experience that is properly distinct from knowing an object. Thus, while the notion of self-consciousness will add another element to our overall theological understanding of Christ's mind, it cannot dispense with the fact that his supernatural knowledge must involve either faith or vision.

Another possible solution might be found in the 'hypostatic vision' proposed by Weinandy. His proposed vision he calls 'hypostatic' because it is the Son's 'personal' human vision of the Father. If a *clear* vision, it would presumably exclude faith, but again it would not be identical with the beatific vision, which Weinandy refuses to Christ, as we saw in Chapter 3. Weinandy calls the hypostatic vision a 'human cognitive vision of the Father, which would manifest, in a human manner, that his identity, who he is, is that of being the divine Son of the Father'. In an echo of 1 John 3.2, which may be unintended, he says that by this vision the Son comes to know the Father 'as the Father truly exists'.[78] How, though, can the Son have such knowledge of the Father, just as he is, without such knowledge of the divine essence with which the Father is identical? By what adequate means can the Son have such knowledge of the Father, if not by way of a communication to the Son in the order of human knowledge of that means by which the Father knows himself? Certainly Weinandy assigns a role to the Holy Spirit, who illuminates Jesus' human mind, revealing to the incarnate Son 'the true nature of the Father'. However, he does not go so far as to identify the Holy Spirit himself as that means of knowledge by which the Son knows the Father, replacing any human *species* or images or whatever it might be.[79] The illumination by the Spirit is in fact dependent on Jesus' general mental advancement, which indicates that it takes place through the finite means fitted to ordinary human knowing and only once those means are in place.[80] Weinandy speaks of Christ having his hypostatic vision by his human prayer and pondering of the Scriptures.[81] His means of vision are thus neither the divine essence nor a divine person, but finite means that can hardly render his vision of the Father a clear one, and Weinandy is in any case quite happy to concede imperfection in Christ's vision.[82] But, if this is the case, the hypostatic vision is once again an example of indirect knowledge, where the Father is not in fact clearly seen by the Son, and this 'vision' is thus incapable of substituting for faith within the soul of a non-beatific Christ. Christ would not be exempted from believing what he knew by his hypostatic vision.

78. 'Jesus' Filial Vision of the Father', p. 193.
79. Ibid., p. 196.
80. Ibid., p. 197.
81. 'The Beatific Vision and the Incarnate Son', p. 613.
82. 'Jesus' Filial Vision of the Father', pp. 198–9.

The failure to find a third way between faith and vision leaves us in the position of saying that Christ's supernatural knowledge must be interpreted theologically, at least in part, either by faith or by the beatific vision. If Christ had faith while on earth, he did not have the beatific vision; and vice versa. Earlier in this chapter we established that Scripture does not ever clearly ascribe faith to the earthly Jesus, and went on to ask whether we might immediately conclude without further ado that Christ did not have faith. Having now shown that faith and vision are mutually exclusive, we would be in the position of concluding to vision from the absence of faith. To deny faith to Christ we were unable to do with such speed, however, once we recalled that neither does Scripture ever clearly ascribe the beatific vision to Christ. As Scripture makes no bold proclamation of Christ's faith, so it also makes no bold proclamation of his beatific vision. In the last chapter I had suggested that, despite the latter silence, we might nevertheless explore Christ's knowledge in the light of Aquinas's understanding of the beatific knowledge of the saints, following the analogy of faith. Why then should it not also be legitimate by the same analogy to explore Christ's knowledge in the light of the knowledge that comes to Christians by faith, despite the silence of Scripture? Why should one not attempt a theological theory of Christ's knowledge, as it is presented in Scripture, which explains it at least partly in terms of faith? Might not a theory of Christ's faith be just as plausible a partial explanation of the data of Scripture, if not one more plausible, than the theory of his vision?

To some extent this application of faith to Christ had already happened in a very attenuated way within medieval scholasticism's endorsement of Christ's vision. Peter Lombard argued from the fact that the saints did not have the 'virtue of faith' (*fidem-virtutem*) in God, because they had direct knowledge of God, to the fact that the earthly Christ, who also possessed the gifts of our heavenly homeland, did not have this virtue either. He accepted talk of Christ and the saints believing, so long as this was not understood to be through the virtue of faith in God. Thus he allowed that Christ 'believed' (*credidit*) in his own future resurrection, as the souls of the saints believe in their future resurrection, but this was not via the obscurity of the virtue of 'faith' (*fides*), but through direct vision of what was to come. Christ saw what he was said to believe in.[83] There was, however, some openness among Peter's successors to apply even the word *fides* to Christ, so long as it could indicate only what was perfect in faith and not what was imperfect, so long as it could point to faith's luminosity rather than its obscurity, so long as one could distinguish Christ's perfect faith from our imperfect faith. Alexander of Hales, who was first to comment on the *Sentences*, entertained the view in his *Summa* that Christ had 'faith' (*fides*), but qualified this as a 'lucid' (*lucida*) faith, which had the perfections of faith, such as certitude, but not the imperfection of obscurity.[84] Alexander seems to have been postulating a form of knowledge that somehow attained to clarity despite the fact that it remained indirect: knowledge in a mirror but not in a riddle. This approach tended to trace any imperfection in

83. *Sententiae*, 3.26.4.
84. *Summa Theologica*, 2, 4.3.3.2.2.1.1.

faith to sin rather than to the finitude of its means of knowledge and the indirect character of this knowledge, such that Alexander could also attribute a *fides lucida* to Adam before he sinned.[85] The hypothesis could not really last, however, once a more careful examination of the finite means of ordinary human knowledge by Aquinas reinforced the perception that obscurity was always present in faith's indirect knowledge of God, however perfect that faith and however sinless the believer may be.[86] In any case Alexander himself later returned in the *Summa* to the view he had already expressed in his commentary on Peter Lombard's *Sentences*, that the clarity of Christ's vision excluded faith in God from him altogether.[87] Later, Bonaventure conceded that faith was in Christ insofar as it was perfect and not imperfect, but in another place he refused faith to Christ altogether on the grounds of its inherent imperfection.[88] Finally, while Aquinas straightforwardly denied that there was faith in Christ, he also said that 'whatever perfection is in faith' is in him 'most perfectly'.[89] This would allow us to have all the various elements of faith that bespeak perfection to be present in Christ, but not faith taken as a whole, because of its element of cognitive imperfection. In this way scholasticism remained close to the vocabulary of both Scripture and the Fathers by its wariness of attributing faith to Christ.

The more recent attempts to speak of Christ's faith may be compatible with these more modest medieval moves, insofar as they are in part motivated by the desire to attribute to Christ what is of perfection in faith.[90] Here they explicitly include those elements of faith other than the cognitive element that had largely been the object of scholastic analysis, elements such as fidelity and obedience.[91] But some more recent speculations on Christ's faith, like those of Sobrino, have also included in it the element of cognitive imperfection, yielding a Christ who in his human mind believed in what he did not see there. All that is left to distinguish Christ's faith from ours essentially is the fact that while ours is also a faith *in* the incarnate Christ, Christ's is a faith in God alone. He could be said on a Chalcedonian reading to have faith in himself only to the extent that in his humanity he believed what he saw in his divinity, his divine knowledge being numerically the same knowledge as exists in the Father. On this application of the analogy of faith, Christ would have been speaking, when he taught, of what he had *not* seen in his humanity, bearing witness to what was *not* thus evident to him, but was known humanly to him with certainty by faith, just as it is to us. He would lack that unity in means of knowledge between his humanity and divinity that we noted in Chapter 4 is found in the theory of his beatific vision, where

85. Ibid.

86. Cf. *Summa*, 2a.2ae., q. 5, a. 1 ad 2.

87. *Glossa in Quatuor Libros Sententiarum*, 3.13; *Summa Theologica*, 3, 2.1.4.

88. *Commentaria in Quatuor Libros Sententiarum*, 3, 13.1.3 ad 3; 36.1 ad 1.

89. *Summa*, q. 7, a. 10 ad 1.

90. Balthasar, 'Fides Christi'. For a critique of Balthasar's theology of Christ's faith, see Pitstick, *Light in Darkness*, pp. 148–66.

91. E.g. O'Collins, *Christology*, pp. 270–4.

the divine means of knowledge was shared with his human mind. Instead Christ would merely believe in his humanity what he saw in his divinity, giving assent in his human mind on the basis of the authority of divine knowledge.

But if Scripture is silent on both Christ's faith and a vision in his human mind, and either one or the other must be included in any account of his knowledge, how can we decide which theological explanation is best to pursue as the more plausible? I suggest that it is of relevance here that the 'silences' of Scripture on Christ's faith and vision are of diverse significance. In the case of the beatific vision of the saints, while the doctrine has an ultimate importance in the overall shape of the Scriptural narrative, it is hardly the subject of a great deal of biblical discussion in general. In Chapter 2 we saw that it appeared in only a handful of texts. This suggests that the fact that no New Testament author spent time speculating that Christ may have possessed this knowledge is of little significance for determining whether or not he had the beatific vision. In contrast, faith is a matter of some considerable general concern among these authors. The verb 'to believe', for example, appears more than a hundred times in John's Gospel alone, and more than fifty times in the Pauline corpus. In the light of the pervasiveness of the concept of faith and believing in Scripture, nothing could have been easier for its writers than to have attributed it to Christ. Moreover, there would have been many reasons to motivate the authors to attribute faith to Christ, quite apart from giving an explanation of the knowledge he taught. As we have seen, there are many elements to the meaning of faith – obedience, fidelity, endurance, and so on. This would have made 'faith' useful for interpreting and drawing together many of these features, which can be seen throughout Christ's life and in his death, as well as for relating him more closely to us as our Saviour, as one who lived out faith on our behalf and whose faith would be an example to our faith.

In the light of the pervasiveness and richness of meaning in the term, it may be argued that there is a crucial significance to Scripture's silence on Christ's faith, which is lacking to its corresponding silence on Christ's beatific vision. To speak of Christ's faith in this context, that is, the context of its pervasiveness and potential usefulness, would have been so obvious a thing to do that it may be thought at first sight quite surprising that the writers of Scripture did not do it. The inspired authors never explain their omission, but the fact that they did not attribute faith to Christ in circumstances so favourable to its attribution may even suggest that their omission was deliberate or at least instinctive on their part. At the very least they may have perceived that faith somehow did not fit the character of Christ's knowledge, and so were wary of calling him a believer. Be that as it may, the texts' silence over Christ's faith in these circumstances can be regarded as possessing a certain sort of authority, something that cannot be claimed for the silence over vision, where the circumstances were quite different. All this may be confirmed by the fact that the Fathers give no support to the idea of Christ's faith, but some slim support to his vision. Augustine's teaching in the *Contra Maximinum* that Christ has a vision of the Father in his humanity coheres neatly with the fact that he denies in the same work that Christ had faith. Christ could only have had one or the other, and if he had vision, then this would explain why he did not have faith.

We may conclude then that the different characters of Scripture's silences put a considerable weight against the theory of Christ's faith but no special weight against his vision. Furthermore, given that Christ's knowledge must include either faith or the beatific vision, the fact that Scripture's silence puts considerable weight against the theory of Christ's faith must in turn put considerable weight in favour of his beatific vision. Christ's beatific vision is thus not merely a plausible theological explanation, or part explanation, of the knowledge in his human mind, but a more promising line of enquiry than a theory that involved him having faith: the weight of probability is in its favour. In these circumstances, we need to ask what would be capable of tipping the balance back in favour of faith. It seems to me that we would have no option but to return to a theory of Christ's faith and to struggle with the difficulty raised by Scripture's silence about it, only if the theory of his beatific vision could be demonstrated to fail to cope with features of Christ that may definitely be traced in Scripture and Tradition. Should there yet prove to be good reason to exclude beatific knowledge from Christ, we would find ourselves having to explore yet further the possibility of his faith, whatever the reticence of Scripture. It is to these further objections to Christ's vision that we shall devote our remaining chapters.

Chapter 6

'BUT JESUS DIDN'T KNOW!'

In the last chapter we considered an objection to Christ's beatific vision from the alleged presence in him of the supernatural knowledge of faith. In this chapter we look at an objection from the presence in Christ's human mind of *natural* knowledge gained from the world in the normal human way. O'Collins asks: 'how can one reconcile the knowledge of vision … with Jesus' human knowledge of the world?'[1] O'Collins' implication is that one cannot: most opponents of Christ's earthly vision charge that it simply cannot be reconciled with his ordinary human knowing and its natural limitations, with features such as gradual growth in knowledge and ignorance. Balthasar claimed that to introduce the beatific vision into Christ's soul would render it no longer a credible human soul.[2] To teach Christ's beatific vision would then lead not to a kind of Nestorianism, as Weinandy supposes, but to a kind of Monophysitism, where such features of the human reality of Christ's knowledge are denied. It is argued that since Scripture in fact shows Christ's knowledge of the actual creation to be thus limited, he therefore could not have possessed the perfection of beatific vision. We shall begin by looking at the evidence for Christ's possession of a natural limited knowledge, before passing on to investigate how far the beatific vision and natural knowledge are mutually exclusive. While the impression is often given that the beatific vision introduces a problem for Christ's natural knowledge, we shall argue that it in fact resolves a tension between the Fathers' emphasis on the perfection of Christ's knowledge and the limitations we find portrayed in the Bible.

The Gospels make no straightforward statement that the earthly Christ possessed 'natural human knowledge' with some or all of its limitations. In order to ascertain whether or not he enjoyed natural human knowledge, we need to identify those limitations that would manifest such knowledge in Christ, and ask whether they appear in the Gospels. One serious limitation someone might suggest for Christ is error. Error, after all, is something we all experience in our own mental lives, though we may reasonably hope to be freed from it and so from its deleterious effects in heaven. It could be urged by our objector that so great an

---

1. *Christology*, p. 267.

2. *The Glory of the Lord: A Theological Aesthetics*, vol. 1: *Seeing the Form* (trans. E. Leiva-Merikakis; Edinburgh: T&T Clark, 1982), p. 328 n.141.

imperfection as positive error is incompatible with the perfection of knowledge of God and creation that this vision would deliver. Should Christ then be convicted of error on any point during his earthly lifetime, of holding what was false to be true or what was true to be false, that would cast serious doubt on his earthly possession of beatific knowledge. Error fits more easily with the attribution of faith to Jesus, and Sobrino put forward the view that Jesus made mistakes when arguing that he had faith.[3] In general, however, those Catholic theologians who are inclined to devote their energies to attacking the theory of Christ's vision are generally disinclined to argue to their conclusion from error, and are normally wary of attributing positive error to Christ at all. The reasons for this must surely derive from their reading of Scripture in the light of Tradition. There is no passage in Scripture that explicitly asserts that Jesus was in cognitive error on any point. Not that this silence in itself proves that Christ was never in error, though it does sit rather easily with what we saw in Part One of the perfection of knowledge ascribed to Christ by Scripture and Tradition. In fact this silence in itself does not exclude the possibility of demonstrating error in Christ's human mind from Scripture, if one could show from there that Christ fully assented to something *we ourselves know to be false*. However, although there are several candidates for such erroneous assent, it does not turn out on inspection to be easy to identify any particular passage where Christ *definitely* does such a thing.

One possibility that has been proposed comes from when Jesus tells a story of King David entering God's house. His recounting of it differs in various details from the account we know in the Old Testament.[4] One of these is his locating of the story in salvation history by reference to Abiathar the High Priest (Mk 2.26), when the priest who appears in the Old Testament account is in fact Abiathar's father, Ahimelech (1 Sam. 12.21). Should Jesus have held that Abiathar was actually High Priest at the time of the incident and not Ahimelech, he could easily be convicted of an error about the contents of Scripture. And he would indeed be convicted if we translate the preposition ἐπί as 'when', such that the incident happened 'when Abiathar was High Priest' (ἐπὶ Ἀβιαθὰρ ἀρχιερέως). The fact that the phrase was considered potentially misleading is suggested by its absence from some manuscripts and from the versions of the story given in Matthew 12.1–8 and Luke 6.1–5. One suggestion is that the phrase even came originally from a marginal comment by a scribe that was erroneously incorporated into the words of Jesus by another scribe.[5] An alternative translation, however, takes ἐπί as indicating merely the *lifetime* of Abiathar the High Priest, which is even clearer in those manuscripts that also have the definite article before 'High Priest', something a scribe may have added to give clarity to the Greek: ἐπὶ Ἀβιαθὰρ τοῦ ἀρχιερέως. On this translation Jesus would be locating the incident in the *lifetime* of Abiathar

---

3. *Christology at the Crossroads*, p. 101.

4. J. R. Donahue and D. J. Harrington, *The Gospel of Mark* (Collegeville, MN: Liturgical, 2002), p. 111.

5. Lagrange, *Évangile selon saint Marc* (Études Bibliques; Paris: Lecoffre, 1929), p. 54 n.26.

the High Priest rather than in the specific period of his high priesthood.[6] That Jesus should speak in this way is arguably not without plausibility: Abiathar's name would have been very well-known to his hearers, more so than Ahimelech's, and thus an effective way of letting them know whereabouts in the Samuel scroll the incident occurred (cf. 12.26). Moreover, there does appear to be some leeway for speaking more loosely in identifying someone as High Priest: despite having been succeeded by Caiaphas, Annas is still called High Priest more than once in the New Testament (Lk. 3.2; Jn 18.12–24). Given these complications, we are left without a case where we can say for certain that Christ was in error.[7]

The results are similar in other instances.[8] The most discussed of these is the contention of some scholars that Christ himself held that his Second Coming would take place very soon after his earthly lifetime, when we of course know it did not. Sobrino makes this very point in his treatment of Jesus' faith – this is a perspective on Christ that allows for him to be wrong.[9] Key texts here include the words of Jesus in those passages just before the Transfiguration is recounted in the Synoptic Gospels (Mt. 16.28; Mk 9.1; Lk. 9.27), words that differ slightly in each case. In Mark 9.1 Jesus says, 'Amen, I say to you that there are some of those standing here who will not taste death until they see the kingdom of God come with power.' Luke similarly has Jesus say, 'Truly I say to you that there are some of those standing here who will not taste death until they see the kingdom of God.' But to what does the kingdom of God and its coming in power refer? Given that there seems to be no reason to suppose the coming of the kingdom must consist in only one event, to which event or indeed set of events does this language point? The possibilities include the Transfiguration itself, which follows on immediately in each of the three Gospels, the crucifixion, the resurrection of Christ and those events that surround it, such as the Ascension, which Luke recounts, the destruction of Jerusalem in AD 70 and events leading up to it, the general resurrection and last judgement enacted by Christ, or all of the above or some combination thereof. Any of these events could be interpreted as a powerful arrival of God's kingdom that could give fulfilment to Christ's words, and not all of them are to be found at a considerable temporal distance from Christ's ministry.

Finding a definite answer as to which event or events is meant is by no means as easy as might be supposed. As Augustine noted, sayings of Jesus that may seem to refer to the last judgement may in fact be ambiguous or relate more to

6. Cf. J. Winandy, 'Le logion de l'ignorance (Mc XIII, 32; Mt XXIV, 36)', *RB* 75 (1968): 63–79; W. L. Lane, *The Gospel of Mark* (The New International Commentary on the New Testament; Grand Rapids, MI, Eerdmans: 1974), pp. 115–16.

7. For ancient solutions to the problem, see C. A. Evans, 'Patristic Interpretations of Mark 2:26: "When Abiathar was High Priest"', *VC* 40 (1986): 183–86.

8. For a presentation of the various possibilities, see Raymond E. Brown, *Jesus God and Man* (London: Chapman, 1968), pp. 49–79, and *An Introduction to New Testament Christology*, pp. 36–59.

9. *Christology at the Crossroads*, p. 101.

the coming of Christ in the Church or to the destruction of Jerusalem.[10] Thus Matthew's saying at this point – 'Amen, I say to you that there are some of those standing here who will not taste death until they see the Son of Man coming in his kingdom' – hardly settles the issue, since again it is by no means clear that this particular apocalyptic language, which also occurs in the preceding verses in all three Gospels, refers only to one particular event. The imagery arguably derives from the prophetic vision in chapter seven of the book of the prophet Daniel, which describes the coming of 'one like a son of man with the clouds of heaven' (v. 14) to the Ancient of Days from whom he receives 'dominion and glory and kingdom' (v. 15). The primary function of this imagery in Matthew 15.28 is thus to interpret the event or events to which the words of Jesus refer in the light of whatever theological significance is found in the content of Daniel's vision, rather than to give a literal description of a single future event.[11] The same may be said of other applications of 'coming of the Son of Man' imagery and of similar language of an apocalyptic nature, which can involve prediction of events within the lifetime of Jesus' hearers (e.g. Mt. 10.23).

This language, however, came to be most often interpreted of Christ's Second Coming in particular, partly because the latter still lay in the future for the Church and so became of greater religious concern than events that had already come to pass. It was an exclusive focus on the Second Coming by exegetes at the end of the nineteenth century, who took Christ's apocalyptic language to be a literalistic description of his expectations, that raised those doubts about Christ's knowledge that were rejected by the Catholic Church as part of Modernism.[12] In the light of studies of apocalyptic, exegetes today can scarcely have the same confidence in explaining this language solely and narrowly in terms of the Second Coming. Some indeed even refer it almost exclusively to proximate events such as the destruction of Jerusalem,[13] while others identify a point of transition in Jesus' apocalyptic discourse about the future where he passes from what is to take place in the near future, in the present generation, to a day and hour that lies farther off (Mt. 24.34–35; Mk 13.30; Lk. 21.32).[14] In this situation, it is once more impossible to conclude that we have a definite instance of error on the part of Jesus, since we can hardly be certain that he foretold the temporal proximity of any identifiable event that we know not in fact to have taken place.

In his presentation of various biblical texts illustrating Christ's knowledge and possible errors, Brown admits that his evaluation of the evidence of the Gospels 'does not predetermine the theological interpretation to be drawn from

---

10. *De Civitate Dei*, 20.6.

11. For recent scholarship on these issues, see D. Allison, *Jesus of Nazareth: Millenarian Prophet* (Minneapolis, MN: Fortress, 1998) and I. H. Marshall, *New Testament Theology: Many Witnesses, One Gospel* (Downers Grove, IL: Intervarsity, 2004).

12. See, e.g. A. Loisy, 'L'Apocalypse Synoptique', *RB* 5 (1896): 173–98, 335–59.

13. Wright, *New Testament and the People of God*, pp. 339–67.

14. Lane, *The Gospel of Mark*, p. 474.

it'.[15] As always, readings of Scripture are shaped to one extent or another by the tradition in which Scripture is read. The reader who holds Jesus to be merely human would have no difficulty in interpreting various passages as implying error in him, and would surely be somewhat inclined to do so, because an erring Jesus more obviously fits the pattern of one who is merely human and not God. Our objectors to Christ's beatific vision, however, read Scripture in the light of Chalcedonian tradition, and are hence in various ways disinclined to attribute error to Christ, even if he were to lack beatific knowledge. One difficulty would be the attribution of error, albeit in a human mind, to someone who is a *divine person*, something that may be considered by theologians to be unfitting or even necessarily incompatible with the hypostatic union. Furthermore, Galot considers that Christ's human moral integrity would have ruled out his making any affirmation that exceeded what he knew, such that he would never have contradicted the truth.[16] Moreover, there is a question arising from the fact that error can hardly be considered *essential* to human knowledge, given that it would appear to be logically possible for there to be an instance of a human mind that never failed in this way. This raises the question of *why* Christ would co-assume liability to error along with natural human knowing (supposing that it would be metaphysically possible to do so): how could error rather than truth be conducive to Christ's saving mission? Given such concerns, objectors to Christ's beatific vision tend to focus their case on limitations that would seem to be *essential* characteristics of our natural human knowing, namely, growth in knowledge and lack of knowledge, characteristics without which the normal process of human knowing could not take place at all.

While no biblical text explicitly attributes error to Christ, our objectors can without any difficulty find texts that clearly say that he 'grew' in knowledge and that he did 'not know' something, indicating the presence of natural human knowledge with its essential limitations. O'Collins refers to the fact that Luke 2.52 states of Christ that, after his return to Nazareth as a boy, he 'grew in wisdom' (προέκοπτεν σοφίᾳ).[17] Though this might be taken to refer to a growth in extraordinary wisdom of the kind Christ soon demonstrates in the Gospel narrative and has already indicated in the temple during his boyhood stay in Jerusalem (v. 47), its immediate connection with the fact that Christ grew 'in stature' suggests it includes a natural childhood acquisition of knowledge. To this testimony to childhood growth are added indications in the Gospels that Jesus continued to acquire knowledge as an adult through asking questions. Not that the very fact that Jesus asked questions and received answers proves that he was thereby increasing in knowledge, something that has been evident to exegetes since patristic times.[18] The asking of questions is after all a common teaching method, where the teacher already knows the answer to the question. The point is to bring

---

15. *Jesus God and Man*, p. 99.
16. *Who is Christ?*, p. 351.
17. *Christology*, p. 268.
18. E.g. Origen, *Commentarii in Matthaeum*, 10.14.

others to knowledge, and Christ was able to make use of this technique as much as any other teacher. However, there are occasions when his questioning can strike one from context as a genuine seeking out of knowledge for himself rather than a pedagogical exercise in bringing his hearers to some special knowledge, and some of these are indicated in the *Catechism of Catholic Church*, which, as we noted in Chapter 1, emphasizes the reality of his acquired knowledge.[19] For example, when he arrived at Bethany after the death of Lazarus, he asked where the tomb was located (Jn 11.34).[20] The *Catechism*'s use of this example to illustrate acquired knowledge clearly departs from the exegesis of Pope Gregory the Great, who had taught that Christ already knew the answer in his humanity.[21] Then there is also the fact that the Gospels sometimes say that Jesus 'wondered' at something – for example, he marvelled at the words of the centurion in Matthew 8.10, which suggests surprise at something that was new for him, that he did not know before. Finally, Jesus is said to have left Judea for Galilee when he 'knew' (ἔγνω) or 'came to know' that the Pharisees had heard about the extent of his ministry, leaving the clear impression that Jesus had obtained a new piece of information (Jn 4.1).

It is not difficult for opponents of Christ's beatific vision to point out that a growth of knowledge in Christ must presuppose some kind of prior absence of knowledge in him. They are, however, careful to avoid the implication that this absence of knowledge could be construed as a culpable or sinful ignorance, the lack of knowledge of something Christ *ought* already to have known. Rather this 'ignorance' is a case of what theologians have sometimes called 'nescience', a purely innocent absence of knowledge for which someone cannot be blamed.[22] Finally, such 'innocent ignorance' is claimed to be something that never leaves the earthly Christ. O'Collins cites words of Jesus from the last week of his earthly life: 'But concerning that day or that hour no one knows, not the angels in heaven nor the Son, but only the Father' (Mk 13.32).[23] Christ would then advance to such knowledge only after the conclusion of his earthly lifetime.

This picture of Christ's natural knowledge is often supported by an appeal to Chalcedon. Admittedly the Council itself said nothing explicit about the exact character of Christ's human knowledge, whether beatific or naturally acquired or whatever it might be. However, there can be no doubt that Chalcedonian tradition affirms the reality of Christ's human mind and its proper knowledge. The Definition itself stated that Christ is 'perfect in humanity', possesses a 'rational soul', is 'consubstantial with us as to humanity, like us in all things, except sin', and that the 'proper character' of the human nature is preserved in the union of his two natures in one person. Moreover, Leo the Great had taught that Christ's human nature had its own proper activity,[24] and we have so far argued with

---

19. *Catechismus*, 472.
20. Other examples given are Mk 6.38 and 8.27.
21. *Sicut aqua frigida*.
22. E.g. Aquinas, *Summa*, 1a., q. 101, a. 1 ad 2.
23. *Christology*, p. 268.
24. *Tomus ad Flavianum*, 4.

Aquinas that this proper activity includes the beatific vision. Objectors to Christ's beatific vision take it as obvious that, since Christ was 'like us' in his rational soul, he would acquire and grow in knowledge as we do, and indeed this fits with the testimony of the Gospels. Despite the Fathers' general tendency to emphasize the perfection of Christ's knowledge, which we observed in Chapter 3, even one sixth-century author (who did not wish to treat the question himself) opined that the members of the Council, despite the fact that Chalcedon did not treat the issue as such, would seem to have accepted a lack of knowledge in Christ, given that they taught that he was 'like us'.[25]

Although opponents of Christ's beatific vision make his natural knowledge the starting-point of one of their objections, we should note that not all theologians who affirm his natural knowledge find in it a basis for rejecting his beatific vision. In his *Summa Theologiae*, Aquinas himself is at one with objectors to Christ's beatific vision in teaching that Christ acquired knowledge.[26] By teaching that Christ had genuinely acquired 'science', Aquinas departed from his earlier position and that of many theologians of his own day. Aquinas had initially accepted the view common among his contemporaries that Christ did not acquire conceptual knowledge through the usual channels. Whatever novelties there might be in the daily impact of the world on his senses, in specifically cognitive terms he gained nothing new from it.[27] Now Aquinas never made the suggestion that it was not within God's power to cause an incarnation where there was no actual acquiring of intellectual knowledge, but he came to envisage the incarnate Word in fact co-assuming the natural acquisition of 'science' so as to bring the natural equipment of his human mind, which included the mental apparatus for abstracting intellectual knowledge from sense data, to its own proper perfection, in keeping with the perfection that Christ's humanity required for our salvation.[28] As we saw in Chapter 4, Aquinas's concern with the means of human knowledge had an important effect in his theory of the beatific vision of the saints, and now we see that his 'Aristotelianism' likewise had an effect on his understanding of Christ's natural knowledge. He argued from the fact that, should Christ not have acquired knowledge through the senses, his 'active intellect' would have been without its proper activity and hence redundant. However, his active intellect did not in fact remain redundant, and during his lifetime Christ acquired 'science' from the world around him through the senses, and hence had the capacity to wonder at what was new for him in this respect.[29]

---

25. Leontius the Scholastic, *De Sectis*, 10.3. Though not by Leontius of Byzantium, this work has been included among his writings. There is a discussion of the question of authorship in Grillmeier and Hainthaler, *Christ in Christian Tradition*, 2/2, p. 493.

26. See my 'Christ's Acquired Knowledge according to Thomas Aquinas: How Aquinas's Philosophy Helped and Hindered his Account', *NB* 96 (2015): 255–68.

27. *Super Sent.*, 3.14.3.5 ad 3; 18.3 ad 5. For another example of the consensus, see Bonaventure, *In Sent.*, 3.14.3.2.

28. *Summa*, 3a, q. 9, a. 4.

29. Ibid., 3a., q. 15, a. 8.

Despite breaking important new ground on the question of Christ's experiential knowledge, we should note that Aquinas is widely held as failing to convince in some of the details, in places where his account diverges from the one more commonly accepted by theologians today. A first point concerns the immediate source of Christ's acquired knowledge: Aquinas thought that Christ would not have learned anything 'scientific' from other people.[30] In general Aquinas valued acquiring such knowledge for oneself from the world over learning from others.[31] He concluded that, on account of his saving role as Teacher, Christ would not learn from any angel or any other human being, not even from Mary and Joseph, at least not in terms of the kind of knowledge of the world that Aquinas considered 'scientific', but was always one step ahead of any teacher. Nicolas points out that Christ certainly had no 'Master' who revealed to him the Father – Christ had no Teacher in any such sense.[32] However, it is now widely held to be implausible that his assumption of genuine human nature for our salvation, including its infancy and natural development, did not involve his learning from his mother Mary, from Joseph her husband and from others, just as is natural for the children of the race he had come to save.[33]

A second point concerns the absolute perfection of Christ's acquired scientific knowledge, which Aquinas evidently takes to be achieved by adulthood, his early modern Carmelite commentators of Salamanca specifying the age of twelve.[34] For Christ's active intellect to be perfect, it had to have acquired everything it could possibly know in that way, whether through direct experience or by reasoning from what he had experienced. In some ways this claim to so extensive a knowledge would hardly have struck Aquinas as implausible just as it now strikes us as implausible. It may have seemed to him to have been the case that the ancient philosophers and contemporaries, like his own teacher, Albert the Great, had acquired for themselves a very large proportion of what could be known by scientific investigation, and hence it was hardly implausible that the earthly Christ had completed this work. Our view of the universe and the extent of possible scientific knowledge are of course immensely different, rendering this kind of perfection in Christ's knowledge quite implausible to us. Indeed it would also seem unnecessary, given the nature of his mission, which was hardly to increase the human race's scientific understanding. The perfection of Christ's acquired knowledge can, however, be presented in another way, by extending to his whole earthly life the kind of perfection Aquinas attributes to him during his childhood. Prior to his attainment of a knowledge absolutely perfect for human nature, Aquinas envisioned Christ's knowledge as increasing in such a way that it was always perfect relative to the needs of any particular moment.[35] To think of Christ's

30. Ibid., 3a., q. 12, a. 3.

31. On Aquinas's educational theory, see V. Boland, *St Thomas Aquinas* (Continuum Library of Educational Thought, vol. 1; London and New York: Continuum, 2007).

32. Cf. Nicolas, 'Voir Dieu dans la "condition charnelle"', p. 387 n.7.

33. E.g. Y. Congar, *Jesus Christ* (trans. L. O'Neill; Chapman: London, 1966), pp. 54–8.

34. Salmanticenses, *Cursus Theologicus Summam d. Thomae Complectens*, 21.22.2.2.

35. *Summa*, 3a., q. 12, a. 3 ad 2.

knowledge *throughout his life* in terms of this relative perfection was suggested by theologians in the nineteenth century.[36] If we then modify Aquinas's position by applying this relative perfection of dynamic growth throughout Christ's earthly life, we can establish a certain common ground on the fact of Christ's natural human knowledge between those who reject Christ's beatific vision and those who hold to a broadly Thomist account. While in the last chapter we rejected the premise of the opposing argument that Christ had faith, here we positively endorse the premise of our opponents, namely, that Christ had what was essential to natural human knowing. This means that, while in the last chapter we endorsed the mutual exclusivity of faith and vision, in what follows we shall defend the mutual compatibility of the beatific vision and natural human knowledge.

So where our two parties will differ, despite a basic common ground on Christ's natural knowledge, is on whether the presence of the beatific vision would somehow suppress the reality of this knowledge. Before examining the arguments normally put in favour of the mutual exclusion of the beatific vision and natural knowing, we should note how one can easily get the impression that a theology must go down either one line or the other, having to choose between beatific and acquired knowledge. Aquinas's predecessors and contemporaries, after all, had accepted Christ's beatific vision while rejecting acquired knowledge, and this position continued in later scholasticism and was represented in the school of Duns Scotus.[37] It has been noted how the reality of Christ's acquired knowledge, when affirmed, could sometimes be treated as something almost grudgingly *conceded* rather than as enjoying a positive role.[38] Thus one could easily slip into supposing that, in order to maintain the integrity of Christ's natural knowing, one must abandon or at least drastically curtail his beatific vision. This impression may also be reinforced by the way theologians in the twentieth century further modified or even effectively abandoned Aquinas's account. Karl Adam, for example, while strongly maintaining Christ's acquired knowledge and its relative perfection, adopted a Scotist theory of Christ's beatific vision in place of the Thomist one.[39] On Scotus's account, the finitude of Christ's humanity put more limitations on his beatific vision in practice than Aquinas allowed. This included making Christ's beatific knowledge an *habitual* body of knowledge on which he could draw, rather than one single *act*, as Aquinas had conceived it.[40] Though, for Scotus, Christ could in principle know *anything* in his human mind that he knew in his divine mind, even things Aquinas excluded from the beatific vision, in practice what he knew in the beatific vision was limited, because he could not actually call all of it to mind all at once. By turning his back on the standard

36. Cf. Schell, *Katholische Dogmatik*, 3, pp. 105–20; Rivière, 'Le problème de la science humaine du Christ: Positions classiques et nouvelles tendances'.

37. See Leeming, 'The Human Knowledge of Christ', p. 144.

38. Rivière, 'La problème de la science humaine du Christ', p. 344.

39. K. Adam, *The Christ of Faith* (London: Burns, Oates & Washbourne, 1957), pp. 266–76.

40. *Ordinatio*, 3, d. 14, q. 2, nn.20–1.

Thomist account and restricting Christ's actual vision in this way, Adam seems to have been trying to 'make room' for his natural knowledge, as though beatific and acquired knowledge must be in tension, competing over the same territory, so to speak. His adoption of the Scotist account was not without problems, however. For example, it meant the loss of Aquinas's sense of how happiness, precisely because it is one's *ultimate perfection and end*, is a matter of *actual* knowing and not merely habitual knowledge.[41] It is worth noting with Moloney that Bonaventure, Scotus's Franciscan predecessor and Aquinas's contemporary, at one stage abandoned an earlier reliance on applying the concept of 'habitual knowledge' to the beatific vision for a theory more akin to Aquinas's.[42]

While some theologians drew in this way on Scotus or on Bonaventure,[43] others elected to modify Aquinas's own understanding of Christ's beatific knowledge, but seemingly with a similar end in view, that is, modifying Aquinas's account to 'make room' for natural knowledge. Some did this by introducing a certain compartmentalization into Christ's human mind, where his beatific vision would be not merely inexpressible but also somewhat *inaccessible* to his ordinary consciousness. It is true that Aquinas gave no specific attention to the more modern question of the interrelation and interaction of Christ's different kinds of knowledge in his single human consciousness. However, there is nothing in Aquinas's distinctions of knowledge that demands a psychological partitioning up of the mind, any more than does an ordinary distinction between knowledge of literature and knowledge of chemistry in our case, or the distinction between faith and reason, or Rahner's distinction between different levels of unthematic and thematic knowledge. Lonergan has argued that among the reasons why different kinds of knowledge did not break up Christ's consciousness is the fact that the acts of various kinds of knowledge, whether humanly expressible or inexpressible, whether supernatural or natural, were all ordered to one another within his single mind or consciousness.[44] However, given that Aquinas does talk of higher and lower 'parts' of the soul, thereby distinguishing reason and the passions, and of the higher and lower reason insofar as reason can have both eternal and temporal objects, some have been encouraged to suppose, either approvingly or disapprovingly, that different kinds of knowledge must introduce relatively isolated 'areas' within the soul's 'higher part'. Balthasar seems to think that something of the sort must follow from the presence of the beatific vision in Christ's mind.[45] Here we

41. *Contra Gentiles*, 3.60.2.

42. *The Knowledge of Christ*, p. 56. But see Z. Hayes (ed.), *Works of St. Bonaventure*, vol. 5: *Disputed Questions on the Knowledge of Christ* (Bonaventure Texts in Translation Series; St Bonaventure, NY: Franciscan Institute, 2005), pp. 43–4.

43. Gutwenger, 'Das menschliche Wissen des irdischen Christus', *ZKT* 76 (1954): 170–86, before adopting a more Rahnerian position in *Bewusstsein und Wissen Christi*; R. Haubst, 'Die Gottesanschauung und das natürliche Erkenntniswachstum Christi', *TQ* 137 (1957): 385–412.

44. *De Verbo Incarnato*, p. 405.

45. *Glory of the Lord*, I, p. 328 n.141.

have the danger of somehow marooning Christ's beatific vision within an 'apex' of his soul or mind. Maritain effectively did this very thing by introducing a quasi-Freudian concept of a 'supraconsciousness'.[46] This certainly made the beatific vision not merely inexpressible for Christ's consciousness but largely inaccessible to that consciousness, where his ordinary knowing took place. Maritain's compartmentalizing of Christ's mind won his theory little support. Nicolas has pointed out that it seems to suggest more than one subject in Christ, one (supraconsciously) enjoying the beatific vision and the other (consciously) not, which pushes in a Nestorian direction.[47]

While such compartmentalization of Christ's mind may have served to reinforce an impression that Christ's ordinary knowing will be suppressed by Christ's beatific knowledge, unless somehow shielded from it, some of those who have better retained the unity of Christ's mind have nevertheless done the same. Nicolas, in his defence of a generally Thomist account of Christ's beatific vision, restricted the range of objects seen in Christ's single earthly act of vision, thereby leaving knowledge of what was not at all known through the beatific vision to be gained through natural means. Nicolas achieved this by making Christ an exception to Aquinas's mature position that the ultimate end of the beatific vision does not in any way grow.[48] For Nicolas, the secondary content of Christ's beatific knowledge on earth thus matched the needs of his earthly mission (which did not include communicating the day and hour of the last judgement), and increased in extent after the resurrection for the purposes of his exercising universal judgement.[49] One problem with this modified version of Aquinas's theory is that it becomes difficult, for all its avoidance of the quasi-Nestorianism of Maritain, to see how it can satisfy the teaching of Gregory the Great and avoid Agnoetism, because it altogether denies knowledge of the last day *in* the earthly humanity of Christ. In distinction from Maritain's supraconciousness, which allows for the presence of such knowledge in Christ's human supraconsciousness, for Nicolas there is no sense at all in which the earthly Christ can be said to know the day and the hour *in his humanity*. It might also be thought problematic for Nicolas that Christ would in respect of this kind of knowledge come to know the Father more perfectly at the resurrection than he did during his earthly lifetime, given that on Thomist principles a wider range of objects seen in the beatific vision follows from a more intense knowledge of their cause. We shall return to this difficulty in the next chapter, when we consider its implications for Christ's will.

For now we note that such (unsatisfactory) attempts at departing in one way or another from Aquinas's theory for the sake of encompassing natural limitations in Christ's human knowledge have only served to confirm an impression that Aquinas's own theory of Christ's beatific vision must not be able to cope with

46. *Grace and Humanity of Jesus*, pp. 47–93. Maritain's theory has received support most recently from Oakes, *Infinity Dwindled to Infancy*, pp. 219–21.

47. 'Voir Dieu dans la "condition charnelle"', pp. 388–89.

48. Ibid., p. 391.

49. Ibid., pp. 390–2.

the latter's natural knowledge and its essential features. While acknowledging that the reality of Christ's acquired knowledge has suffered among some scholastic theories, I suggest that the *Thomist* theory of the beatific vision was never the real culprit, and that, however much we may need to modify some of its details for different reasons, there is no good reason to abandon the theory so easily or subject it to completely unnecessary modifications, as did Adam, Maritain and Nicolas. We can begin to appreciate how it was not Aquinas's theory that introduced the threat to Christ's natural knowledge by recalling that the latter's essential features, such as growth in and acquisition of knowledge, were *already* vulnerable at a time when a vision in his humanity was only occasionally hinted at. As we saw in Chapter 3, a consensus emerged among the Fathers that, since he was God Christ had a full knowledge of creation, including knowledge of the timing of the last judgement, and that, while his humanity was not the source of this knowledge, it did not fail to benefit from it. This led to difficulties in interpreting, for example, Jesus' not knowing the timing of 'that day' in Mark 13.32, and a number of somewhat inadequate interpretations of the text emerged.[50] These interpretations shared the undisputed assumption that he did not reveal what he knew here because that was not part of his mission, it not being conducive to our salvation to have this information, as illustrated by Christ's words before the Ascension: 'It is not for you to know times or seasons which the Father has set by his own authority' (Acts 1.7). From there different interpretations of Mark 13.32 (and its parallel, Matthew 24.36) diverged.

Christ's words were often taken *not* to be saying that he did not know, but in some complicated way or other to be saying that he *did* know. His *not* knowing was often relegated, somewhat implausibly, to conditions that did not in fact obtain. For example, he was taken to be saying that he *would* not know but for the fact that the Father knew and had made it known to him,[51] or that he would not have known, had he been a mere man.[52] Abstracting from the hypostatic union, he would not have had this knowledge in his humanity, but on account of the union he did.[53] However, it is one thing to say that these assertions are in themselves theologically acceptable, but another to say that they give us a plausible theological interpretation of the particular meaning of *this* saying. The same may be said for Augustine, who put forward an interpretation that had Christ speaking not about what he did not know or even directly of what he did know, but about what he was not *making known*. Augustine was aware that 'know'

---

50. For analyses of the Fathers on this verse, see L. R. Wickham, 'The Ignorance of Christ: A Problem for the Ancient Theology' in L. R. Wickham and C. P. Bammel (eds), *Christian Faith and Greek Philosophy in Late Antiquity: Essays in Tribute to George Christopher Stead* (Supplements to Vigiliae Christianae, vol. 19; New York: Brill, 1993), pp. 213–26 (223–5); F. X. Gumerlock, 'Mark 13:32 and Christ's Supposed Ignorance: Four Patristic Solutions', *TJ* 28 (2007): 205–13.

51. E.g. Basil, *Ep.*, 236.2.

52. E.g. Gregory of Nazianzus, *Orationes*, 30.15.

53. E.g. Maximus, *Quaestiones et Dubia*, 66.

could be used in a different way from a claim to knowledge: when someone says they 'do not know' someone, they may be expressing rejection of that person, as Jesus says he will do to many in Matthew 7.23: 'I never knew you.' Augustine effectively invented a further figure of speech to fit the case of Mark 13.32: when Christ said he did not know the day, he was in fact saying that he was not *making it known* to the disciples. Thus when he also said that the Father *did* know, he was actually meaning that the Father had in fact *made it known* to the Son.[54] In contrast to all these positions, Epiphanius had the merit of speaking both of Christ's genuine not knowing and of this within the circumstances that did really obtain.[55] However, by interpreting Christ to be saying that he did not know the day and hour in terms of his actually bringing it about, that is, as an experienced present reality produced by his own action, Epiphanius unfortunately reduced Christ's words in their context to a rather trivial statement: that this or any other of the events foretold in Christ's discourse was not yet known to him in terms of his actually bringing them about could hardly have been news to the disciples, who were looking for knowledge of the future (v. 4). Finally, several Fathers saw Christ as speaking of an ignorance that was effectively feigned.[56] On account of his assumption of human nature, which could not be the source of knowledge of the future, they supposed that Christ could legitimately pretend to his disciples that he did not know what he in fact knew from a non-human source.[57]

Similar difficulties were encountered in the interpretation of those passages that bear witness to Christ's growth in knowledge. Sometimes the Fathers seemed to accept a real growth in Christ's knowledge, when they quoted Luke 2.52 against those who in some way denied Christ's humanity, such as the Apollinarians. Commenting on this passage, Ambrose said that infancy 'through lack of human wisdom knows nothing of those whom it has not learned to recognise'.[58] However, in many other passages, the Fathers explicitly set aside a real growth in Christ's knowledge for a growth in a *manifestation* of his wisdom,[59] a change in attitude towards his wisdom from those who encountered it,[60] or a growth in the wisdom of his hearers.[61] It has been a matter of debate whether Ambrose abandoned a mere growth in manifestation for a real growth, and whether Cyril abandoned a real growth in wisdom for a growth in manifestation and the appreciation given by others.[62] The Fathers' principal problem in all this was their difficulty in

---

54. E.g. *De Diversis Quaestionibus LXXXIII*, 60.

55. *Ancoratus*, 21.

56. E.g. Basil, *Ep.*, 8.6.

57. On the theory of Christ's '*de iure* ignorance' in Cyril and Athanasius, according to which he was entitled to *say* he did not know, even though he did, see Moloney, 'Approaches to Christ's Knowledge in the Patristic Era', pp. 41–4, 52–7.

58. *De Incarnationis Dominicae Sacramento*, 7.74.

59. E.g. Gregory of Nazianzus, *Orationes*, 43.38.

60. E.g. Cyril, *Thesaurus*, 28.

61. E.g. John of Damascus, *Expositio Fidei*, 3.22.

62. For the different positions on Cyril, see Most, *Consciousness of Christ*, p. 107.

seeing how to square an increase in knowledge or a lack of knowledge with that fullness of Christ's knowledge to which they considered themselves doctrinally committed. In this difficulty of seeing how one full of wisdom could increase in it, we see how Christ's natural knowledge was already at some risk, even before his beatific vision had become commonly accepted.

Opponents of Christ's beatific vision tend to be uncomfortable not only with this scholastic theory but also with the patristic tradition that lies behind it. Not only do they understandably reject the various interpretations of verses of Scripture by the Fathers as unsatisfactory, but they also routinely set aside the wider patristic picture of Christ possessing a fullness of knowledge in his humanity. This is because they rightly sense a tension of some kind between the Fathers' attribution of perfect knowledge to Christ and Scripture's picture of Christ as exercising limited human knowledge, a tension which is betrayed in the Fathers' unsuccessful attempts at interpreting verses such as Mark 13.32 and Luke 2.52. Unable to find a way of resolving this tension, our opponents again understandably favour *Scripture's* limited knowledge over the *Fathers'* fullness of knowledge, and so abandon the consensus that emerged by the end of the patristic period. This, however, is not without its problems for a Catholic theology, which, as we have seen in previous chapters, ought not to interpret Scripture contrary to a patristic consensus. Moreover, in seeking an apologia for disregarding the patristic witness, some have treated it as involving a kind of intrusion of a 'Greek' overvaluing of knowledge into Christian thought.[63] This move at least flirts with the well-known problematic tendency in modern theology that regards the encounter between the Gospel and Greek philosophy as one that essentially distorted rather than helped to clarify the meaning of the Gospel. Finally, it is difficult to see how the interpretation of Mark 13.32 with which we are left, despite the effort to avoid Nestorianism, can be adequately distinguished from Agnoetism, since Christ is left without any kind of knowledge of the day and the hour in his humanity. However, the challenge for Catholic theology, with its commitment to Scripture and the consensus of the Fathers, must surely be to search out a resolution of the tension between Scripture's limited knowledge and the Fathers' fullness of knowledge, avoiding Agnoetism and seeking out a convincing exegesis of verses such as Mark 13.32.

Although the idea of Christ's beatific vision was then not responsible for originating this tension and its problems, most of the alternative theories of his beatific vision we mentioned above have done little more than continue to reformulate these difficulties. For example, the restriction of the secondary objects of Christ's vision, such that the earthly Christ had no knowledge at all of the day of judgement in his humanity, is again difficult to distinguish adequately from Agnoetism. Though Adam's Scotist theory clearly avoids this position, since Christ had habitual knowledge of the day and hour in his humanity, Adam's speculative exegesis of Mark 13.32 is no more convincing than its patristic predecessors. According to Adam, Christ knew the timing of the last day habitually, but

---

63. Cf. Gutwenger, *Bewusstsein und Wissen Christi*, pp. 103–4.

not actually.[64] In other words, this knowledge was there for him to call to mind, much as anyone's personal knowledge of a foreign language, for example, is there to call to mind. And just as I may not be in the act of recalling my knowledge of the details of French verbs at some particular moment, so Christ could refrain from the act of considering his knowledge of that day and hour. However, is it plausible that his denial of knowledge of the day and hour can be construed as denying only that he was not *actually considering* knowledge that he in fact possessed habitually in his human mind all along? Should someone assert that he does not know French, merely because he is not actually considering his knowledge of the language at that very moment, we would surely take him to be speaking a falsehood. When a plain denial of this kind is made, we invariably expect it to be a denial of habitual as well as actual knowledge, even if we have not ourselves reflected on the conceptual distinction between habit and act. Should we elect to interpret Mark 13.32 in Adam's way, we would surely have Christ perpetrating an unworthy deception on the disciples. Only Maritain's theory fares reasonably well in this respect because, while escaping Agnoetism by granting Christ knowledge of the last day in his human supraconsciousness, it takes his denial of knowledge to extend only to conscious knowledge. Since the disciples were presumably only concerned with Christ's conscious knowledge, being quite oblivious to the very existence of supraconscious knowledge, his denial can escape the charge of deception. However, passing this particular test hardly compensates for the fundamental difficulties with Maritain's supraconsciousness theory, which we mentioned above.

I shall suggest that, in contrast to all these theories, it is an advantage of the *Thomist* theory of Christ's beatific vision that it does not land the Catholic theologian with such problems, but instead provides a coherent theory that can resolve the apparent tension between the Fathers' general picture of Christ's perfect knowledge and Scripture's witness to the limitations of his natural knowledge. Not only then did Aquinas's position not introduce into theology a problem for Christ's natural knowledge, but it offers a resolution of a significant tension that predates his scholastic theory, escaping Agnoetism and possessing the potential to suggest a convincing exegesis of such verses as Mark 13.32. This it does on the basis of a beatific vision and an acquired knowledge that are *not* mutually exclusive. Opponents of Christ's beatific vision, however, see Aquinas's theory as only reinforcing the Fathers' tendency to underplay the limitations of his natural knowledge in favour of the perfection of his earthly knowledge, because the beatific vision and natural knowledge *are* mutually exclusive. We shall now critically examine the various ways in which they argue for this mutual exclusion, before finally suggesting how Aquinas's position can successfully resolve the apparent tension between Christ's fullness of knowledge and his natural knowledge with its essential limitations.

Sometimes opponents make their argument through a further appeal to Chalcedon, despite the fact that Chalcedon had nothing explicit to say about

---

64. *The Christ of Faith*, pp. 275–6.

Christ's beatific vision one way or the other, and the further fact that the theory of Christ's vision actually arose within a Chalcedonian context. O'Collins says that the Council's insistence on Christ's humanity retaining its proper character 'should make one cautious about attributing special properties (in this case, the quite extraordinary knowledge of the beatific vision) to his human mind'.[65] Thus the impression is sometimes given that the Council not only endorsed Christ's natural knowing, but also somehow implicitly ruled out his beatific knowing. One possible line in favour of this conclusion would be to recall that Chalcedon said that Christ in his humanity is 'like us in all things except sin'. From here an objector to Christ's vision could argue that, since he is like us in all things except sin, then he will be like us in knowledge, and therefore not *unlike* us in knowledge. While Christ's being like us in knowledge will be satisfied by his gaining knowledge in the natural way as we do, to possess the beatific vision would render him *unlike* us in knowledge, since we – at least while on earth – do not see God just as he is. The question is whether by saying Christ was 'like us in all things except sin', the Council Fathers thereby excluded from him such perfections as we do not now possess, such as the beatific vision.

Although the Council took the words 'except sin' from Hebrews 4.15, the Letter itself hardly helps us, since it was making not a general point about Christ's likeness to us but no more than the point that Christ was *tested* as we are yet did not sin. However, when we look at the general picture of Jesus the Fathers took from Scripture, we see that it involves many individual ways in which Christ was unlike us. For example, he was conceived by the Holy Spirit, was uniquely anointed by that Spirit, worked miracles by means of human touch and taught with an unparalleled authority. Were Christ to be like us in all such areas, he would have been conceived by the act of a human father, not outstrip us in his receipt of the gift of grace, be unable to work miracles through the instrument of his humanity and be no more enlightened than us in teaching the things of God. It is inconceivable then that the Council Fathers could have taken the view that they were excluding such individual differences from Christ. The likeness they were defining is to be understood in terms of the Council's rejection of the Monophysite heresy of Eutyches, who denied that Christ was 'consubstantial with us'. Thus the Council was declaring that Christ was 'consubstantial (ὁμοούσιον) with us in regard to humanity, like us in all things except sin'. What is at issue here is Christ's likeness to us in terms of the general make-up of his human nature, a body like ours and a rational soul like ours, only untouched by sin, which is generally a feature of the human nature we possess. There is no concern with and so no deliberate exclusion of any individual perfections Christ may have had over and above others. Hence we cannot see Chalcedon's proclamation of Christ's likeness to us as necessarily excluding a certain unlikeness in terms of knowledge. In principle, there is no contradiction between him being like us in one respect of his knowledge and unlike us in another. He certainly was like us in the natural knowledge pertaining to his rational soul, but there is no definite exclusion by the

---

65. *Christology*, p. 268.

Definition of his being unlike us insofar as his soul was individually blessed with the perfection of a higher knowledge also. We cannot then assume that what it meant for the earthly Christ of Chalcedon to be perfect in humanity can be just read off from an examination of how humanity exists in us.[66]

Any individual perfection, however, can surely only be attributed to the Christ of Chalcedon, so long as that perfection is itself compatible with what follows from Christ's likeness to us in human nature. What, however, if the perfection in question were excluded of necessity by the presence of natural knowledge? Is the beatific vision compatible or incompatible with the fact of Christ's human knowledge and its natural features, which Chalcedon teaches? O'Collins presents one objection that relates specifically to the early stages of Christ's human development. As we saw in Chapter 1, those who teach Christ's beatific vision hold that he was never humanly without it. O'Collins retorts that Jesus having this vision from conception has its own special difficulties. He argues from the fact that, although the mind is not to be reduced to the brain, mental life depends on the brain, and concludes that Jesus could not, at a single-cell stage of embryological development, have supported such an advanced knowledge as the beatific vision.[67] O'Collins is certainly right to maintain that Jesus' body developed in the womb in the normal human way. In contrast Aquinas had made Christ an exception to what he understood to be the rule. Following the Fathers, Aquinas held that the Word took flesh at the Annunciation by the angel and the overshadowing of Mary by the Holy Spirit. Hence Aquinas required there to be present from this moment what he could identify as the Word's human nature, which according to him had to be a *completely* formed body with all its developed organs, informed by an intellectual soul. To have assumed a less than fully formed body would have been unfitting, but in the normal way of things that is what Aquinas held the Word would have assumed, since on Aquinas's biology a completely formed body was ordinarily delivered only after a lengthy process of conception and bodily formation. What happened in Christ's case, according to Aquinas, was that Christ's body was perfectly formed instantaneously, which was possible because it took place by the power of the Holy Spirit rather than the limited power of sperm provided by a human father. Christ's development in the womb would thus have been unlike that of any other unborn child, with fully formed organs from the beginning and growth limited to size alone.[68] However, in view of the fact that advances in modern embryology have inclined the Catholic Church and theologians away from limiting the presence of human nature to any later point in the development of the embryo after conception, there would seem to be no theological reason why Christ should not share in the usual development of a human embryo.

But if Catholic theologians can agree that Christ's embryological development after his conception by the Holy Spirit followed the normal pattern, what

---

66. Cf. Ols, 'Réflexions sur l'actualité de la Christologie de Saint Thomas', *DC* 34 (1981): pp. 58–71 (64–7).

67. *Christology*, p. 267.

68. *Summa*, 3a., q. 33.

conclusions can be drawn from this about his knowledge? There is definitely one conclusion to be drawn about his natural knowledge, insofar as it is recognized that a developed body has a crucial role to play in such knowledge, namely, that Christ could not have exercised it without the requisite physiological developments having taken place, whether in the brain or in the senses or whatever it might be. Though Aquinas held an act of intellect to be an act of the immaterial soul and not a bodily act per se, he recognized the crucial roles of both bodily senses and bodily images to this act in a human being, who is a unity of body and soul. Hence we can no more think of the unborn Christ making natural human cognitive acts before the necessary developments had taken place in his body than we can think of this of any other human embryo. This is not, on a Thomist account, because of anything lacking in the intellectual soul but because of what is still lacking in bodily development.

We should be wary, however, of drawing any similar conclusion about Christ's beatific knowledge, since this vision can come about neither through the bodily senses nor with the support of finite bodily images. As we saw in Chapter 4, nothing finite of any kind can be the means through which the infinite God is known just as he is, and certainly nothing bodily. What role could this possibly leave for the brain in supporting such a vision? O'Collins seems to suppose that until Jesus' brain had developed somewhat, he could not have supported the beatific vision. However, it is surely the case that, however far any human brain were to develop, it could never make any contribution to support the beatific vision on account of its materiality, and this is the case with Christ's brain too. Christ's beatific vision can only be an act pertaining to his immaterial soul, elevated by the light of glory to knowledge of the Father through his very essence. To this act itself the development of the body and brain can contribute nothing. This is confirmed by the Catholic teaching, to which we referred in Chapter 2, that souls separated from their bodies, and hence from their brains, are admitted to the beatific vision. Should Christ then have possessed the beatific vision at all, the reality of his physical development presents no reason why the vision should not have begun from the very first moment of the existence of his intellectual soul. We may of course be deflected from accepting this conclusion, if we imagine it to involve the embryonic Christ cogitating and reflecting in the manner of natural human thinking, as if he were already an adult. But that would only be to create a truly mythological picture of Christ by confusing the wordless gaze of beatific knowledge with the mundane processes of natural human knowing. For Christ intuitively to behold his Father is one thing; to begin to acquire knowledge humanly and think it over is another. The question then is whether, if Christ is already in possession of the beatific vision in his soul, that fact would somehow obstruct the natural knowledge that should naturally arise with the growth of the body.

It is hardly controversial to suggest that different kinds of knowledge can co-exist in a single mind.[69] The objections made against Christ's earthly vision

---

69. Cf. Tekippe, 'The Vision of Christ', pp. 94–5.

on the grounds of his natural knowledge generally suppose some particular level of mutual exclusion between the beatific vision and natural knowledge. Now if this mutual exclusion were the case, and Christ has natural knowledge according to his humanity, the presence of the beatific vision would put the genuineness of this humanity under threat. The concern appears to presuppose something like there being insufficient 'space' in Christ's single human mind to encompass both beatific and natural knowing, as though his act of vision would either eliminate or at least hinder or render superfluous the limited natural workings of his human mind. O'Collins appears to envisage the latter when he expresses concern that beatific knowledge would place Christ beyond the normal limits of human knowing, and so cast doubt on his humanity's authenticity.[70] Allowed the broadest terms, a charge of this kind risks implying that the beatific knowledge of the saints must also detract from the genuineness of their humanity. If Christ's beatific vision were destructive of genuine human nature, then why not that of the blessed? Does the beatific vision then eliminate or make superfluous the natural workings of the minds of the saints? Are we to picture them as so mesmerized by the vision of God that they no longer know humanly? As we saw in Chapter 3, there were hints of such a (Platonist) position in Origen. However, though we too might easily slip into thinking in this way, it would certainly be unacceptable to Catholic theological principles to suggest that divine grace is destructive rather than perfective of human nature. Aquinas often stated the axiom that God's grace does not destroy our nature but perfects it.[71] Since the state of glory is itself the consummation of the life of grace, grace being the 'seed' of glory, Aquinas equally well stated that '*glory* does not destroy nature but perfects it'.[72] This means that whatever pertains to the beatific perfection of a nature presupposes the continuing reality of that nature for its very existence. Hence nature and thus the capacity for natural knowing must be at least *preserved* and possibly even *enhanced* by the perfection of the beatific vision, rather than suppressed.[73] Without an overriding reason why this capacity should not be actualized, we should surely be open to its possible use in heaven. Should, however, the beatific vision obstruct the natural knowledge of the blessed, we would find it difficult to affirm that nature was perfected by glory after all, both in their case and in the case of the earthly Christ.

Aquinas himself held that, glory preserving nature, the blessed angels and saints exercised both beatific and natural knowledge.[74] While he held that supernatural faith and the beatific vision could not co-exist in the same mind, natural knowledge and the beatific vision could and did. As we saw in the last chapter, in the case of faith and vision, this mutual exclusion was because there was a real point of opposition between them, namely, the fact that faith had of itself an object that was *unseen*. However, in the case of the beatific vision and natural creaturely

---

70. *Christology*, p. 268.
71. E.g. *Summa*, 1a., q. 1, a. 8 ad 2.
72. *Super Sent.*, 4.45.3.1.
73. Cf. *Summa*, 1a., q. 62, a. 7.
74. Ibid., 1a., q. 58, a. 6.

knowledge, no such point of opposition could be found. Thus both a beatified soul separated from its body and a human person inhabiting heaven at the resurrection would continue to exercise their appropriate natural knowledge as well as the vision of God. Aquinas increasingly came to realize how the soul's loss of its body diminished its ability to exercise the knowledge that is proper to it by nature, since it was natural for the soul to be united with its body, and this had its implications for human knowledge.[75] Nevertheless, he held that before the resurrection the soul would be able to exercise, in addition to the beatific vision, a mode of knowing 'natural' to its separated state and similar to that of the angels, though weaker in power. Following Augustine's exegesis of the opening verses of Genesis, Aquinas distinguished two kinds of knowledge in an angel: evening knowledge and morning knowledge. According to Aquinas, 'evening knowledge' is the natural knowledge an angel possesses from its creation, and 'morning knowledge' the beatific vision it receives immediately following on its initial act of supernatural faith and charity. With its finite creaturely intellect, angels by nature have finite means of knowledge like human beings, but being purely immaterial they had never abstracted their *species* from images received through bodily senses.[76] Rather the presence of these *species* in the angelic intellect is connatural to it, and through these non-abstracted *species* they are able to know individuals as well as universals,[77] something the separated soul could only manage in a confused way. Thus by natural knowledge the angel knows through finite *species*, and by beatific knowledge through the divine essence taking the place of the *species*. As well as the single act of beatific knowledge by which the angel participates in God's eternal knowledge, both the angel and the separated soul can make a succession of acts of knowledge by means that are proportionate to its own finite nature, including a certain knowledge of God derived from knowledge of creatures.[78]

In all this we can observe something of how Aquinas understands natural knowledge to be preserved along with beatific knowledge. He can detect no opposition between angels and separated souls exercising the beatific vision and exercising natural knowledge. He considers, for example, whether it might be simply impossible for the intellect of an angel to make a beatific and natural act together, at the same time, as it were. Behind his rejection of this position lies the fact that, nature being ordered to glory, there is a kind of referral of natural knowledge to the beatific vision. Just as our own intellects in this life can each have two operations at the same time, where one is referred to the other, so can the blessed. Aquinas is thinking of our present ability at the very same moment both to perceive certain principles and certain conclusions through those principles. Likewise, evening knowledge is referred to morning knowledge in the angels, and nothing hinders them being exercised together.[79] Moreover, infinitely different as

75. Ibid., 1a., q. 89, a. 1.
76. Ibid., 1a., q. 55, a. 2.
77. Ibid., 1a., q. 57, a. 2.
78. Ibid., 1a., q. 12, a. 10 ad 2.
79. Ibid., 1a., q. 58, a. 7 ad 2.

the two means of knowledge are, the divine essence and a finite *species*, Aquinas can detect nothing here that would introduce any opposition between the angel's two acts of knowledge, even where the same object is concerned. Just as we might know the same conclusion from two quite different but compatible arguments, one compelling and one merely probable, so the angel can know the same object by two means, one beatific and one natural. Thus an angel may know a particular creature both in its divine cause (through the beatific vision) and in itself (through a finite *species*).[80] Finally, each mode of knowledge contributes something the other does not: while the beatific vision provides a knowledge of God just as he is that no finite knowledge, however exalted, can supply, the angel's knowing via *species* furnishes it with a mode of knowledge in proportion to its own nature. The same compatibility holds for beatific knowledge and natural human knowledge, both for souls separated from their bodies and for risen persons where the soul is reunited with its body.

Aquinas does hold that, since the resurrection body is to be perfectly subject to the soul, the soul will not experience the dependence for knowledge on the body and bodily images that it did on earth.[81] Nevertheless, the resurrection will restore to the soul its natural capacity to know via the bodily senses. For Aquinas, it is not just that glory perfects nature, but that 'the glory *of the body* does not destroy nature but perfects it'.[82] Among the implications of the resurrection body for eternal life is the fact that a risen person is in possession of perfected bodily senses, the glory of the senses not destroying nature but perfecting it. In the last chapter we saw how, on Aquinas's account of prophecy, an imperfect divine light enhanced a prophet's judgements about what he learned through the senses. Hence we should suppose that the perfect light of glory will likewise equip the saints for knowledge of the new creation, not merely preserving their knowing via the senses but enhancing it. Aquinas envisions the risen saint, who sees the Creator just as he is, as also able to observe the new creation and consider how the Creator's likeness is expressed in his created effect which he perceives.[83] Again, there is an ordering between the two acts of the intellect, knowledge of the Creator and knowledge of the creature, which means that they can be exercised together. The saint's knowledge of creatures through sight or indeed any other kind of contemplation of them will not hinder his contemplation of their Creator, but rather glory perfects nature and the beatific vision enhances natural knowledge. So we should conclude that, on Aquinas's eschatology, neither mode of knowledge, whether beatific or natural, impedes the other, but, as Kromholtz comments, 'a person's sensing of God's creatures and his contemplation of God himself will be mutually reinforcing'.[84]

80. Ibid., 1a., q. 58, a. 7 ad 3.

81. Ibid., 3a., q. 11, a. 2.

82. *Super Sent.*, 4.44.2.4.1 ad 3.

83. *Compendium*, 1.170.

84. Kromholtz, *On the Last Day: The Time of the Resurrection of the Dead According to Thomas Aquinas* (Fribourg: Academic, 2010), p. 463.

Were we to apply these principles to the earthly life of Christ, we could scarcely conclude that his possession of the beatific vision would exclude natural knowledge acquired through the senses. On the contrary, we would more likely conclude that glory would once again perfect nature, and that Christ's light of glory perfecting his mind would enhance his natural knowledge of the world, even in the absence of the glorification of his body. Of course Aquinas's account of Paul's being caught up to the third heaven may make us exercise a momentary caution. As we saw in Chapter 4, Aquinas interpreted this experience as a passing glimpse of the beatific vision, even though Paul was still in this life and his body not yet glorified. The fact that Paul says he did not know whether or not he was in the body for the period of his heavenly experience (2 Cor. 12.13) suggests he was abstracted from his bodily senses. While Aquinas allowed that Paul could form finite *species* from his vision, he thought of him as withdrawn from the bodily senses and hence from drawing *species* from the world in the usual way.[85] But if this was the case for Paul in a merely transient passing glimpse of the divine essence, why should it not be the same for the earthly Christ's continuous vision of the Father?[86] For Aquinas, Christ was no mere pilgrim of this life, as Paul was, but was also a *comprehensor*.[87] Lonergan points to the radical difference between Paul who had a sudden experience of being caught up from natural knowledge through the senses to the vision of God, and Christ who had seen the Father in his human mind from the very first moment of his existence, even before he could acquire knowledge naturally.[88] In Christ's case all natural knowledge was nurtured within the context of his fundamental vision of God, which Lonergan sees as the integrating factor within Christ's human consciousness. There is thus no possibility of any clash but only harmony between the supernatural act of vision and the natural acts of acquiring knowledge through senses. As with Torrell's theory of a 'Christic light', which we encountered in Chapter 5, the beatific knowledge of God would enable Christ to judge well and discern a divine meaning in what he perceived around him. Lonergan envisaged that in this way what was seen in Christ's inexpressible vision could be given human expression through knowledge drawn from the senses.[89] This principle was taken up and developed by several of Lonergan's admirers.[90]

Having concluded then that, where it is admitted that grace and glory perfect nature and do not destroy it, Christ's beatific vision will not in fact suppress his

85. *Summa*, 2a.2ae., q. 175, a. 4.

86. Cf. Allen, *Christ's Faith*, p. 66.

87. *Summa*, 2a.2ae., q. 175, a. 4 ad 2.

88. *De Verbo Incarnato*, p. 337.

89. Ibid., pp. 407–9.

90. E.g. Tekippe, 'Vision of Christ', pp. 97–8; F. E. Crowe, 'Eschaton and Worldly Mission in the Mind and Heart of Jesus' in *Appropriating the Lonergan Idea* (Buffalo TOR and London: University of Toronto, 2006), pp. 193–234 (209–14); Mongeau, 'The Human and Divine Knowing of the Incarnate Word'; R. S. Rosenberg, 'Christ's Human Knowledge: A Conversation with Lonergan and Balthasar', *TS* 71 (2010): 817–45 (836–9); Wilkins, 'Love and Knowledge of God in the Human Life of Christ', pp. 90–9.

natural knowledge, we still need to face the objection that it will instead render his natural knowledge practically superfluous. On this view it will be the case that Jesus' acquiring knowledge, though it may give added perfection to him through the use of his active intellect, will nevertheless be *superfluous* in terms of the knowledge actually acquired. If Jesus already possesses knowledge of the world in the beatific vision, then what knowledge can he acquire through ordinary means that he does not already have? How can this acquired knowledge be new and surprise him, if he already knew its content in another way? Unless we curtail the range of Christ's vision, it is indeed true that what he comes to know through the senses he already knows in the vision of God. Acquiring knowledge will not extend the overall range of the knowledge in his human mind. But what also needs to be considered is again how very different the two means of knowledge, finite and infinite, are. What Christ always knew of the world in the inexpressible vision of God's essence by way of that transcendent essence, he now knows through finite images and concepts properly proportionate to the created objects known and the finite nature of the human mind. It is easy to forget that the vision of God cannot be adequately expressed in human language, images or concepts, and hence that this vision does not of itself articulate what is known of God's power and so of what he creates. It is easy to slip into imagining that the vision of God consists in this kind of articulated, expressed knowledge, but it does not. Such knowledge of the world and analogous knowledge of God, proportioned to the finite, can come only by some further act, such as the acts of 'translation' we discussed in Chapter 4 and the drawing of ordinary human knowledge from the world. This acquisition of knowledge will appear superfluous to us if we confuse the inexpressible vision of God through infinite transcendent means with the kind of knowing with which we are constantly familiar. But if we refuse to confuse them, we can see that acquired knowledge truly gives Christ the possibility of knowledge of a kind that the beatific vision in its very self does not give, of knowledge of things by finite means, properly expressed in human concepts and images, a knowledge naturally proportioned to the human mind and its perfection.

Aquinas is evidently so convinced of the difference between the two kinds of knowledge that he does not even bring an objection based on Christ's wordless beatific vision against Christ's acquisition of knowledge in the *Summa*. However, it is telling that he does bring another objection against acquired knowledge, namely, that the knowledge Christ could have acquired by it he already possessed by the way of supernaturally infused knowledge, which Aquinas attributes to Christ's humanity along with beatific and acquired knowledge.[91] Now infused knowledge clearly differed from beatific in that it meant the imprinting of finite *species* onto Christ's mind.[92] While this knowledge could not extend to knowing the infinite God just as he is, since its objects were known by finite means, it did deliver an habitual knowledge of finite creatures (and thus presumably a limited, analogous knowledge of God). Just as Aquinas came to give greater importance to Christ's

91. *Summa*, 3a., q. 9, a. 4, obj. 2 and 3.
92. Cf. ibid., 3a., q. 9, a. 3.

acquired knowledge during his career, so he also gave a more important role to his infused knowledge. While he previously restricted infused knowledge to what could be known naturally of the world, in the *Summa* he extended it to knowledge of human hearts and of the future, which would include knowledge of the timing of the last day.[93] Thus, prior to the working of Christ's active intellect there was already contained in Christ's 'passive intellect' many habits of knowledge, made up of finite *species*, applying to all creation across space and time, on which he could later draw.

All this enabled Aquinas's Carmelite commentators to state that Christ was 'by habit not only the best dialectician, philosopher, mathematician, doctor and political scientist, but also musician, grammarian, rhetorician, carpenter, farmer, navigator, painter, soldier, and other such things'.[94] And, on the same logic, we today would also suppose him to have possessed a complete body of knowledge of Chinese grammar, of the details of quantum physics, of how to fly a jumbo jet and other such things. Not that he would necessarily have consciously thought about any of these subjects during his earthly lifetime, but he *could* have done so, had he had reason to do so. We saw in Chapter 5 how some opponents of Christ's beatific vision, such as Galot, retain Christ's infused knowledge, so as to give him prophetic knowledge beyond what can be acquired through the senses, while they avoid the embarrassment of a kind of omniscience by limiting its content to what Christ actually needs for his saving mission, thereby allowing some scope too for ignorance of the last day. Indeed some of those who have supported Christ's beatific vision have argued similarly for a restriction on Christ's infused knowledge.[95] It seems to me also that it is Aquinas's account of a very extensive infused knowledge rather than his account of the beatific vision that is truly the more vulnerable to criticism.

The objection, putting it now more precisely, that Aquinas makes against his own mature position on Christ's acquired knowledge is that by his infused knowledge Christ already possessed a mind *full* of *species*, such that there was no possibility of experience adding any more. His answer was that, while the new *species* drawn from the senses do not give the mind new cognitive content that was not available through infused *species*, it did add the new perfection of sense images to which the mind can turn.[96] Thus new habits of knowledge, connected to such images, can be added to the infused habits, which were themselves *not* connected to such imagery, their own *species* being infused rather than abstracted through the senses.[97] Thus the *species* of infused knowledge were considered by Aquinas more akin to those natural to angels, though they were more powerful than theirs. So, while Christ had by the beatific vision a knowledge natural to God alone, and by acquired knowledge that natural to human beings, by infused knowledge he

93. *De Veritate*, 20.6; *Summa*, 3a, q. 11, a. 1.
94. *Cursus Theologicus*, 21.22.2.4.
95. Durand, 'La science du Christ', p. 502.
96. *Summa*, 3a., q. 9, a. 4 ad 2.
97. Ibid., 3a., q. 9, a. 4 ad 3.

had a way of knowing 'proportioned to the angelic nature'.[98] Whether it is truly fitting for God, in becoming *human*, to possess not only knowledge proper to divine and human natures, but also that proper to the angelic, is another worry that has been raised against Aquinas's view.[99] Moreover, the fact that, despite the contributions of sense and imagination, the production of *species* by acquired knowledge does not in fact add any new *cognitive* content to Christ's knowledge does suggest that infused knowledge renders acquired knowledge superfluous in that important respect. If that is the case, and there were no compelling reason for Christ to enjoy such a range of infused knowledge, might it not be better to explain the knowledge in Christ's humanity for the most part in terms of beatific and acquired knowledge? While we made a case in Chapter 4 for Christ's beatific vision, and in the present chapter reviewed a case for his acquired knowledge, we must now turn briefly to the case for infused knowledge.

Some followers of Aquinas have given the impression that there is almost a kind of necessary connection between beatific and infused knowledge, where the very purpose of infused knowledge was to add *to the vision* a communicability that Christ would otherwise lack. The presence of infused knowledge has sometimes been thought of as necessary for Christ so that he could receive the transcendent and inexpressible knowledge *given by the vision* in a way that was connatural to his human mind and expressible, however inadequate the expression might be. This was the view taken by Maurice de la Taille and Alexandre Durand.[100] Noting how Poinsot had argued that infused knowledge enabled Christ to know higher realities in a manner proportionate to his human nature (which the beatific vision did not), Maritain also took the view that Christ *had* to have this infused knowledge in order to do so.[101] He saw the beatific vision as used by God instrumentally in order to cause the infused habits of *species* at the moment of the creation of Christ's soul.[102] Beatific knowledge was even sometimes conceived as somehow *automatically* the cause of infused knowledge in Christ. Bernard Leeming spoke of infused knowledge as 'connaturally consequent' upon the beatific vision, an infused knowledge thus had not only by angels but also by blessed souls and by the soul of Christ.[103]

All this is important here because, even though it may be granted that Christ's acquired and beatific knowledge were in themselves perfectly compatible, if infused and acquired knowledge are at some level incompatible, any necessary connection between beatific and infused knowledge would render natural and beatific knowledge somehow incompatible after all. On this scenario, it would

98. Ibid., 3a., q. 9, a. 4, corp.

99. Cf. Cessario, 'Incarnate Wisdom'.

100. M. de la Taille, *The Mystery of Faith Regarding the Most August Sacrament and Sacrifice of the Body and Blood of Christ*, p. 242 n.6; Durand, 'La science du Christ', p. 502.

101. Maritain, *Grace and Humanity of Jesus*, p. 90 n.2; cf. White, 'The Earthly Christ and the Beatific Vision', p. 516.

102. Maritain, *Grace and Humanity of Jesus*, p. 101.

103. Leeming, 'The Human Knowledge of Christ', p. 140.

be a 'cascade' of infused knowledge caused by the beatific vision (rather than the beatific vision itself) that would put Christ's acquired knowledge at risk of being rendered superfluous. Maritain sidestepped this conclusion by making infused knowledge inaccessible to Christ's consciousness, placing it along with the beatific vision in the supraconsciousness, for it to be gradually made available to consciousness during Christ's lifetime as need required so that he could express and communicate what he knew supraconsciously in the beatific vision. But if Maritain's notion of a 'supraconsciousness' is already problematic, as we suggested above, it cannot offer a genuine solution to the problem. Durand surely did better by restricting infused knowledge to what Christ required for his mission.[104]

The kind of approach found in these authors, however, is not that of Aquinas. There is nothing in Aquinas's texts to suggest that the beatific vision need be considered the automatic cause of infused knowledge in Christ or the saints. Again, there is nothing in Aquinas's texts to suggest that he thought the *very purpose* of Christ's infused knowledge was to give him his communicable expression *of his beatific knowledge*. As we saw in Chapter 4, Aquinas has a quite different explanation of how the saints can give a finite (and inadequate) expression to what they see in the vision of God. While Nicolas conflated the latter account with Aquinas's account of Christ's infused knowledge,[105] Aquinas himself did no such thing. As we saw in Chapter 4, he understood the blessed, Christ included, to be able to form similitudes of what they see in the divine essence, so that they are thereby equipped with *species* by which they can reformulate in a limited and finite way what they see there. He does not envisage them as almost automatically endowed with *species* caused by the beatific vision. Given that Christ, being in possession of the beatific vision, would be able to 'translate' such similitudes from his vision, we can appreciate that his need to know and express by finite means what he knows beatifically is *not* Aquinas's rationale for the existence of his infused knowledge. Christ's need to do all this is instead met by his ability to draw similitudes from the vision. Aquinas in fact gives a different, independent rationale for infused knowledge, which stands – or falls – independently of his arguments for beatific (and acquired) knowledge. Should we find his argument wanting, if only for the great range he ascribes to this knowledge, we have the possibility of dispensing with at least Aquinas's own *extensive* account of infused knowledge and so of any possibility that it would make acquired knowledge superfluous.

Taking the familiar starting-point of the perfection of the Saviour's humanity, Aquinas argues that Christ's passive intellect needed to be fully actualized, and for that reason there was from the creation of his soul the presence in it of *species* proportioned to the human mind of all that could be known in that way.[106] Their infusion is thus 'independent' of the gift of the beatific vision, and these *species* do not have the same continuity with the beatific vision as do those that have been drawn from the vision by the blessed. The fundamental question, however, is

---

104. 'La science du Christ', p. 502.
105. Nicolas, 'Voir Dieu dans la "condition charnelle"', p. 386 n.5.
106. *Summa*, 3a., q. 9, a. 3.

whether the human mind of Christ truly demands the kind of *perfection* infused knowledge is meant to give, such that Christ would have possessed what was in fact an angelic knowledge. In the case of acquired knowledge, we argued that Aquinas exaggerated the perfection proper to the human mind by wanting Christ to have acquired by adulthood all knowledge that could be acquired. In place of this, we extended the application of the principle of perfection Aquinas applied to Christ's childhood, namely, that the human mind's proper perfection was relative to each moment. If this is indeed the dynamic perfection proper to a human mind as such, it would seem to be sufficient for the perfection of Christ's earthly mind so as to render the perfection of a whole panoply of infused knowledge superfluous. In the normal course of things, his passive intellect could thus have its proper perfection according to the need of each moment by receiving *species* abstracted by the active intellect's acquiring of knowledge.

To be sure one cannot conclude from this that Christ definitely had no infused knowledge from God at all, and that no argument for its presence is possible. Pius XII taught that, along with beatific knowledge, it had a role in shaping Christ's human love (though that role could theoretically be reassigned to *species* derived from the vision).[107] The fact that it has made this (albeit brief) appearance in ordinary papal teaching means at the very least that it deserves a proper consideration in its own right from a Catholic theologian for which we do not have the space here. However, certainly in terms of the *range* that Aquinas accords it, it seems easily dispensed from a theological account of Christ's knowledge. It is absolutely required neither for the proper perfection of Christ's human mind nor even for this mind's reception of supernatural knowledge, whether infinite in means or finite. Without wishing to dismiss infused knowledge without proper consideration, we can affirm that beatific and acquired knowledge would seem in themselves to be sufficient for Christ to be able to know reality in a normal human way and to have access to a saving knowledge beyond natural human abilities, such that he could with authority teach human beings the things of God. His unique history of mental development throughout his earthly life would thus at least include drawing expressible knowledge both from the world around him and from his vision of the Father.

Without the added complication of an exhaustive infused knowledge, we can better appreciate the vast difference between the knowledge Christ acquires from the world around him and the knowledge afforded in the act of vision. Thus, no more than did the divine vision, his inexpressible beatific vision did not prevent it from being true that Christ also really did grow in wisdom and knowledge, that is, in knowledge both expressible and communicable. We need not then shy away, as Aquinas also did not, from a theological interpretation of Luke 2.52 as indicating a *real* growth in such knowledge, since we may understand it to be something perfectly compatible with and indeed enhanced by Christ's beatific vision. His advance in wisdom may be interpreted as growth in his articulation of knowledge in communicable terms, effected by his drawing on his experience of the world,

---

107. *Haurietis Aquas*, 56.

as well as on his beatific knowledge of the Father. Moreover, these principles could even offer the advantage of a speculative exegesis of various incidents in the ministry of Christ, where he is moved to act or speak in some significant way after prayer (Mk 1.35–29; 6.45–52; Lk. 3.21–22; 6.12–16; 9.18–22; 9.28–36; 22.39–46), through reading the Scriptures (Lk. 6.16–30) or through experiential knowledge of the needs or intentions of others (e.g. Jn 2.1–11; 11.1–4; 12.20–36). For our purposes, however, we need to see how these principles can offer us an exegesis of Mark 13.32 that moves beyond the impasse of Agnoetism and an orthodox, but unconvincing, account of Christ's not knowing.

Mark 13.32 we could interpret on our principles as indicating the fact that Jesus did not have a humanly articulated and communicable knowledge of the day and the hour, not even one present by any infused *species*. In this sense he just did not know it, though of course he knew it in another way in his humanity by seeing it in the inexpressible vision of God. Hence, in his human mind he both knew it and did not know it. It would be false to say that he did not know it *at all*, as did the Agnoetes, but he did not know it in a very significant and relevant way. It is true that Aquinas himself did not apply his theory to Mark 13.32 in the way we are suggesting. Aquinas would not even have felt the need to search for such exegesis, because he already accepted on Augustine's authority that when Christ said he did 'not know', this was a biblical idiom for 'not making known'.[108] Aquinas's theory of Christ's knowledge was, however, applied to this verse in the twentieth century in the way we are suggesting, that is, through the use of the distinction between inexpressible and expressible knowledge. De la Taille, Durand and Lonergan each argued that Christ knew the day and the hour, in his humanity, inexpressibly and not expressibly.[109] Thus, not only is Christ's beatific vision and his natural knowledge perfectly compatible on Aquinas's account, but the distinction of expressible and inexpressible knowledge can offer us a plausible theological interpretation of Scriptural verses such as Mark 13.32, which resolves the tension between patristic teaching on the fullness of Christ's knowledge and the limitations on his knowledge witnessed by Scripture.

That the same thing may in different ways be known and not known in the same human mind is not without analogies. Let us imagine that, sitting back at school in class, I am presented with what would be for me a long and complex mathematical problem, full of multiplications and divisions and mathematical operations of still greater complexity. If faced with such a challenge, I can easily say straight off that I do not know the answer to the sum. That would remain true, so long as I had not worked out the answer. But someone – say, my mathematics teacher – could easily reply to my denial, 'But you *do* know.' He could say that quite truly because, despite the fact I do not have the answer ready to recall, I do know my numbers, how to multiply, how to divide and so on. In that virtual sense I *do* know, because I have the knowledge of the mathematical principles

---

108. *Catena aurea in quatuor Evangelia*, Mt. 24.36.

109. De la Taille, *Mystery of Faith*, p. 242 n.6; A. Durand, 'La science du Christ', p. 502; Lonergan, *De Verbo Incarnato*, p. 412. Cf. E. Durand, *L'Offre universelle*, pp. 169–71.

with which to work out the answer, but in another sense I do *not* know, because I have not in fact worked it out. And if we reverse the situation, and have a member of the class fire back another complex string of mathematical operations at the teacher, even the teacher may truly say, 'I do not know,' if he has not worked out the answer. And equally the class could chorus back, 'But you *do* know.' And both would be right. In an analogous way, we can say Christ the Teacher does know the day and the hour, that is, in the beatific vision, but does not know it because he has not 'worked it out', has not drawn expressible and communicable knowledge of it from his inexpressible knowledge of the Father. And so he truly said to his hearers, 'I do not know.' And the Church Fathers then chorused back, 'But you *do* know.' And both were right.

We can make theological sense of the fact that both are right with the help of Aquinas's theory of Christ's beatific vision, at which a few Fathers do no more than hint. Christ knows the day and the hour in the wordless beatific vision, but does not know it in any humanly 'worked out', communicable fashion. Of course, on Aquinas's theory he was *able* to 'work out' the timing of the last day in such a form by drawing it, 'translating' it, from the knowledge he enjoys in the vision of his Father. He did not do so, however, because to reveal it was not part of his earthly mission. Given that his human will was perfectly attuned to the divine will, he had never drawn such knowledge from the beatific vision. Had it been the Saviour's mission to do so, he would surely have chosen to do it, and it would have been one of the words he heard from the Father (cf. Jn 15.15; 17.8), but that was not his mission. And so, just as the mathematics teacher might have priorities in his teaching other than answering the pupil's question, so did Jesus. Just as the teacher could then legitimately say, 'I do not know,' and move on, so could Jesus.

But can this interpretation count as a convincing theological exegesis of these words of Christ that he did not know? It certainly has the advantage of not having Christ instead mean that he *does* know or mean anything else other than that he – in a sense – *does not know*. I suggest that the interpretation is acceptable because its sense of the word 'know' here is one which would have been easily grasped by the disciples and thus easily meant by their Teacher, even without any epistemological reflections on the nature of *species* and the means of the beatific vision and so on. One pertinent question is whether this interpretation would have Christ deceive the disciples, given that he in fact knew the day and the hour in his wordless beatific vision. No more, it would seem, than if Christ did *not* possess the beatific vision, since *he* would still have known by divine knowledge, if not in his humanity. But on that view, it would hardly be deceit if, in saying he did not know, Christ were speaking to the disciples of the kind of knowledge with which they were familiar – human knowledge rather than divine. For Christ to say of something that he did not know, it would surely be most easily taken, and therefore perhaps most easily meant, as applying to knowledge in the human mind. The disciples were hardly likely here to be considering Christ's divine knowledge as though they had now grasped the details of Chalcedon. Likewise, given that Christ did in fact enjoy beatific knowledge in his humanity, for him to speak to the disciples of not knowing something would most easily be taken, and therefore likewise meant, of the kind of articulated, expressible knowledge with which they were familiar rather than a transcendent beatific knowledge of which they surely had no inkling.

So what, more precisely, is this communicable knowledge that Christ was denying? Certainly the disciples could not have supposed that Christ was making the trivial point that he did not know it by way of the ordinary knowledge of human experience they all shared, since future events like the last day are closed to that means of knowledge. Rather they would have surely supposed him to be denying some extraordinary prophetic knowledge of the timing of the last day, and yet one that was expressible and communicable, just as Christ had in their recent experience already communicated to them much that was at the same time both extraordinary *and* expressible. He spoke to them of 'not knowing' in a sense with which they had become familiar throughout his ministry, a knowledge both extraordinary *and* communicable. He spoke to them of 'not knowing' in a sense that was entirely compatible with a knowledge of which they themselves were as yet ignorant, that of seeing God by the very same means that God knows God, the vision of the Father just as he is. Thus there was no deception at all, and the difficulties that accrue, say, to Adam's exegesis of Mark 13.32 in no way apply here. In this way Aquinas's theory can resolve the apparent tension between the words of Scripture and the teaching of the Fathers, avoiding Agnoetism and manifesting the truth that glory perfects nature.

At the conclusion of the last chapter, we suggested that the disinclination of Scripture and Tradition to ascribe faith to the earthly Christ, despite the centrality of 'faith' in the pages in the New Testament, puts the weight of probability in favour of Christ's beatific vision as a theological explanation of his extraordinary knowledge. Had this beatific vision proved incompatible with the fact of his natural knowing, we might now have had cause to revise that conclusion. However, our examination has shown the beatific vision to be not only quite compatible with Christ's natural knowledge, but also to afford us the positive advantage of a way of being theologically faithful to both the witness of Scripture on the limitations in Christ's knowledge, including the fact that he did *not* know, and the general consensus that emerges among the Fathers on his overall human fullness of knowledge, the fact that he *did* know. Were we instead to have dismissed Christ's beatific vision on the ground of his natural knowledge, we should have not only lost out on that positive advantage, but would have had to set ourselves at variance with the consensus that emerged in the patristic period and uncomfortably close to the Fathers' opponents. In view of these problems and the positive advantage afforded by Aquinas's theory, we can state at the conclusion of this chapter that the balance of probability in favour of the earthly Christ's beatific vision can only be weightier still.

Chapter 7

'BUT JESUS WAS FREE!'

O'Collins has stated that the beatific vision 'raises problems for the free operation of Jesus' human will.'[1] In this chapter we are moving from objections to Christ's beatific vision based on intellect to objections based on will. Put simply, it is charged that possession of the beatific vision would have stifled the earthly Christ's freedom of will, because the two are incompatible. Specifically he would not have been free in several crucial areas, namely, the freedom to engage in the world, the freedom to grow in knowledge, the freedom to grow in grace, the freedom to be tempted to sin and to experience a difference of will from the divine will, and the freedom to merit a reward from the Father. On the assumption that freedoms of this kind are essential to Christ's saving acts, it is concluded that he could not have enjoyed the vision of heaven. As Galot writes, 'The existence of this freedom poses insurmountable problems for those who affirm the beatific vision.'[2] In what follows, we shall argue instead that Christ's beatific vision in fact provided the very freedom our Saviour required.

We can have no quarrel with the fact of Christ's fundamental freedom, despite its being hardly a matter of explicit reflection for the writers of the New Testament. When attention was drawn by them to his freedom, it was because something extraordinary was in view, such as his laying down his life 'of himself' (Jn 10.18), which may be taken on a Chalcedonian reading to indicate that *divine* power would have enabled him to avoid death at the hands of others. However, the fact that Christ performs specifically human acts throughout the Gospels is sufficient to imply that he possessed *human* freedom. If we suppose that human acts as such are free, then we must suppose that Christ's, given that they are true human acts, are free. A Chalcedonian reading of Scripture confirms this picture, since it has Christ 'like us' in all things strictly pertaining to the make-up of humanity, which we should surely take to include freedom of will. That Christ had a human will in addition to the divine will was indicated in Scripture in his prayer to the Father in the Garden of Gethsemene: 'Not my will (θέλημα) but yours be done' (Lk. 22.42). That his complete human nature included a human will was confirmed by the decree of the Third Council of Constantinople, in response to the suggestion by

1. *Christology*, p. 267.
2. *Who is Christ?*, p. 389 n.15.

some that he had only one will, which we observed in Chapter 3.[3] Thus we may conclude that the earthly Christ was master in his humanity of his human acts, as human beings are in general the masters of their own human acts.

Opponents of Christ's beatific vision charge that Aquinas's account of it would undermine this picture of Christ's freedom in a number of ways. That Aquinas's theory of the beatific vision should have implications of some kind for the will is obvious, once we pay attention to the close relationship that obtains between intellect and will in his philosophical psychology.[4] Here we find a close interpenetration and mutual interplay between human knowing and willing, which includes an element of dependence of willing on knowing. Aquinas accepted Augustine's principle that nothing can be loved unless it is known, concluding that there is no act of the will that is not informed by the intellect.[5] For an object to be enjoyed or merely desired or loved by the will, there must be at least some knowledge of it as an appropriate good in the intellect, however inadequate and unspecific that knowledge might be. Developing Aristotle, Aquinas treated this rational will as intellectual appetite – the mind's response to an intelligible object. Given such a close relationship between intellect and will, *any* claims about knowledge must have implications for the will, and so claims about Christ's human knowledge bring issues for the theologian about his human will and freedom. Hence the knowledge reported of Christ in the Gospels typically raises questions about its effect on his human freedom, such as his knowledge that it is *necessary* for him to suffer and die before entering the glory of the resurrection (Mk 3.31), and that the Father had *commanded* him to undergo this saving death (Jn 10.18). In view of such knowledge, how can Christ's death be considered truly voluntary? Such issues of course remain for theologians, whatever explanation they give to Christ's extraordinary knowledge, whether beatific, prophetic or whatever it might be, simply because of the general interpenetration of will and intellect. Critics of Christ's beatific vision, however, allege that in this particular case special problems arise for his earthly freedom of will, meaning that this freedom must exclude all *beatific* knowledge from his soul. It is these specific questions that we shall be considering in this chapter.

On Aquinas's understanding then, beatific knowledge will inevitably involve a certain communication of beatitude to the will. While the essential core of beatitude pertains to the intellect – it is by knowing that the soul finally apprehends the divine essence – this apprehension engages the will in a new way.[6] So, when the blessed see God just as he is, an act of heavenly love necessarily arises

3. Third Council of Constantinople, *Definitio de duabus in Christo voluntatibus et operationibus*. For Aquinas on Christ's two wills, see Barnes, *Christ's Two Wills in Scholastic Thought*.

4. For attempts to follow through the implications of the beatific vision for Christ's wider psychology, see Sarrasin, *Plein de grâce et de verite*; Brownsberger, *Jesus the Mediator*.

5. E.g. *Summa*, 1a.2ae., q. 3, a. 4 ad 4; citing Augustine, *De Trinitate*, 10.1. See M. S. Sherwin, *By Knowledge and By Love: Charity and Knowledge in the Moral Theology of St. Thomas Aquinas* (Washington, DC: CUA, 2005), pp. 18–118.

6. Ibid., 1a.2ae., q. 3, a. 4.

from their heavenly knowledge of God. The consummate grace of the Holy Spirit thus unites the blessed with God not only by knowledge in the intellect but also by love in the rational will. This love is a perfect charity, though not perfect in the sense that by it God would be loved to the extent that he is fully loveable. Since God is infinite, only an infinite act of love – in other words, strictly divine love – can match him, just as only divine knowledge can comprehend his being, as we saw in Chapter 4. While Christ, being God, loves the Father with such love in his divinity, the perfect love he bears him in his finite humanity has a different kind of perfection. According to Aquinas, the blessed may be said to have perfect charity in the sense that each one loves to the full extent that one can. As a consequence, the saint's 'whole heart is always actually borne towards God'.[7] This unending act of charity does not involve further desire to reach God since he is now known just as he is, and the will is engaged in regard to God in a new way that is not such desire. The soul's search for its essential happiness is now fulfilled, and its desire has been brought to 'repose' or 'rest' in the dynamic acts of beatific knowing and loving. Since the will's desire has now come to rest in possession of the Supreme Good, the will is said to have perfect 'enjoyment' (*fruitio*) of the divine essence known through the intellect.[8] Should Christ have already possessed this vision on earth, he would have exercised this love, one that trained his whole heart permanently on the Father, where desire for the Father was always already fulfilled in his beatific knowledge and possession of God. And, just as Aquinas would have the earthly Christ blessed with the highest beatific knowledge in the actual order of things, with the saints participating in the heavenly vision of their Head, so Christ's supreme charity is the principle in which the beatific love of the blessed participates.

For critics of Christ's beatific vision, all this raises problems by limiting his freedom of will in certain respects. Before looking at the ways in which it might do this, we should note that, as with the case of natural knowledge in the last chapter, the principle that grace and glory do not destroy nature but perfect it should make us wary of assuming that heavenly beatitude will eliminate natural human freedom. Rather, on Catholic principles glory, like grace, should preserve and even enhance our freedom, just as it preserves and enhances our natural knowledge. Sometimes even supporters of Christ's beatific vision leave the impression that this vision is ordinarily 'paralyzing' of human activity.[9] However, should anyone suppose that heavenly glory suppresses our freedom, they would surely be presupposing either that glory destroys nature or that freedom is not truly natural to humanity but pertains only to an imperfect version of it. But this is a position no Catholic theologian can legitimately take. One therefore needs to distinguish carefully between the freedom of heaven, perfected by glory and for which we hope, and the as yet unperfected freedom in which we now live on earth. Freedom is thus no straightforward notion.

7. Ibid., 2a.2ae., q. 24, a. 9.
8. Ibid., 1a.2ae., q. 11.
9. Cessario, 'Incarnate Wisdom', p. 338.

While Scripture again makes no explicit reflections here, the Fathers, considering the different states of salvation history, typically distinguished different levels of freedom, including a heavenly level that is distinct from all earthly levels.[10] Such distinctions made their way into the work of medieval theologians.[11] So heavenly freedom is, for example, a freedom from misery, which earthly freedom is not. Servais Pinckaers has argued that, on this patristic and medieval view, human freedom is to be conceived dynamically as able to be developed towards new levels of perfection, as disciplined learning of a language or how to play a musical instrument open up new freedoms to communicate and to perform more and more difficult musical compositions.[12] On this view, the beatific vision brings an eschatological perfection to the development of freedom in this life.[13]

The more careful critics of the earthly Christ's beatific vision therefore argue not that heavenly glory will altogether eliminate Christ's human freedom, but that heavenly glory would bring a perfection to Christ's freedom that does not correspond to what befits his work of salvation on earth. According to O'Collins, Christ's beatific vision would 'rule out the possibility of human freedom under the conditions of earthly history'.[14] He supposes that, while on earth, Christ must have a merely earthly freedom to the exclusion of the heavenly freedom that would be provided by the beatific vision. However, what is precisely at stake is whether it is fitting for our Saviour while on earth to possess an imperfect, earthly freedom or rather to possess the perfect freedom of heaven. As we have argued that the earthly Christ possessed a heavenly *knowledge* for the sake of our salvation, so we ourselves could argue that the earthly Christ might possess a heavenly *freedom* to our benefit. In order to investigate this question, we need to clarify exactly what might be the relevant qualities that human freedom has in this life that will be removed by the perfect freedom of heaven. Only so shall we be in a position to conclude which level of freedom it would be fitting for the Saviour to co-assume.

One view seems to be that Christ's beatific vision would cancel out all freedom to do anything else but know and love the Father. It is sometimes imagined that the vision of God will so mesmerize those who enjoy it that they will be completely distracted from all else. On this view, while the saints are free to gaze on the essence of God for all eternity, this heavenly freedom will exclude the freedom to engage in any further human acts. Caught up in their beatific vision, the saints will be left without the motivation that would make further acts possible, because their arrival at their final end will exclude the need for further acting. Nicholas Lombardo

10. E.g. Augustine, *De Civitate Dei*, 22.30.

11. E.g. Anselm, *De Libertate Arbitrii*, 1.

12. S. Pinckaers, *The Sources of Christian Ethics* (Edinburgh: T&T Clark, 1995), pp. 354–6.

13. See Gaine, *Will there be Free Will in Heaven?* For these issues in relation to the earthly Christ, but where there is a distinction made between divine essence and energies and no vision of the divine *essence*, see J. P. Farrell, *Free Choice in St. Maximus the Confessor* (South Canaan, PA: St Tikhon's, 1989).

14. *Christology*, p. 267.

has suggested that Aquinas's system must require some kind of limitation on the effects of the beatific vision in Christ's case so that he can 'do anything at all, rather than just being completely absorbed in his beatific knowledge'.[15] A mesmerized Christ could hardly have done any of the human acts to which the Gospels bear witness, because he could have attended to nothing but his immutable vision of the Father. If this were the case, he could hardly have been our Saviour, since he would not have been free to do whatever acts were needed for our salvation. We should then be in the position of asking whether the attribution of faith to Christ, for all its difficulties, would prove the preferable opinion, since we know from our own Christian experience that faith allows there to be a whole range of actions open to an earthly, yet supernatural, freedom.

Now Lombardo is surely presuming that the absorption he attributes to a beatified Christ and its consequent lack of freedom to do anything else is the normal effect of this vision on the blessed. One could take some encouragement in this view from the fact that Aquinas thought of Paul as caught up out of the state of natural knowledge when he had his glimpse of the essence of God. Christ too could have been similarly without the freedom to attend to the world around him through the senses. However, as we noted in Chapters 4 and 6, Christ's case was entirely different because he enjoyed the beatific vision from the first moment of his conception, meaning that he was not caught up out of the senses by it but that his sense knowledge came to life in the context of his primary ineffable knowledge of the Father. Again, the fact that Aquinas spoke of a certain 'immobility' on the part of the intellect and will of the saints at rest in God may encourage the impression that they were not free to place their attention elsewhere.[16] However, that was certainly not Aquinas's position.

As we saw in Chapters 4 and 6, Aquinas envisaged the blessed as engaged in a succession of further acts, as well as in the single immutable act of seeing the Father, which was measured by a participated eternity. For Aquinas there is no 'competition' between the beatified will's adhesion to God, clearly seen, and its choice of such acts as intercession, movement from place to place, appearing in some way to those still on earth according to divine providence, and observation of the new creation.[17] He taught that, since God is known by the saints to be the principle of all that they do, none of their actions can impede divine contemplation and vice versa.[18] When the saints attain to the vision of God, though they no longer act so as to come into possession of that end, they now act 'from their attainment of the end'.[19] Even on earth, we act not only to attain an end but, once we have attained it, to share it out of love with others.[20] In heaven, the blessed

---

15. N. E. Lombardo, *The Logic of Desire: Aquinas on Emotion* (Washington, DC: CUA, 2011), p. 216.

16. *Compendium*, 1.149.

17. *Summa*, 2a.2ae., q. 83, a. 11; *Compendium*, 1.171; *Super Sent.*, 4.45.1.1.3.

18. *Super Sent.*, 4.44.2.1.3 ad 4.

19. *Summa*, 2a.2ae., q. 53, a. 2 ad 1.

20. Ibid., 1a., q. 19, a. 2.

are not then left without a purpose for acting but, motivated by the end to which they have been brought, they exercise their heavenly freedom in a heavenly environment to 'spread abroad the goodness and glory of God for all eternity'.[21] Should this heavenly freedom be granted to Christ in his earthly environment, his possession of the beatific vision would be the basis of an immense freedom of action as Saviour of the world. While others on earth would act from desire to attain the Supreme Good, Christ would act out of perfect love to diffuse it. According to Lonergan, the very fact of his perfection of knowledge and intensity of love would guarantee that his free action on account of this end would be the more efficacious.[22] Far from reducing his freedom to act by abstracting him from the world around him, by plunging him more thoroughly into engagement with that world, his vision of the Father would enhance his freedom to act for our good.

However, even if we grant that the beatific vision would bless Christ with a powerful further freedom for action, we still need to ask if there are particular aspects of the range of earthly freedom that would be excluded by this vision to the detriment of his mission. Should any aspect of earthly freedom that *would* be required for our salvation (in the form God has willed it) be excluded by beatific knowledge, we should be forced to reconsider the possibility that the Saviour was a man of faith rather than sight. The particular freedom O'Collins takes to be threatened by Christ's vision is his freedom to grow in *knowledge*. The reason why the beatific vision will allegedly exclude this freedom is that the latter is necessarily based on the fact that natural knowledge, unlike the beatific vision, is *limited*: 'Here and now the exercise of freedom requires some limits to our knowledge and some uncertainties about the future'.[23] What, though, might O'Collins mean by that statement?

Rahner had maintained that a lack of knowledge or 'nescience' plays a positive role as a significant 'opening out of space for freedom and action'.[24] This connection between nescience and human freedom was opposed by Most with the counter-example of divine freedom: there is no nescience in the omniscient God, and Rahner can hardly deny that God is free.[25] Lack of knowledge is therefore scarcely essential to freedom. Rahner's point, however, was not meant to cover every freedom and certainly not the infinite freedom of God, but is definitely aimed at 'the freedom of a finite being'. As applied to our earthly freedom, nescience 'renders the finite person's exercise of freedom possible within the still continuing drama of his history'.[26] In other words, a limited knowledge allows for a range of objects the person is then free to come to know within their historical development. What Rahner had in mind was our freedom gradually to 'come to ourselves' in the course of experience, to learn to express to ourselves

21. Gaine, *Will there be Free Will in Heaven?*, p. 136.
22. Lonergan, *De Verbo Incarnato*, p. 337.
23. *Christology*, p. 267.
24. 'Knowledge and Self-Consciousness of Christ', p. 201.
25. *Consciousness of Christ*, p. 150. Cf. Tekippe, 'The Vision of Christ', pp. 85–90.
26. Rahner, 'Knowledge and Self-Consciousness of Christ', p. 202.

what we are, to bring to objectified knowledge what is already present in our subjective consciousness. Without prior nescience of such things, one is not free to grow in knowledge of them. According to Rahner, his own theory of Christ's 'immediate vision' of the Word in no way excluded this specific freedom. Instead, Christ's unobjectified, pre-conceptual self-consciousness allowed for the free development over time of an objectified, conceptual articulation of this very self-consciousness.[27]

It appears to be a freedom of this kind that O'Collins takes to be excluded by the beatific vision, although he seems just as concerned with Christ's freedom to develop knowledge about the world around him as with his self-knowledge. As we saw in the last chapter, when we reviewed the biblical evidence for such growth in knowledge and the implied lack of knowledge, O'Collins took the view that the possession of beatific knowledge would cast serious doubt on Christ's possession of natural knowledge with such inherent limitations. If O'Collins were right that a blessed Christ could not possess natural knowledge, and that the latter was essential for the exercise of this-worldly freedom, then the beatific vision would indeed deprive Christ of such freedom. However, would such a freedom to develop articulated knowledge about oneself and the world be excluded any more by the beatific vision than by a Rahnerian self-consciousness? As we argued in the previous chapter, the earthly and blessed Christ did in fact possess natural human knowledge with its inherent limitations. Since natural and beatific knowledge have very different means of knowledge, finite and infinite, they are quite compatible. What Christ knows wordlessly and inexpressibly in the vision of his Father by means of the transcendent divine essence, he is free to come in time to know and express by finite means naturally proportioned to his finite human mind. Thus the blessed Christ was quite free on earth to make unhindered enquiry about the universe through the senses and so on, to build up his acquired knowledge of what he experienced, as well as to discover ways to express knowledge of himself. Hence, he was free to come to knowledge of things in a way that he did not know them before. Thus, in this respect at least, Christ's earthly freedom would not be suppressed by the beatific vision. If it be an element of the incarnation that the Saviour develop knowledge in a natural, historical human way, that would be available to him as much in heavenly freedom as in earthly freedom. Indeed the assumption of a heavenly freedom should put Jesus at an advantage in terms of his saving mission, because the beatific vision would not only preserve but enhance his freedom to grow in natural knowledge, putting at the disposal of historical development finite knowledge drawn from the beatific vision as well as what was drawn empirically from the world around him.

A second area we need to consider is the freedom to grow in *grace*, since Galot has contended that possession of the beatific vision would render Christ unable to grow in holiness.[28] Because the latter state of affairs would contradict the witness of Scripture, he concluded that Christ could not have enjoyed the beatific vision

27. Ibid., p. 211.
28. *Who is Christ?*, pp. 377–8 n.2.

while on earth. Now it is certainly true that Luke 2.52 states not only of Christ as a child that he increased in wisdom and stature, but also that he increased 'in grace' (χάριτι). At the same time it is also true that Aquinas denied that Christ's 'sanctifying grace' (*gratia gratum faciens*) increased. Now this grace of the Holy Spirit was that stable habit by which Christ's soul, on Aquinas's account, was made holy.[29] Just as this grace does not increase in the blessed, since they have reached their final end, so nor did it increase in Christ, who had always already reached his final end.[30] The denial that his habit of grace grew was of a piece with Aquinas's denial that Christ grew in his beatific knowledge and love of God. Though Aquinas did not identify the habit of grace with charity, as would Scotus, he saw them as closely co-ordinated in the sanctification of souls. As the power of the will was rooted in the essence of the soul, so the habit of charity was rooted in the habit of sanctifying grace. While charity perfected the will, sanctifying grace perfected the essence of soul, giving a certain participation in the divine nature, just as charity bestowed a participation in the divine love.[31] Moreover, just as Christ's love was perfect and did not admit of increase, so likewise his habitual grace was perfect and did not admit of increase. Unlike the habitual grace of others on earth, which could grow as an unconsummated participation in the grace of Christ their Head, the latter grace always existed in a consummate state, such that Christ could make the heavenly acts of knowledge and love that Aquinas held were required for our salvation. Though God could have willed things otherwise, absolutely speaking, in the actual order of things that God had established there was no possibility of an increase in his habits of grace and charity. On this view, Christ was indeed not free to grow in habitual grace, as those justified on earth are free to grow in this grace.

It might be easy to conclude from this that the growth in grace to which Luke refers must be not a real growth but a growth in manifestation only. In other words, Christ's habit of grace did not increase, but a constant grace was only revealed more and more as was appropriate to his growth in age. This has proved unconvincing to those who take Luke plainly to mean that Christ *really* increased in grace, just as he *really* advanced in stature and (at least in some significant way) in wisdom. Some have gone on to suggest ways in which the habit itself might be said really to grow from some particular point of view. Maritain took a solution from how the recipient of a virtue supernaturally infused by God might be said to grow in that virtue which, while perfect in itself from the moment of infusion, is progressively *rooted* in the soul through individual acts.[32] Thus, as Christ's mission required of him acts stemming from charity that were greater in themselves, so the habits of grace and charity were the more deeply rooted in his soul.[33] Though this may be true, we should take seriously the possibility that the growth to which Luke bears witness may not concern sanctifying grace at all, at

29. *Summa*, 1a.2ae., q. 113.
30. Ibid., 3a., q. 7, a. 12.
31. Ibid., 1a.2ae., q. 110, aa. 3–4.
32. Ibid., 1a.2ae., q. 24, a. 4 ad 4.
33. *On the Grace and Humanity of Jesus*, pp. 77–8.

least not directly, as Galot himself admitted. Should this be the case, the witness of Scripture can hardly demand that Christ be free to grow in *habitual* sanctifying grace. Now it would be anachronistic to suppose Luke was consciously referring to a gift that had been clearly distinguished from other gifts of grace only after some considerable scholastic reflection. Although by Aquinas's time, *gratia* had come to be normally taken to denote the habit of sanctifying grace, it also had a wider reference to a whole series of divine gifts, and Aquinas distinguishes several meanings of the word.[34] Moreover, χάρις also had a wide range of reference in the New Testament, although the basic meaning appears to be one of divine favour. From context it would appear that we are directly concerned in this verse with such *favour*, since Luke says that Jesus grew 'in favour' (χάριτι) before God *and his fellow human beings*. Now the 'grace' that Jesus would have received from other people was surely their favour, and so the divine grace in which Jesus is said to grow may surely be the favour of the Father.

What it means for Jesus to have *grown* in human favour is relatively straightforward. People noticed what was good in Jesus, even from a young age, and so in response bestowed their favour upon him in various ways with various effects. The more his wisdom and virtue would have been revealed in his actions, the more they would have responded to him with their favour. The same cannot quite be said of God whose own knowledge and love are perfect and immutable and do not depend on creatures, but rather he is the Creator on whose knowledge and love creatures depend.[35] It is not that God learns about something in us or in Christ and as a consequence becomes more favourable to us or to him. Rather, whatever good there is in us is the result of his favour, and by his eternal will he can cause different effects of his favour at different points in time, such that we can be said to be more favoured at one point than we are at another. In our case God can favour us in such a way that by his eternal will our habit of grace grows and we are more favoured at one point than we were beforehand and better disposed to a further growth in grace and to heavenly glory.[36] Now although Jesus cannot increase in God's favour in that way, there were other ways in which he could be more and more in receipt of divine favour. For example, he was favoured by God in all sorts of natural ways through certain natural effects, namely, growing up, acquiring knowledge, making friends, and so on. He could also be favoured in supernatural ways through the greater effects of his habit of grace in the greater acts he performs throughout his earthly life, in his teaching, his miracles and even his death on the cross for our salvation.[37] Thus, though already consecrated, Jesus could consecrate or sanctify himself in a new way for his passion (Jn 17.19).

We should not jump to the conclusion that there is no real growth in grace here but merely a growth in grace's manifestation. It should not be easy to forget that such supernatural works as Christ did and we do in Christ are not only the

34. *Summa*, 1a.2ae., q. 111.
35. Ibid., 1a., q. 20, a. 2.
36. Ibid., 1a.2ae., q. 114, a. 8.
37. Ibid., 3a., q. 7, a. 12 ad 3.

fruits of the habits of grace and charity, but these acts themselves are graces and also the effects of divine favour. Aquinas sees divine grace as at work not only for the existence of habits that order us to act but for the very acts themselves, which also outstrip the power of our nature.[38] So, in the case of Christ, God's favour can be said to grow as through divine grace he performed acts that were greater and greater in themselves. Thus growth in the habits of sanctifying grace and charity is hardly necessary for Luke's words to have a significant theological explanation. Though Christ was not free to grow in the habit of grace, he was free to grow with regard to the acts of grace he performed from childhood to the cross. This may make the Saviour's growth in grace different from ours, but Galot cannot be against such differences in principle, since he denies that Christ's growth in holiness could have involved amendment of ways or receiving the forgiveness of sins, which are bound up with the progress in grace of us sinners.[39]

A further set of free acts, which would definitely be excluded by a heavenly freedom, are those that are sinful. All mainstream Christian accounts of heaven rule out the possibility of sin in one way or another. This is part of the fact that heaven is presented in Scripture as without end (e.g. Rom. 2.7). Should we be free to sin, we would have the power to bring an end to heaven, at least for ourselves. Augustine distinguished the heavenly state as one in which the blessed are unable to sin, while those on earth can sin or in some cases not stop themselves from sinning.[40] As Aquinas understood the beatific vision, sinful acts are incompatible with the enjoyment of it. Since God is clearly seen by the blessed to be the Supreme Good, it is impossible for the saints to want to turn away from him. There is nothing about God that is lacking in goodness, nothing in the perfection of his goodness that is unfitting for human beings in any way, and all this is seen for what it is and cannot be construed to the contrary. In this heaven there is a true fulfilment of the human desire for happiness, which Aquinas thinks one cannot truly will against on earth, even though one can misconstrue it in this life and choose what will not really make one happy. When God is clearly seen by the blessed to be their happiness, without any possibility of thinking it otherwise, the saints cannot will in any way against his goodness, they cannot will against their true happiness, they cannot sin.[41] Thus when heavenly freedom opens up a whole range of possibilities for the saints' activity, a fact we have already noted, it also closes down certain possibilities that belong to the imperfection of freedom, leaving that imperfection to the freedom we experience on earth. Should the earthly Christ have already experienced this heavenly freedom by way of the beatific vision, he too would have been unable to sin. If, to the contrary, he were able to sin, he could not have enjoyed the perfect vision of God and would be better thought of as a man of faith.

It is not so easy to make a case that Jesus was able to sin as it might be thought. It is certainly not possible to think of Christ as a sinner, despite his

---

38. Ibid., 1a.2ae., q. 109, a. 8.
39. *Who is Christ?*, p. 379.
40. *De Civitate Dei*, 22.30.
41. *Summa*, 1a.2ae., q. 5, a. 4.

identification with sinners, so long as one accepts the witness of Scripture as reliable. Christ's sinlessness is explicitly taught by several New Testament authors (2 Cor. 5.21; Heb. 4.15; 1 Pet. 2.22, 3.18; Jas 5.6; 1 Jn 3.5), and John's Gospel has Jesus lay down the challenge, 'Which of you convicts me of sin?' (8.46). The implied answer is of course that none could truly do so. Rather than his sinlessness impede his solidarity with sinners, Jesus is able to come close to them precisely because his sympathy is not blunted by any sin or inclination to sin in him, because he is sinless. Catholic theologians have generally gone further by teaching explicitly not just Christ's sinlessness but that he was always *unable* to sin, that he was and is impeccable. More recently, however, in a time when the theory of the earthly Christ's beatific vision has been widely dropped, there have been Catholic theologians who have entertained the possibility that the earthly Christ was peccable. Their claim is not that Christ ever sinned, but that he was able to, though he never did.[42] The basis of this claim cannot be that freedom to do good always requires the freedom to do evil, since that would mean that God, the angels and the saints would not be free – the freedoms of all of these are capable of a range of good acts but not of any evil ones. A beatified Christ then, like the other blessed, would be able to make free choices from among various goods.[43] So the basis of an opponent's claim would have to be that the ability to do good is connected to the ability to do evil *in this case*. The opponent's argument could be better supported by a further claim that it would not make sense for the earthly Christ to be tempted to do evil, unless he could have done evil and so failed the test, unless he were able in mind to choose what are in themselves or in the particular circumstances sinful acts, to choose unbelief as well as belief.[44] If that were the case, then Christ's freedom must have been an earthly rather than a heavenly one, and he could not have possessed the beatific vision.

For someone to be 'tempted' is to be 'tried' or 'tested'. That we are not the only ones who are tested, but that Jesus was tested too, is clear from the New Testament. As the Letter to the Hebrews has it, 'We do not have a high priest who is unable to sympathise with our weaknesses, but one who was tested (πεπειρασμένον) in everything likewise – without sin' (4.15; cf. 2.18). His temptation was thus both like and unlike our own experience: unlike ours because in his case it was always sinless, and like ours because of the full range of testing. According to patristic interpretation, the full range of matter for sin is reflected in the three temptations of Christ in the desert (Mt. 4.1–11; Lk. 4.1–13), where at the end of Luke's account we are told Christ had undergone 'every testing' (πάντα πειρασμὸν).[45] Though Christ is also said in the Gospels to be 'tested' by the Pharisees with their questions

---

42. E.g. E. Lyons, 'His Own Person or Divine Puppet?' in M. A. Hayes and L. Gearon, *Contemporary Catholic Theology: A Reader* (Leominster: Gracewing, 1998), pp. 251–8 (257–8).

43. *Summa*, 3a., q. 18, a. 4 ad 3.

44. Cf. Sobrino, *Christology at the Crossroads*, p. 97.

45. Ambrose, *In Lucam*, 4.35.

(Mk 8.11; 10.2) and likewise by a lawyer (Mt. 22.35), in the desert the source of his testing is the devil, who makes three suggestions to him. In the order Matthew gives them they are the temptation of a hungry Christ who has fasted forty days to command stones to become bread, the temptation to throw himself down from the Temple, given that angels would bear him up, and the temptation to receive from the devil all the kingdoms of the world and their glory on condition of falling down and worshipping him. We may presume that Jesus, with his extraordinary knowledge, whether it is interpreted as beatific or not, would have had a profound insight into the attractiveness of all things, including all merely apparent goods, such as were presented to him by the devil. It would be impossible for us to read the narratives as implying that Jesus had no clue of whatever the desirability might variously be of turning stones into bread, receiving the kingdoms of the world or being rescued by angels. The narratives, however, do not give any clue that Jesus might have been actually attracted in any degree to what was suggested to him, nothing to imply that he actually experienced any positive desire of them. Rather, each time he is tested, he apparently passes the test with ease: Jesus is the stronger one (cf. Mk 3.27), who always conquers his adversary directly with a quotation from Scripture.

Should Christ – or anyone else – possess the beatific vision, as Aquinas under-stood it, their impeccability would have guaranteed the passing of the devil's test and excluded the very possibility of failure. Though their beatific knowledge would provide them with a thorough grasp of the particular attractiveness of any merely apparent goods, it would also provide them with a vision of the Supreme Good from which they would not be able even to want to depart. The question is whether these testings in the desert would be genuine, any more than mere shows, if Christ would not have been able to fail.[46] It seems to me that a test can be a true one, even if one is bound to pass. Should someone test me right now on my ten times table, I am confident that there is no possibility of me failing, and yet there is no reason to deny that a test would have taken place. Of course someone may object that the inevitability of my passing makes the test trivial, and that to see the temptations of Christ in this way would be to trivialize them. It seems to me, however, that though testing me on my ten times table may be trivial in itself, in certain contexts it would not be trivial at all. For example, were someone to test me as a way of encouraging a child to learn his ten times table, the act of testing would have an important significance. Likewise, if an impeccable Christ were to be tested so as to equip him to sympathize with us when we are tested, or to provide us with an example in refusing temptation, it would have an important significance in terms of our salvation. Aquinas gives a number of ways in which Christ's temptations work to our benefit: they strengthen us against temptation, warn us not to think that we are safe from temptation, teach us how to overcome the devil and give us confidence in his mercy (cf. Heb. 4.15).[47] But if we can give an account of the meaningfulness of Christ's temptations such as this, that

46. Cf. O'Collins, *Christology*, p. 267.
47. *Summa*, 3a., q. 41, a. 1.

weakens the argument that Christ was peccable and so could not have possessed the beatific vision.

Giving an account of how Christ would be able to choose the sinful acts suggested by the devil or indeed any sinful acts is not without its own difficulties. From what we know of Jesus in the Gospel accounts, it is difficult to think of him as the kind of man who would be positively attracted by the idea of an earthly kingdom, let alone one gained by worshipping the devil. The whole flow of the narratives tells against it. A Jesus who is so focused on the will of his Father would surely be vehemently disinclined to sin, and a sinless Jesus would not suffer the effects of past experiences of sin that would mean he would be pulled internally in that direction again. Aquinas's account of Jesus' great virtue, the absence in him of even any inclination to sin, such that there was no source of temptation for him from within, only from without, meaning that Jesus' humanity would have been thoroughly disposed to act according to the will of the Father, matches the picture of Christ we find in the Gospels. For Aquinas the very purpose of the incarnation excluded sin from Christ, and the perfect grace and virtue that fitted this purpose themselves excluded any inclination to sin.[48]

Opponents of Christ's beatific vision are often disinclined to make an argument against the beatific vision because it would make Christ impeccable, on account of the fact that they are already committed to Christ's impeccability in some other way. For many, the fact that, on a Chalcedonian reading of Scripture, Jesus is true God brings a most powerful difficulty for supposing that he would be able to fail a temptation, even in his human nature. For Jesus to be peccable would mean that a divine person would be peccable, that God could be actively opposed to God, and that is widely thought to be impossible. In the *Summa*, however, Aquinas appears to have been entertaining the possibility that a divine person could in theory co-assume sin and the inclination to sin *in his human nature*, presumably because he had earlier explained the impeccability of the divine persons by reference *to the divine nature*.[49] However, Aquinas had elsewhere appealed to Christ's divinity in arguing for his impeccability, and his school has generally followed him here by making the hypostatic union the formal reason for Christ's impeccability.[50] This would mean that peccability – and impeccability – could not possibly be something an incarnate divine person could *co*-assume. An incarnate divine person must always assume a humanity that is impeccable by way of the hypostatic union, and which can be considered able to sin only in abstraction from the hypostatic union. What Christ *co*-assumes are those gifts that befit the impeccability that necessarily follows on from his divine identity – whether or not these gifts can include the beatific vision is of course what is at issue, but they are not themselves the formal reason for impeccability. So, as far as Galot and

---

48. Ibid., 3a., q. 15, aa. 1–2.

49. For some reflections on this in connection with Christ's beatific vision, see Ols, *Le cristologie contemporànee e le lóro posizióni fondamentali al vaglio della dottrina di S. Tommaso* (Studi Tomistici, 39; Vatican: Libreria Editrice Vaticana, 1991), pp. 172–6.

50. *Super Sent.* 3.12.2.1.

llins are concerned, it is metaphysically impossible for God to sin, even in ... ...uman nature: a divine person cannot sin on account of the absolute holiness of God.[51] Thus Galot and O'Collins brought no argument against Christ's beatific vision based on his need to be free to sin. It would seem to be valueless to object to Christ's beatific vision on the ground that it would render him impeccable when he is already impeccable by way of his divine personhood. So, just as the opponents of Christ's beatific vision rarely argue from the attribution of error to Christ, as we saw in Chapter 6, so they rarely argue from the attribution to him of peccability.

Though he does not go so far as to characterize it as sinful, Lombardo does suggest that there is an actual example of Christ's human will being contrary to the divine will in the Gospels. This is Christ's prayer to the Father in Gethsemene: 'Not my will but yours be done' (Lk. 22.42). In these words we have an element present in the narrative that was not present in the accounts of the temptations in the desert. The difficulties involved in the conflict of wills we have here lead Lombardo to suggest that one way out may be 'to reconsider the claim that Christ experienced the beatific vision of God in his human soul during his earthly life'. This is based on the fact that 'Aquinas's analysis of Christ's prayer is difficult to reconcile with his claim that Christ experienced the beatific vision in his soul.'[52] However, it is unclear why this should be so. Aquinas identified Christ's own act of will here as his wanting to remain alive and avoid death. As Mark has the words of Jesus: 'Abba Father … take this cup away from me; yet not what I want (θέλω) but what you want' (14.36; cf. Mt. 26.39).

From John of Damascus Aquinas appropriated a patristic practice of distinguishing between various levels of willing.[53] From the rational will he distinguished the appetite shared by human beings in common with animals, which we would not normally term the will, and here Christ shared the natural human animal spontaneous desire for life and recoiling from death. Aquinas did not think, however, that Christ's spontaneous desire to live and avoid death remained only at that sensory level: it also engaged his rational will. Here Aquinas further distinguished the single rational will by his terms 'will as nature' (*voluntas ut natura*) and 'will as reason' (*voluntas ut ratio*). The rational will, he held, is a single power that can be considered in terms of its act from two points of view, namely, insofar as it is natural and insofar as it is rational, *ut natura* and *ut ratio*.[54] An example of this would be someone who in one sense did not want to take some bad-tasting medicine when considered in itself, but in another sense wants – and chooses – to take it for the good of his health. By the same rational will the person both wants

---

51. Galot, *Who is Christ?*, p. 386; O'Collins, *Christology*, p. 281.

52. *Logic of Desire*, p. 220.

53. John of Damascus, *Expositio Fidei*, 2.22. On Aquinas's sources, see P. Gondreau, *The Passions of Christ's Soul in the Theology of St. Thomas Aquinas* (Beiträge zur Geschichte der Philosophie und Theologie des Mittelalters, Neue Folge 61; Münster: Aschendorff, 2002), pp. 309–17.

54. *Summa*, 3a., q. 18, a. 3.

to take the medicine and does not want to take it, though in different respects: he does not want to take it by his will when considered as nature, but does want to choose it by his will considered as reason. What happened in Gethsemene as regards the rational will was that from one point of view Christ wanted to die and from another point of view he did not. Quite naturally he wished to live and to avoid death as an evil in itself, but from the point of view of his rational choice he wanted to die for the sake of our salvation. So when Christ prayed that he did not want to die, that expressed his rational will considered as natural. But when Christ prayed that the Father's will be done, he was expressing his own human will as reason, choosing in harmony with the divine will that he should die on our behalf. As someone may not want in one way to take his medicine but in another way want to take it for the sake of his health, Christ wanted to live rather than die insofar as life and death are considered in themselves, but chose to die in obedience to the Father precisely so that we might be saved. Aquinas held that there was no problem of contrariety between the divine and human wills raised here, because the human will as nature was not in the position of rejecting the reason for which the divine will and the will as reason willed the passion, namely our salvation, and the divine will and the will of reason were not impeded by the will as nature. Moreover, neither did the divine will nor the will as reason impede the natural will in its wanting to live and avoid death: rather, by his divine will and his will as reason Christ wanted his natural will to be moved in this perfectly natural way.[55]

Lombardo is content that objections to the coherence of Aquinas's account of different levels of willing can be given a satisfactory response.[56] However, he thinks the account difficult to reconcile with Christ's possession of the beatific vision, because he was willing something on the level of *voluntas ut natura*, namely, that he not die, which did not accord with the object of the divine will, that being that he should die.[57] However, it is unclear what more serious problem is raised by the compatibility of the beatific vision and the will to avoid death than is already raised by the more basic question of how Christ's human will to avoid death can be compatible with the divine will. But if there is no ultimate problem with the compatibility of the divine and human wills in Gethsemene, which Lombardo recognizes, then there can hardly be an outstanding problem for the compatibility of Christ's human will with his vision of God, since all that the beatific vision would add is that Christ would know in the beatific vision that it was the divine will that he should by his rational will want on one level to live and avoid death. Now Aquinas seems to have understood Christ's prayer according to his natural will not to be something God merely permitted, as though it were sinful, but as something God positively willed.[58] God willed both that Christ should want to avoid death, as is natural to human beings, and that he should

55. Ibid., 3a., q. 18, a. 6.
56. *Logic of Desire*, pp. 212–15.
57. Ibid., p. 220.
58. Cf. *Summa*, 1a., q. 19, a. 9.

choose to suffer death for our sake. And for this there could be very good reasons: first, that it should be manifest that Christ had a true human nature that worked in the proper way, that is, as naturally orientated towards the preservation of its life, and secondly, to show that it is in general not necessarily sinful for human beings to want on some levels what God does not want, simply speaking.[59] But if we can accept that God, who willed that Christ should die for our salvation, also positively willed that Christ should according to his will as nature want to avoid death, then Christ's beatific knowledge that this divine willing was the case could be no trouble for his willing on any level. Rather this knowledge could only assist him in his human willing, since he would know in the beatific vision what was right according to each level of his rational willing. His will to avoid death would only be difficult to reconcile with his beatific vision if it were difficult to reconcile with the divine will. But, given that it can be reconciled with the divine will and this willing is something God positively wanted, it can equally well be reconciled with possession of the beatific vision.

Finally, there is the charge that Christ was not free to do good so as to *merit*. The objection arises from the key role the concept of merit has played in Catholic theology. Although the term is not found in Scripture, the Fathers were able to speak of Christ's meriting the reward of his glory because this idea was manifest in the logic of a number of New Testament passages. For example, Paul taught that the state of exaltation was granted Christ as a consequence of his humbling in the condition of a slave all the way to death on the cross: 'Therefore God highly exalted him ...' (Phil. 2.9). Thus God rewarded the humbling and death of Christ by raising him on high, such that Christ by his humbling and death deserved or merited his resurrection. The pattern is found elsewhere, for example in the Letter to the Hebrews: Christ is crowned with glory because of his passion and death (2.9). Furthermore, as well as his meriting something for himself, the logic of the story of salvation also suggests that Christ merited *on our behalf* as our Saviour. When Paul compares Christ to Adam, he compares justification coming to all from Christ's act of obedience with the condemnation of all stemming from Adam's disobedience (Rom. 5.12–21). This means that as universal death came as a just punishment for sin, so life comes to all as a reward for Christ's righteousness: in other words, by his passion and death Christ merited our salvation. Thus Christ's merit was a crucial theme at the Council of Trent.[60] Aquinas had of course already taught both that Christ merited his own bodily glory, and that as our Head he merited for us to share his glory (cf. Jn 17.10).[61]

Galot however writes, 'The glorious state would be incompatible with the merit attributed to Christ in the work of salvation, inasmuch as anyone who possesses the glorious vision can no longer merit.'[62] Galot did not question that Christ, as Aquinas presents him, possessed most of the qualities required to merit on our

59. Cf. ibid., 3a., q. 21, a. 2.
60. *Decretrum de iustificatione*, 7.
61. *Summa*, 3a., q. 19, aa. 3–4.
62. *Who is Christ?*, pp. 356–7.

behalf. Catholic theologians normally require that the meritorious act be good, exercised while in the body, freely done and the fruit of divine grace, without which there can be no merit of a supernatural reward. In all these there is no problem, except that Christ, though free in a more general way, was allegedly unfree in respect of meriting, because he did not fulfil the further requirement of living in a state of being able to merit rather than in a state of reward. Galot, like Aquinas, understood this life to be the state where we are able to merit our reward, and the actual state of reward to exist only the other side of death. However, given that the beatific vision belongs to the state of reward and Aquinas's Christ had that vision throughout his earthly lifetime, he could never have been in a position to merit. Since Galot wanted to guarantee that Christ was able to merit our salvation, he felt he had to place him in the state of merit, and so argued that he never possessed the beatific vision until after his death.

Aquinas did not agree that the earthly Christ was in a state where he was unable to merit. The fact that his body was mortal meant that, though he was a *comprehensor* in regard to his beatific knowledge, he was a pilgrim in regard to the body.[63] This meant that, since the body's glory was still to be achieved, he was in a perfect position from that point of view to merit the resurrection and glory of his body. Moreover, the fact that, as well as being a pilgrim in regard to the body, he was already a *comprehensor* in respect of his possession of the beatific vision, did not render him unable to merit. The fact that the other *comprehensores*, the blessed in heaven, are unable to merit is no reason to suppose that the earthly Christ could not merit, because of a key difference between him and them. While the blessed have indeed received their vision of God as a reward for what the action of divine grace in them achieved in this life, Christ just did not receive the beatific vision as a reward in any way at all.[64] We have argued that he was uniquely blessed with beatific knowledge as a gift that would enable him to be a fitting Saviour for us, not as a reward for something done in faith. We cannot think then of him as unable to merit, just because he was a *comprehensor*, since he enjoyed beatific knowledge for a reason which was quite different from that of every other *comprehensor*, who themselves are ultimately rewarded by their beatific vision and are no longer able to merit. Of course Christ was not free to merit the beatific vision for himself, since he always already possessed it, and this is altogether consistent with the patristic denial of faith in Jesus. As Augustine wrote of Christ in the Scriptures: 'We do not read that he merited through faith to acquire a goodness he did not already possess.'[65] But the fact that Christ enjoyed the beatific vision from the very beginning did not prevent him from being able to merit it *for others*, for our salvation. Rather, as Scheeben opined, it was his very possession of the beatific vision that enabled him – or we might say, freed him – to merit it for us.[66]

63. *Summa*, 3a., q. 15, a. 10.
64. Ibid., 3a., q. 19, a. 3.
65. *Contra Maximinum*, 2.23.7.
66. *Mysteries of Christianity*, pp. 447–52.

We should then consider the possibility that, while Christ may not have been free to merit the beatific vision for himself, at the same time his beatific vision opened up for him the very freedom he needed to bring about our salvation. In this an earthly Christ of heavenly freedom can compare well with one merely of the freedom that pertains to earth. Had Christ possessed only faith and not vision, he would still certainly have been blessed with charity, but it would not have been the *perfect* charity that arises from beatific knowledge. Rather than his will reposing in the Father, he would have been in the position of needing to come closer to God, of desiring to know and love him better. Only after his death would this Saviour have possessed perfect love of the Father in his humanity. Only after having saved us through his passion would he likewise love us with a perfect love. On this view the beatific vision would be something he merited for himself rather than purely for others. His saving us would somehow improve his soul by bringing him the perfection of his knowledge and love as a reward for the cross.

We can see this too, but to a lesser extent, in Nicolas's theory of a greater range of objects seen in Christ's beatific vision after the period of his earthly life, which we encountered in the last chapter. On the Thomist principles we considered in Chapter 4, such an increase in range must depend on an increase in intensity of knowledge of their cause, that is, God the Holy Trinity. The implication of Nicolas's position is that Christ knew the Father to a greater degree after the resurrection than he did on earth, and will also surely mean an increase in his beatific love for God, which arises from beatific knowledge. This introduces a tension for Nicolas, because he maintained at the same time that Christ died with an act of *unsurpassable* beatific love that no resurrection or exaltation could render 'more pure, more intense, more complete' (*plus pur, plus intense, plus total*).[67] However, if Christ knew his Father more intensely after the resurrection, would he not then have *loved* more intensely than he did at the moment of his death?

A danger in approaches such as these is that what Christ does on our behalf becomes a moment in his own inner development, something by which he enjoys self-improvement in his inner life. I suggest that this bears a striking similarity to the idea of a mutable God who grows in love and who becomes perfected in love through creating us and redeeming us. Just as theologians like Weinandy have in recent years come persuasively to the defence of the unchanging God of love whose love for us cannot be improved, who saves us not to any possible benefit of his own but to ours,[68] so it seems that a Christ who dies out of an unsurpassed beatific love rather than one who gains greater love through dying stands in need of a comparable theological defence. I suggest that, just as a Christ of imperfect and increasing love would seem fitted to reveal a mutable God, so a Christ who acts out of unsurpassable beatific love would seem better fitted to reveal a God whose love is so perfect that it cannot change. Just

---

67. 'Voir Dieu dans la "condition charnelle"', p. 393.

68. E.g. Weinandy, *Does God Change? The Word's Becoming in the Incarnation* (Still Rivers, MA: St. Bede's, 1985).

as God's divine love is in itself constant and unchanging and not to be bettered or somehow increased, so in its own order is the act of beatific charity by which that divine love is embodied in Christ's human heart. And if the earthly Christ was already in possession of perfect knowledge of the Father and of us, perhaps this would also open up for him a greater freedom to redeem us out of pure love with no benefit for himself in terms of the knowledge and love of God, but only benefit for others.

Should the earthly Christ have possessed the beatific vision, it would have enabled him in his humanity to know not only God but also to know in God all those for whom he was to undergo his saving death. As well as knowing in his divinity all those for whom he was to die, he would have known them also in his humanity, not as though he were limited to thinking over them and imagining them one after the other by finite means of knowledge, but by knowing them all together in his single wordless knowing of the divine essence. And not only would this have enabled him to know in his humanity each and every one of those for whom he was to die, but it would have enabled him to love each one in his humanity also, to love each one personally with the love of his human heart. It was thus Christ's vision of God that enabled him to love perfectly both God and those for whom he was to undergo his saving death, and so die for them out of this perfect love in his humanity, this immense beatific charity that would never be bettered.[69] This then presents us with a theological explanation of Paul's words: 'I live by faith in the Son of God, who loved *me* and gave himself for *me*' (Gal. 2.20). Here we have a Saviour who dies for each one of us out of a supreme charity that embraces each one of us, a love he possesses only because he knows the Father just as he is, knowing us in him. Such a perception of Christ's perfect charity underlies Aquinas's whole theology of how Christ saves us, in particular through his passion, which is the supreme expression of his love for us. Without enjoying the beatific vision, he would not have been free to have loved us in this way and so suffered and died as our Saviour in the way the Father willed.

At the end of Chapter 5, we concluded that it was more probable that a theological explanation of Christ's extraordinary knowledge in his human mind include the beatific vision rather than faith, with the proviso that if the objections put against Christ's beatific vision carried, we should have to abandon vision and reconsider the possibility of his faith. However, in the last two chapters, not only have the objections brought from Christ's natural knowledge and his freedom failed to disprove his vision of the Father, but a richer picture has emerged of a Saviour whose natural knowledge and freedom are enhanced by the beatific vision for the purpose of our salvation rather than suppressed. In this light, rather than find ourselves required to recast Christ as a man of faith, we can consider ourselves approaching a moral certainty that Christ was a man of vision. However, there is still one further objection to be heard, which is often thought to be the

---

69. On how this fulfils the Old Covenant, see M. Levering, *Christ's Fulfilment of Torah and Temple*, pp. 59–60.

most persuasive. Though it may be true that the beatific vision would equip the Saviour with a perfect charity out of which he would suffer and die for us, if the beatific vision were to impede this very suffering, emotional as well as physical, then the beatific quality of Christ's charity would lose its advantage. In the final chapter, we shall turn from Christ's intellect and will to his emotions and body, in order to ask whether a beatific Christ would have been free to suffer.

Chapter 8

'BUT JESUS SUFFERED!'

We have argued in the preceding chapters that while the beatific vision is indeed incompatible with faith, the earthly Christ did not in fact possess faith, and consequently it could have presented no bar to his vision on earth. We have argued too that Christ's natural knowledge and freedom of will were not excluded but enhanced by his vision of the Father. We come now, however, to what is often perceived as the most powerful argument against Christ's beatific vision. At the very beginning of his list of objections to Christ's vision, O'Collins writes, 'First, how could he have genuinely suffered if through his human mind he knew God immediately and in a beatifying way?'[1] Opponents of Christ's beatific vision hold that it and human suffering of any kind, whether physical or psychological, are just incompatible. This is because of what Balthasar regarded as the beatific vision's 'anaesthetic effect'.[2] Were Christ then to have enjoyed the beatific vision, he could not have undergone the negative experiences the Scriptures record of him, especially those towards the end of his earthly lifetime. Hence, it is concluded that the earthly Christ could not have possessed the beatific vision at all. Should this final argument fail to convince, I suggest that the theory of Christ's beatific vision can hardly be in any doubt for the Catholic theologian, in view of the advantages that we have seen accrue to this theory, together with the difficulties that come with the alternative.

Aquinas's opponents begin from two teachings that are undeniably part of the Christian confession, namely, the sufferings of Christ and the joys of the blessed. Scripture presents Christ not only as suffering pain through injuries done to his body but as undergoing various emotions or passions of the soul that arise in response to evils perceived by him. For example, he is reported to have been angry at the hardness of heart of the Pharisees (Mk 3.5). Though anger and other feelings, such as pity, are sometimes attributed by Scripture to God by way of a figure of speech, suggesting that a Chalcedonian reading might refer them to Christ's divinity as opposed to his humanity, there seems to be no good reason for an orthodox account of Christ's humanity to deny their human reality. The physicality of the descriptions of this man's feelings given in the Gospels leaves

1. *Christology*, pp. 266–7.
2. Von Balthasar, *Theo-Drama* V, p. 259.

little doubt that they were experienced in his humanity (e.g. Mk 1.41). Without denying their revelatory power, we can say that by his physical tears Christ manifested human sorrow over the death of his friend Lazarus (Jn 11.35) and over Jerusalem, which did not know the things that made for peace (Lk. 19.41). In the Garden of Gethsemene he is said 'to be greatly distressed and troubled' (ἐκθαμβεῖσθαι καὶ ἀδημονεῖν; Mk 14.33), and he declares to Peter, John and James that his soul is 'very sorrowful' (περίλυπός) until death (v. 34). All this appears to be a world away from those who will enjoy the heavenly vision of God and the Lamb, where God 'will wipe away every tear from their eyes, and death will be no more, neither will there be mourning nor crying nor pain anymore, for the former things have passed away' (Rev. 21.4–5). It is suggested by Christ's parables that the kingdom of heaven is a place where one enters into the joy of the Lord God (Mt. 25.23), to be compared to a feast celebrating a wedding (Mt 22.2). The Fathers too proclaimed the joys of heaven.[3]

Opponents of the earthly Christ's beatific vision take it from this radical difference between the two states that the joy of the beatific vision and the experience of negative emotions are mutually exclusive, and conclude that Christ, who possessed earthly emotions, could not at the same time have enjoyed a heavenly vision. While there may be some divergence between them on the exact nature of Christ's sufferings,[4] for most of them this incompatibility is nevertheless obvious, and needs little more than to be stated. Since heavenly joy, and thus the beatific knowledge that gives rise to it, must drive out all negative emotions from the blessed, the Saviour could not have enjoyed the beatific vision or else he would have been unable to undergo experiences of pain and sorrow to which the Gospels bear witness. The objection is not so much that anticipatory knowledge of what is to come – the resurrection – must drive out present sorrow, and Tepikke has argued from our own experience that knowledge of bliss to come does not necessarily exclude from us present pain.[5] Rather, it is the joy arising from a present knowledge of the Father – and all it contains – that is alleged to drive out all negative emotion.

Galot is encouraged by the fact that even theories that defend Christ's beatific vision seem to concede the fundamental incompatibility of joy and sorrow in him. He cites Maritain's idea of Christ's supraconsciousness,[6] which we have already mentioned in Chapter 6. On this theory, in which Maritain placed Christ's beatific vision in his supraconsciousness rather than his normal consciousness, Christ would ordinarily not be conscious of his joy but thus open to suffering and sorrow. Maritain has Christ's earthly consciousness as forbidden even limited access to the supraconsciousness during his passion, but then full access at the

---

3. E.g. Cyprian, *Epistulae*, 58.10.

4. For a critique of Balthasar's views on Christ's suffering in relation to the beatific vision, see Pitstick, *Light in Darkness*, pp. 173–90.

5. 'The Vision of Christ', pp. 90–3.

6. 'Le Christ terrestre et la vision', pp. 435–6.

very moment of his dying.[7] As we have seen in preceding chapters, the appeal of such compartmentalizing of Christ's consciousness has been limited. For Galot, any such manoeuvring would in fact confirm the suspicion that Christ could not have experienced the beatific vision and suffering simultaneously.

Galot also made passing mention here of the early modern scholastic theory that Christ's joy was somehow suspended during his passion so as to leave room for his sorrow. This was the proposal of the sixteenth-century Dominican, Melchior Cano. He was seeking a solution to the problem that the sources of theology led him *both* to the conclusion that Christ possessed the beatific vision *and* to the conclusion that he suffered the greatest sorrow. Joy and sorrow, however, he considered to be 'absolute qualities' (*qualitates absolutae*) that could not co-exist in the same subject.[8] This was the case whether these had the same object or even different objects: either someone is joyful at some particular moment *or* he is sorrowful – he cannot be both, and cannot even be joyful and sorrowful about different things at the same time. This mutual exclusion of these 'absolute qualities' must be even more the case in Christ during his passion, who could hardly have been both joyful and sorrowful over the very same thing, namely, his death, and who would furthermore have possessed *either* the greatest joy *or* the greatest sorrow. So the question is put: was his will joyful or sorrowful? Cano answered that the fact that there was great sorrow in Christ (which he took on the basis of his prayer in Gethsemene to be in the rational will) meant there could be no joy, despite the undeniable fact that Christ possessed the beatific vision. What Cano proposed was a 'miracle': though it was natural for anyone who possessed the vision of God to rejoice in it, this joy was suspended in the case of Christ, at least for the period of the passion. Cano compared Christ to someone who cannot take pleasure in the food he eats on account of illness. Christ saw the Father, and attained to him, but by way of a miracle took no joy from all that. Galot of course, being *unconvinced* of Christ's beatific vision, would simply take this vision and the joy that would flow from it as altogether absent – there would be no need to invoke the miraculous to secure Christ's sorrow, merely the absence of the beatific vision. The fact that Cano even felt the need for a miracle was evidence for Galot that the beatific vision and suffering are just mutually exclusive.[9]

We should beware, however, of simply assuming that beatific joy and great sorrow are absolutely incompatible, because we cannot for example *imagine* what such simultaneous joy and suffering must be like. We cannot imagine for ourselves what beatific joy would be like, nor the immensity of the Saviour's physical and psychological sufferings, let alone what it would be like to experience them together. All that we can imagine are the kinds of mixed feelings we experience in this life. Some have come to the defence of the compatibility of Christ's vision and negative emotions by pointing out that human affectivity in general is no simplistic affair, where one could only experience one affection at a time. Mansini

---

7. *On the Grace and Humanity of Jesus*, pp. 134–44.

8. *De Locis Theologicis*, 12.13.

9. 'Le Christ terrestre et la vision', p. 435.

judges the raising of the question of how one can be happy and sad at the same time as too abstract an approach. We need instead, he says, to attend to our own complex experiences:

> Am I not both happy and sad at the same time to send my friend off to Europe? I am happy in the prospect of his education and enjoyment; I am sad to think that I cannot share the common life of friends with him for the next months. It would be very mistaken to think happiness and sadness here are an alternation of acts; no, it is the abiding presence at the same time of two affective states. And lovers, after all, sometimes claim to experience at the same time what in the abstract can only be described as contradictory affective states. Furthermore, it is sometimes the very presence of our happiness in the possession of some good that increases our sorrowfulness over some evil. I think this is well within our ordinary experience.[10]

Others appeal to the experiences of the mystics, who have reported simultaneous experiences of desolation and delight.[11] However, as far as Galot is concerned, since none of these mystics ever experienced the vision of God on earth, their reports, like ordinary mixed feelings, offer no support for the co-existence of beatitude and suffering in Christ's soul.[12] Rather, beatitude must be a wholly exceptional state, in which such complexities are not possible, but joy drives out all suffering and sorrow. However, while Galot very briefly reviewed more modern attempts at dealing with the problem, such as those of Cano and Maritain, he did not really present any real assessment of what Aquinas had to say. We shall turn now to Aquinas's solution and his own account of human affectivity, and the criticisms made of it by those opponents who do take time to engage with it.

While Aquinas rejected his opponents' conclusion, it is worth noting that he did share common ground with them in their starting points, namely, that heaven is kingdom of joy and that Christ was genuinely sorrowful unto death. We shall review what Aquinas had to say about the joy of the saints and Christ's suffering, before passing on to the question of how far they are compatible on his account. In order to do this, we need first to look at his understanding of human affectivity. Aquinas did not speak of 'emotion', which is a relatively recent term in human psychology, but of 'affections', that is, movements of the appetite, some of which he termed 'passions'.[13] Though distinct from any kind of knowledge or perception, all these movements of appetite are intimately related to such knowledge as responses to the objects perceived.[14] Moreover, while Aquinas also spoke of passions that pertain to the body, such as hunger and thirst, he spoke

---

10. 'St. Thomas on Christ's Knowledge of God', pp. 119–20.

11. E.g. Iammarrone, 'La visione beatifica di Cristo', pp. 320–3; Pitstick, *Light in Darkness*, pp. 187–8.

12. 'Le Christ terrestre et la vision', p. 435.

13. *Summa*, 1a., q. 82, a. 5 ad 1.

14. Ibid., 1a.2ae., q. 22, a. 2.

at greater length of passions of the *soul*, which can easily be identified today without too much controversy as emotions: feelings of love, desire, delight or pleasure, hate, aversion, pain or sorrow, hope, despair, fear, courage and anger.[15] These passions of the soul Aquinas sees as those affections that are based not in the higher rational appetite of the human soul (that is, the will) but in the lower sensory appetite, which is shared in common with other animals, as responses to 'sensible' objects apprehended as a good or an evil.[16] Something sensible we perceive gives us pleasure, stirs up our desire, makes us feel angry or afraid. While the passion of pain (*dolor*), though a passion of the soul, has its root in the body, sorrow (*tristitia*) is a kind of interior *dolor* rooted in the soul's perception of a sensory object that saddens it.[17]

The higher affections, which are distinct from the passions, Aquinas places in the rational or intellectual appetite as responses to intelligible objects. Thus he can distinguish pleasure or delight (*delectatio*) in the sensory appetite from that particular pleasure or delight which is in the intellectual appetite, and that he terms joy (*gaudium*). Strictly speaking, a non-rational animal with its purely sensory appetite can experience pleasure or delight, but not joy.[18] About these higher affections of the will Aquinas has comparatively little to say. Like acts of the intellect, they are in themselves immaterial. An angel, which has no body, is said to be joyful when its immaterial will comes to rest in the vision of God.[19] God too may be said to be joyful, though in his case his joy is identical with his very essence, on account of divine simplicity.[20] Aquinas occasionally speaks of sorrow as an affection in the intellectual appetite, attributing it to the fallen angels who will never come to rest in seeing God.[21] These higher affections are 'simple acts of the will' without passion, passionless affections.[22] On Aquinas's own account of human knowledge we ourselves can have difficulty grasping such purely immaterial acts, even in a finite angelic creature, because we are bodily and our immaterial act of knowing is always accompanied by the need of sense images. Whether these purely intellectual affections can rightly be identified as emotions is a matter on which divergent positions have been taken in recent scholarship.[23] Partly this would seem to be because they do not in themselves have a physiological component, which many take to be essential to emotion. For Aquinas,

15. Ibid., 1a.2ae., qq. 22–48.

16. Ibid., 1a.2ae., q. 22, a. 3.

17. Ibid., 1a.2ae., q. 35, a. 2.

18. Ibid., 1a.2ae., q. 31, a. 3. On the lack of a straightforward parallel between joy and sorrow, see Lombardo, *Logic of Desire*, p. 86.

19. Ibid., 1a., q. 59, a. 4 ad 2.

20. Cf. Ibid., 1a., q. 20, a. 1.

21. Ibid., 1a., q. 62, a. 7.

22. Ibid., 1a.2ae., q. 22, a. 3 ad 3.

23. More recently, R. Milner, *Thomas Aquinas on the Passions* (Cambridge: CUP, 2009), pp. 35–8; D. F. Cates, *Aquinas on the Emotions: A Religious-Ethical Enquiry* (Washington, DC: Georgetown, 2009), pp. 95–6; Lombardo, *Logic of Desire*, pp. 75–93.

the soul's passions are psychosomatic and always involve a physiological change.[24] They are much easier for us to grasp, and so we often use them in trying to explore by analogy the immaterial affections, thinking of purely intellectual joy by analogy with sensory delight.[25]

Aquinas has much more to say about the passions than he does about the higher affections. While the passions often have a role in human failure, leading people into sin, he thinks of them as more fundamentally orientated to the life of grace, virtue and right reason, helping human beings towards their beatitude.[26] Indeed, he thinks that, though not rational in themselves, the passions participate in reason, and that perfect moral virtue cannot be had without them.[27] The fact that human beings are composed of body and soul, intimately united, entails the interpenetration of intellectual and sensory appetite – sense and intellect are united, not isolated. Aquinas speaks of a 'redounding' (*redundantia*) between higher and lower powers, a kind of overflow from one to another. On account of such *redundantia*, for example, an act of intellectual contemplation will mean not just intellectual joy in the will, but a resonance of pleasure in the body and sensory appetite too.[28] This explains something a joyful angel could never experience, namely, the physical pleasure we often feel when we solve some specifically intellectual puzzle.

How does this picture of affections and passions apply in the life of heaven? The fact that the higher reason of human beings for what is eternal has come to fulfilment in the beatific vision has consequences beyond the intellect. Taking our cue from beatific knowledge, the essential core of beatitude, we can build up a picture of the complete state of beatitude, beginning with a soul in possession of the beatific vision but separated from the body and thus from the experience of passions. As we saw in the last chapter, Aquinas holds both mind and will to come to rest in the vision of God – in heaven the quest for God has finally come to fulfilment. According to him this means a 'joyful fruition' in perfect contemplation.[29] As any apprehension of a fitting good brings pleasure or delight and intellectual apprehension brings joy, so the intellectual vision of the essence of God gives rise to a consummate affection of joy in the souls of the saints. Since the beatific vision cannot be lost, or else it would not be truly beatific, there can be no fear of losing it, leaving the joy of these souls undisturbed.[30] In other cases, however, our joy can be disturbed. Our natural knowledge on earth, though immaterial in itself, involves the use of bodily senses and sense images, and any of these may be impeded in some way. The very fact that the beatific vision does

24. *Summa*, 1a.2ae., q. 22, a. 3.

25. See Cates, *Aquinas on the Emotions*, pp. 201–2.

26. See P. Gondreau, 'The Passions and the Moral Life: Appreciating the Originality of Aquinas', *TTh* 71 (2007): 419–50.

27. *Summa*, 1a.2ae., q. 56, a. 4; q. 59, a. 5.

28. Ibid., 1a.2ae., q. 24, a. 3 ad 1.

29. *Compendium*, 1.165.

30. Ibid., 1.166.

not rely on such bodily images, however, rules out any such threat to joy. Again, our contemplation on earth, though joyful in itself, can also indirectly bring about some sorrow in the mind, when the object contemplated is apprehended as harmful in some way.[31] This cannot be the case with heavenly contemplation of God, however, since he, who is truth and the supreme good, is clearly seen for what he is. It is only when God is not clearly seen, as on earth, that a human being can construe him as an evil in some respect – for example, God forbids something sinful that I want to do – and that gives rise to sorrow or some other negative affection in the mind.

Though the vision of God himself may not cause sorrow for the blessed, there is still the question of their knowledge of lower matters, to which reason is also directed. Aquinas rejected the idea that knowledge of the sufferings of loved ones on earth can bring intellectual sorrow to the soul that sees God, meaning that just as higher reason cannot be the source of sorrow for the saints, so nor can the lower reason. When examining the knowledge of souls after death in general, he concluded that by the kind of knowledge that is 'natural' to them in their separated state without their bodies, they have no knowledge of the sufferings of their loved ones, removed as they are from this world, which can thus have no impact on them. Taking his cue from Gregory the Great, he counted the sufferings of loved ones as among those things fittingly seen by blessed souls in the divine essence, concerning which the saints can then pray in accordance with God's will. But since this vision is also a vision of divine *justice* (on account of divine simplicity), what is seen in it cannot give rise to sorrow, not even the punishments of those in hell, since everything which comes to pass is seen precisely in the wider context of its relation to the justice and providence of God in which the saints take joy.[32] Moreover, since the wills of the blessed are unable to stray from divine goodness, as we noted in the last chapter, none of their acts, including their acts of knowledge by way of finite *species*, can be such as to be unfitting to their final state of heavenly joy – all their thoughts, of whatever kind, will be joyful for all eternity. On account of their vision of God's goodness, the saints will not want to think any other kind of thought.

Though the separated soul is removed from the physical world by death, at the resurrection the saints will once more live in a bodily environment. However, that which they will perceive by their senses and for which they praise God – the humanity of Christ, the bodies of the saints, the new heavens and earth – will again be no cause for sorrow in them. From Paul Aquinas learns that the body, though sown corruptible, will be raised incorruptible (1 Cor. 15.42). This he connects with impassibility, a quality of the body by which it is immune to any suffering or pain.[33] This perfection also means that there is nothing about the body that can impede the soul's joy in its knowledge, even in its use of the bodily senses, as can happen in this life with tiredness and other conditions. This immutability

---

31. *Summa*, 1a.2ae., q. 35, a. 5.
32. Ibid., 1a., q. 89, a. 8. Cf. 2a.2ae., q. 83, a. 4 ad 2.
33. *Compendium*, 1.168.

and other attributes of the resurrection body Aquinas explains by the fact of glory flowing from the beatified soul into the body, an instance of *redundantia*. Thus the glory of the intellect has repercussions throughout the whole human being, not only on the body but also in the sensory appetite, whose full reality, together with the possibility of experiencing psychosomatic passions, is restored by the reunion of soul and body.[34] The 'overflow' of glory then includes an impact that disallows the possibility of experiencing the negative passions of sorrow and so on. Aquinas knew that in this life, the experience of one passion can in certain cases be overcome by another, a vehement sorrow driving out all delight, and intense pleasure excluding all sorrow.[35] This is what he supposed happens in the case of heavenly beatitude: the repercussions of this vision throughout the sensory appetite would bring a pleasure so intense that all contrary passions would be entirely excluded. Not only then does the beatific vision bring consummate joy to the intellectual appetite, but it brings the most intense pleasure to the sensory appetite, excluding every disagreeable passion.

In contrast, Aquinas learned from Scripture that the incarnate Word possessed a fuller range of human passions, including those we would count disagreeable, such as sorrow. The very fact at least that there can be certain states of humanity, such as heaven, where these passions are excluded, meant Aquinas could not present it as a matter of metaphysical necessity that any incarnation as such must involve these particular passions, even though a sensory appetite was necessarily included in a complete human nature.[36] Hence, in the case of the actual incarnation of Jesus Christ, he needed to seek clarification of why the defect of negative passions in his soul was in fact co-assumed by him, just as he had sought theological understanding in the case of the co-assumption of the perfection of the beatific vision. As with heavenly knowledge, Aquinas envisioned earthly passions such as pain and sorrow, fear and anger, as co-assumed for the purpose of salvation. Just as the passions play a role in the life of virtue of those seeking God, so they play a role in assisting Christ in the fulfilment of his saving mission. Thus, our Saviour 'emptied himself and took on the form of a servant' (Phil. 2.7), assuming not only a mortal body but earthly passions conducive to our salvation, so as to give us an example of virtue and be able to undergo suffering on our behalf. That is not to say that our salvation required Christ's passions to work exactly as ours do, who have an inclination to sin. Instead, always working in tune with reason and never tending towards what is wrong, Christ's passions never led him into sin. Whereas our passions sometimes 'do not remain in the sensory appetite', their proper place on Aquinas's account, but can have the further effect of invading and distracting our reason,[37] Christ's always remained in the sensory appetite, leaving his reason's orientation to the divine will undisturbed.[38] Thus his

34. *Summa*, 1a.2ae., q. 3, a. 3.
35. Ibid., 3a., q. 46, obj. 2.
36. *De Veritate*, 26.8.
37. *Summa*, 1a., 2ae., q. 77, a. 1.
38. Ibid., 3a., q. 15, a. 4.

pain and sorrow, fear and anger, never had the effect of leading him towards sin and away from the Father. Again, this sinlessness matched our need of salvation, to which a reason overrun by Christ's passions could make no contribution but would rather be a hindrance.[39]

Aquinas takes Christ's distress in Gethsemene (Mk 14.33; Vulgate: *pavere*) to involve the passion of fear (*timor*).[40] According to Aquinas, it pertains to the appetitive power not only to pursue good but also to avoid evil, and fear is that passion in the sensory appetite which responds to a future sensory evil that is near at hand and difficult to avoid.[41] This was certainly true of Christ's impending passion, which could in theory have been avoided by the power of his divinity but was not easily avoidable on account of the weakness of his flesh. While Aquinas allowed that fear sometimes involves an element of uncertainty about its object, as when we hear a noise in the night but do not know what it is, that was not the case here. Christ had the kind of fear that knew exactly what was coming, as can be seen from the fact that he had earlier predicted his passion and death. Now that these were apprehended by his lower reason and imagination as *at hand*, his sensory appetite naturally recoiled from the threat of bodily hurt, and hence his soul's passion of fear.[42] Next, Christ declared himself sorrowful (v. 34; Mt. 26.38). According to Aquinas, sorrow takes as its object a present evil. This suggests that by his lower reason and imagination Christ had now apprehended *as though already present* his imminent passion and death as harmful to himself and, as Aquinas says, to those who were in earthly terms responsible for it.[43] After this Christ experienced the distinct positive desire to preserve his life, both in his sensory appetite and, as we saw in the last chapter, in the natural inclination of his rational will, but without any deflection of reason so as by the will actually to *choose* to avoid death. Again, as we saw in the last chapter, in none of this was there anything at odds with the divine will: Christ experienced this series of passions just as the Father wished him to.

Finally, when injury itself came to Christ's body, this gave rise to pain in the soul.[44] Christ's 'whole soul' as such is said to suffer both because the soul is intimately united to every part of the body, and because Christ's lower powers, which are rooted in the soul and whose acts are directed to temporal things, all contained something that brought him pain and suffering. By his lower reason and imagination he apprehended the sins of the whole human race for which he was suffering in making satisfaction, the sinful actions of those responsible for his death and the loss of his bodily life, all of which brought him sorrow.

---

39. *Compendium*, 1.226.

40. See P. Gondreau, 'Aquinas, the Communication of Idioms, and the Suffering of Christ' in J. F. Keating and T. J. White, *Divine Impassibility and the Mystery of Human Suffering* (Grand Rapids, MI and Cambridge: Eerdmans, 2009), pp. 214–45.

41. *Summa*, 1a.2ae., q. 43, a. 1.

42. Ibid., 3a., q. 15, a. 7.

43. Ibid., 3a., q. 15, a. 6; *Compendium*, 1.232.

44. Ibid., 3a., q. 14, a. 5.

Since Christ's body and soul had been perfectly formed by the Holy Spirit, giving him consummate sensitivity in the bodily senses and vehement apprehension of the causes of sorrow by the soul's interior powers, Aquinas argued that Christ's sufferings were more intense than any other earthly suffering.[45] Nevertheless, Christ's reason was again never deflected by such sorrow and so on, which thus remained in the sensory appetite, and Christ remained obedient to the Father's will. Aquinas writes:

> The pain that was in the body itself on account of injury and in the essence of the soul, which is the form of the body, was not able to reach the higher reason inasmuch as it turns to God through its act, such that its turning might be hindered even in the slightest way.[46]

Even as he perceived himself to be delivered up to death by the Father, without legions of angels sent to deliver him, he remained entirely fixed on his Father in prayer, as he cried out, 'My God, my God, why have you forsaken me?' (Ps. 21/22.1).[47]

We may conclude then that, though they are not such as to lead him into sin but to fit him for his saving work, like his opponents, Aquinas affirms that Christ possessed a set of *earthly* passions or emotions. However, this surely differs significantly from the heavenly state of the blessed, who never experience this range of affections. The pictures of heavenly joy and earthly pain drawn by Aquinas himself are very different. Thus, one could easily infer the conclusion that someone must *either* possess the beatific vision *or* the possibility of suffering, fear and sorrow – in this case at least, he cannot have both at the same time. We on earth experience sorrow and not beatitude, while in heaven we shall experience beatitude without sorrow, and Christ would allegedly be no exception. Given his need of such passions for our salvation while on earth, Christ cannot have enjoyed the state of beatitude at that time, but it would be delayed until after his death. What Aquinas required then was a coherent account of how Christ could be an exception to the general rule that the blessed do not experience disagreeable emotions. This he could base in the fact that he was in no way committed to Christ's complete beatitude in every respect. He was certainly committed to his beatific knowledge, but in no way, for example, to a general extension of beatitude to his body before the resurrection – Christ was by the former a *comprehensor* but was also by the latter a *viator*, a 'pilgrim' on the way to beatitude – the extension of beatitude to his body was something he still sought.[48] Now while there certainly would be a mutual exclusivity between beatitude in *all* its respects and Christ's pain and sorrow – a body, for example, cannot be both completely impassible and

---

45. Ibid., 3a., q. 46, a. 6. This contrasts with Balthasar's theology where Christ's sufferings would also surpass all the sufferings of the next life, on which in relation to the beatific vision, see Pitstick, *Light in Darkness*, pp. 175–9, 185–90.

46. *De Veritate*, 26.10.

47. Cf. *Summa*, 3a., q. 47, a. 3.

48. Ibid., 3a., q. 15, a. 10.

capable of suffering – Aquinas found no contradiction between Christ's beatific *vision* as such in the higher reason and his suffering in body and soul. Any contradiction would lie not with this beatific knowledge in itself but in consequences it ordinarily had in heaven, but which did not take place in Christ on earth.

What then is it within the picture of a complete extension of beatitude through the whole human being that introduces a mutual exclusivity between this state and the state of earthly suffering? Different theologians have located the problem in different places. As we saw in Cano's case, it was located in the intellectual joy that naturally arises from the beatific vision. Cano was able to envisage Christ as both possessing beatific knowledge and undergoing great sorrow only by having a miracle suspend his beatific *joy*. Aquinas, however, while agreeing that there *is* a problem somewhere in all this, did not think it was this joy. For Aquinas, just as beatific knowledge in itself and suffering are compatible, so the intellectual joy in Christ's rational will was compatible with his suffering. As we saw in Chapter 6, Aquinas thought there was no contradiction in the intellect possessing both the knowledge of God's essence through an infinite means of knowledge and all sorts of knowledge of other objects through finite means of knowledge – rather, natural knowledge is perfected and enhanced by this supernatural knowledge. One may suppose that, as the resurrected saint will have an enhanced perception of the new heavens and the new earth, so the blessed Christ's knowledge of earthly temporal matters by natural means will be an enhanced one. Aquinas is at any rate clear that, by his higher reason (reason insofar as it has an eternal object) Christ knows the Father just as he is, and simultaneously by his lower reason (reason insofar as it takes temporal things as its object), together with the imagination, he strongly apprehends what is harmful to his bodily life and to others. Since reason can thus take both the eternal and the temporal for its objects, there is no need to divide reason into separated compartments. While the 'higher' reason can take no sorrow from the vision of God, but only intellectual joy, the apprehension of the 'lower' reason and the imagination of the sins of the whole world and so on bring the passion of sorrow, and both negative passion and intellectual joy are experienced simultaneously.[49] For Aquinas, there is no competition for 'space' in Christ's soul between joy and sorrow, for they have very different objects, and they can perfectly well co-exist, the former in the intellectual and the latter in the sensory appetite. Moreover, as we have already noted, Christ's sorrow remained within his sensory appetite so as not to deflect his reason into sin.

If this is the case, however, and Christ is open to what can make him sorrowful through his lower reason, as well as experiencing joy through his higher reason, why should that not be the case with the saints? Why should not the souls of the saints and the saints at the resurrection not also know what can give rise to sorrow in the sensory appetite but does not deflect reason? Just as with the earthly but blessed Christ, perhaps Aquinas could allow that the saints could in theory experience sorrow if they had the kind of knowledge of temporal matters that would enable that to happen. But, on his account, they do not, not because

49. Ibid., 3a., q. 46, aa. 7–8.

they experience intellectual joy and that in itself excludes the possibility of such knowledge, but because of the broader details of their state. As we have already noted, before the resurrection, the souls of the saints, since they are separated from their bodies, are removed from our world from which they can draw no natural knowledge of it that could give rise to sorrow. What they know of things that are sorrowful in themselves they know in the vision of God, which thus brings only joy. Furthermore, without their bodies they cannot experience psychosomatic passions, such as sorrow. Moreover at the resurrection of the body, when natural knowledge through the senses and the sensory appetite is restored, there will simply be nothing in the saints' environment that they could know so as to bring them sorrow or that would bring them pain. Even should there be any such thing, hypothetically speaking, they would be protected from the passions of pain and sorrow by the fact that the glory of the intellect 'redounds' throughout the soul and body of the risen saint.

Where Aquinas *does* locate a problem for Christ's simultaneous joy and suffering is not in his intellectual joy but in the glorious version of the *redundantia* from higher to lower that normally takes place within a human being. As we have just recalled, in his wider picture of beatitude at the resurrection of the body, Aquinas envisaged the glory of the intellect as having repercussions on the resurrected body and the full reality of the restored psychosomatic passions. Just as our intellectual joys on earth can have a pleasurable impact on our sensory appetite, so beatific joy will bring by way of *redundantia* an intense sensory pleasure or delight, together with the impassibility of the body. Should the beatific vision have had all its normal consequences beyond intellectual joy in the case of the earthly Christ, it would thus have rendered him not only incapable of suffering bodily injury but of feeling pain or sorrow or the like in the soul, precisely because of this principle of *redundantia*. What would exclude Christ's sufferings would be not his intellectual joy as such but the pleasure that would result in the sensory appetite as the redounding effect of this joy. This vehement sensory delight would of itself exclude all pain and sorrow and fear, just as the impassibility of the body would exclude all bodily injury. However, since Christ, according to Aquinas, not only possessed the beatific vision on earth but also suffered in body and soul, this vision *cannot* have had its ordinary heavenly effects either on the body or on the soul's sensory appetite. Rather, it is these latter effects, not joy in the intellect, that must be suspended, and Aquinas takes them to be generally suspended throughout Christ's earthly lifetime. This very suspension, then, takes place for our salvation. Just as Christ, according to the economy of salvation (the '*dispensatio*' in Aquinas's Latin), co-assumed the beatific vision and disagreeable passions, so it was by way of divine dispensation that the normal effects of the beatific vision in Christ's body and sensory appetite were uniquely prevented from taking place during his earthly lifetime. Admittedly, this prevention is not within the power of other human beings. It is, however, possible for *this* human being to effect it, since he is also God and possesses the divine power to do so.[50] Aquinas writes:

50. *Compendium*, 1.231.

By the power of Christ's divinity, beatitude was so kept in the soul, according to dispensation, so as not to overflow to the body and his passibility and mortality be destroyed. For the same reason, the delight of divine contemplation was thus by the dispensation of divine power retained in the mind of Christ, so as not to overflow to the sensory powers and in that way exclude sensory pain.[51]

What would have taken place on earth, had glory run its normal heavenly course, did not. The beatific *vision* is in itself no problem for Christ's suffering, but its normal effects in the body and sensory appetite would have been a problem. Therefore, if we accept Aquinas's solution, we cannot conclude from Christ's disagreeable passions that he did not possess the beatific vision, but only that it did not have its normal heavenly effects in the sensory appetite and body. As Christ saw the Father in order to be our Saviour, and took on earthly suffering in order to be our Saviour, so by divine power he uniquely suspended the effects of this glorious vision in his sensory appetite and body in order to be our Saviour.

Thus, while Galot treated the beatific vision as an exceptional state in which there could be no admixture of affections, Aquinas treated the Saviour as an exceptional case among those blessed with the vision of God. We have already said that Galot did not engage with Aquinas's solution. Those opponents of the earthly Christ's vision who *have* explored it nevertheless reject it, because of the very fact that it does what Aquinas intends: it makes of Christ an *exception*. What they do not question is that the solution makes sense. Torrell acknowledged that Aquinas did not ignore the problem of the co-existence of joy and sorrow but gave it a 'coherent response'. Given his starting-points, says Torrell, his method is irreproachable, his solution internally coherent and rigorous.[52] The solution is, he says, 'perfectly logical' (*parfaitement logique*).[53] Gondreau adds that the notion of Christ as at once both apprehending beatitude in one respect and seeking it in another secures for Aquinas

an eminently coherent and sound *raison d'être*, provided one grasp the funda-mentals of his philosophical psychology, whereby the "higher reason" and the "lower powers" of the soul retain logically – and really – distinct objects … Given this formal distinction in object between the higher reason and the sensitive powers, and the diverse operations that ensue from this difference in object, nothing precludes the theologian from holding that Christ's mind can perceive one thing, viz. the very essence of God, through *its own* proper act, while his lower powers can perceive another thing, viz. sense evils (or sense harm), through *their* own proper acts.[54]

51. *Summa*, 3a., q. 15, a. 5 ad 3.
52. 'S. Thomas d'Aquin et la science du Christ', p. 401.
53. *Le Christ en ses Mystères*, vol. 2 (Paris: Desclée, 1999), p. 338.
54. *The Passions of Christ's Soul*, pp. 446–7.

Thus simultaneous joy and suffering in Christ's soul do not 'entangle one in a web of philosophical or psychological inconsistencies'.[55] Aquinas's critics do not challenge the fact that it is possible for God to cause this co-existence of joy and sorrow, as Aquinas describes it. That is not to say, however, that they agree that his solution is acceptable. Rather it is found unacceptable, though not on the grounds of any internal incoherence, but because it is, according to Lombardo, 'of questionable coherency with the rest of Aquinas's account'.[56] In other words, Aquinas's particular solution makes Christ *different* from others, and this is what makes it objectionable. As Torrell puts it, Aquinas has made of Christ a 'blatant exception' (*exception flagrante*) to the rule.[57]

The mere fact of the solution making Christ different from the rest of us can hardly be a serious objection, as Torrell acknowledges.[58] It all depends on *the way in which he was different*. We have seen in previous chapters that, though Christ may be like us in terms of sharing the proper features of our human nature, he enjoys many individual perfections that we do not, such as the fact that he needs no redemption from sin, his ability to work miracles and, we have argued, beatific knowledge. Moreover, unlike us, Christ is God the Son, a divine person, the Second Person of the Blessed Trinity. He is unlike us as well as like us. A successful challenge to Aquinas's solution therefore either requires an opponent to show that Christ was different in a way that undermines his saving mission or that the introduction of this exceptional difference was simply unnecessary. Torrell and Gondreau have taken the latter course, as we shall see below, arguing that the solution is surplus to the requirements of an orthodox Christology. Lombardo, however, has taken the former course, charging that, according to the solution, Christ's affections 'do not operate according to their nature', and that this must 'jeopardise Aquinas's affirmation of the authenticity of Christ's humanity'.[59] Either way, the principal objection is this: Christ's affectivity while on earth worked in a different way from what we usually experience as regards the interplay between higher and lower powers.

Before making an assessment of these criticisms, we need to clarify in what ways and exactly how far Aquinas's solution makes him an 'exception' to the normal laws of human psychology, at least as Aquinas understood them. First we should note that it was Aquinas's direct intention to make Christ an exception *among the blessed*. According to his solution the earthly Christ differed from other human *comprehensores* in the impact their glory has on the sensory appetite and its passions, since this heavenly *redundantia* did not take place in him. The focus of Aquinas's opponents, however, is not so much on this particular difference between Christ and the blessed as on the consequences the solution is thought to have for the difference between Christ *and other earthly pilgrims*. Although we

---

55. Ibid., pp. 447–8.
56. *Logic of Desire*, p. 216.
57. *Le Christ en ses Mystères*, p. 338.
58. 'S. Thomas d'Aquin et la science du Christ', p. 401.
59. *Logic of Desire*, pp. 216–17.

on earth do not enjoy the repercussions of the beatific vision, and so in that very precise respect do not differ from Christ, the principle of *redundantia* is at work in us in a more general way during our earthly lifetimes. Thus, the fact that *redundantia* is removed from Christ's glory in Aquinas's solution allegedly involves him being an exception among us in a wider way that cannot be approved: his psychology is different from ours in terms of the more general relationship that normally obtains between the soul's higher and lower powers.

It is important to appreciate that the lack of heavenly *redundantia* in the earthly Christ fits into a wider picture of how Aquinas conceives Christ's human powers as uniquely related to one another, lower to higher as well as higher to lower. As we noted above, Aquinas also held that Christ's passions remained in the sensory appetite so as not to deflect reason. There was thus a way in which Christ's lower powers did not influence the higher, as well as a way in which the higher powers did not affect the lower. To explain this wider picture, Aquinas took the patristic principle that each of Christ's two natures had its own proper activity preserved, and extended it to cover the preservation of the proper activity of each of the powers within Christ's human nature, so as not to have any one overridden by the others.[60] This principle meant more then than the suspension of the normal effects of glory throughout the soul, which would have prevented Christ from undergoing the disagreeable passions needed for our salvation. It also meant that his passions would not penetrate his reason so as to lead it astray: his fear, anger and sorrow did not deflect his reason from its orientation on the Father, as again was required for our salvation. Each power was allowed its own proper activity, without unwanted influence from the others.

This wider picture is a problem for Lombardo. According to him, it means that the powers would *not* in fact operate according to their own nature. Left to their own nature, they would be engaged with one another, as they are in us. Instead, Aquinas's scenario is one of a 'disengagement', one foreign to our experience, which allegedly 'reifies' Christ's human appetites and 'isolates' them from one another. While we ourselves have an interpenetration of higher and lower powers of the soul that works both ways, in Christ's case it seems to work neither way. Turning first to the influence of the lower powers on the higher, we note that Lombardo treats this aspect of the problem as a consequence of Christ's beatific vision. Lombardo's difficulty is that, while Christ's sorrow remained in his sensory appetite, our sorrow can sometimes involve the intellectual appetite. However, it is by no means clear that Aquinas's position here must necessarily depend on Christ's possession of the beatific vision. As we said above, Aquinas has Christ's passions such as sorrow remain *in their proper place*, that is, in the sensory appetite, so as not to deflect reason. In our case, unruly passions can deflect reason and impede the rational will, leading us into sin. Were Christ's earthly beatific vision to be removed from the overall structure of Aquinas's theology, there would still remain the need to distinguish the effects of Christ's passions from those of ours, because the sinlessness of Christ would still need

60. *Summa*, 3a., q. 46, a. 6.

to be maintained, even if that did not involve his beatific vision. Lombardo would certainly prefer a theory that would allow for sinless sorrow in Christ's intellectual appetite. Nevertheless, however one were to rethink the relationship between the passions, the rational will and sin, one would still need an account of how sorrow in Christ's intellectual appetite did not lead him into sin. The point is that, even if Christ's sorrow were extended into his intellectual appetite, his experience of sorrow must still be different from ours in some way, without a certain engagement between passions and reason that would be present in us. Thus there would still be a discontinuity between Christ's affectivity and ours, the very thing Lombardo wants to avoid. Some kind of discontinuity between the impact of a sinless Christ's passions on his reason and the impact of the passions of sinners on their reason seems to be non-negotiable, even in the absence of the beatific vision. Thus a denial of Christ's beatific vision will be no guarantee that his affectivity will be exactly the same as ours, with the same kind of engagement among powers in Christ that there is in us.

But if we must retain some kind of exceptional lack of impact of the lower powers on the higher in Christ, whether or not he enjoys the beatific vision, how different need a beatific earthly Christ be in terms of the impact of the higher on the lower? Here we are definitely concerned with a direction of influence that has to do with Christ's possession of the beatific vision: there is no doubt that in Aquinas's account the suspension of the *redundantia* of higher onto lower is required precisely because the Saviour who must suffer already possesses the beatific vision. However, in view of the general relationship between higher and lower powers, it turns out that Christ is not so exceptional as he might be thought to be at first glance. Perhaps Aquinas did not think after all that *all* our instances of intellectual joy had an impact on the sensory appetite and that *none* of Christ's did. As for our situation, it has been debated whether or not Aquinas thought that an overflow from higher to lower powers took place in *every* case of an intellectual affection.[61] However, it is clear enough, as we saw above, that Aquinas *did* allow for intellectual affections that did not redound onto the sensory appetite so as to cause passion. This means that the lack of any impact of glory in the case of the earthly Christ could hardly be without any parallel in our normal experience, because there can also be in us instances of the affection of joy where there is no accompanying pleasure in the sensory appetite. In this way he and we are in a certain way alike.

That, however, does not prove that Christ was not exceptional in *any* way with respect to the general impact of higher affections on the sensory appetite. One can grasp how he was truly exceptional by recalling the fact that his intellectual joy was surely *very strong*. Aquinas thought that the more vehement the higher affection, the more it would have an impact on the passions.[62] Doing an act of justice, he says, will lead to joy in the will, but if the joy is increased through the perfection of justice, joy will not be passionless but overflow into the sensory

61. On this debate, see Lombardo, *Logic of Desire*, p. 91.
62. *Summa*, 1a.2ae., q. 24, a. 3 ad 1.

appetite.[63] The intense joy of some act of contemplation would thus also lead to the psychosomatic passion of pleasure (so long as the body was not impeded by illness or something of that sort), but the joy of a milder act of contemplation would remain in the higher will. Now the intensity of joy surely depends on the fact that the object enjoyed has been judged by the intellect to be a great good. Hence, it must be the case that the act of gazing on the essence of the Triune God, which is the supreme good, could scarcely count as among the milder acts of contemplation. Christ would therefore have been truly exceptional because, among all others, he had an experience of *intense* joy arising from intellectual contemplation that did not engage his sensory appetite, while our more intense affections always engage the sensory appetite (except perhaps in cases of bodily illness and so on). However, though he was certainly exceptional in terms of having no sensory repercussions in the case of this one intense affection, was he necessarily exceptional in terms of the impact of higher on lower more generally?

Mention of the many times we may experience the impact of higher affections on the sensory appetite leads us to the question of whether Christ also had such experiences in a general way. Aquinas's opponents seem to suppose that the fact that there was to be no redounding of glory onto Christ's sensory appetite means that there could never be any such repercussions of higher onto lower during his earthly lifetime. On this view, there was a single divinely-willed effect of suspension of *redundantia*, whereby *all* repercussions of higher affections on the sensory appetite were blocked. This could lead to the view that Christ, since he always knew in his vision of the divine essence both sin and his own passion, would always have been grave and sad, never moved to laughter.[64] However, there are in fact occasions reported in the Gospels in which Christ clearly took joy in something. For example, he 'exulted' when thanking the Father for hiding things from the wise and understanding and revealing them to mere babes (Lk. 10.21). For Aquinas, as for us, 'exultation' means the breaking forth of inner joy into an outward manifestation.[65] Unless one is to be sceptical of there being eyewitness reports of Jesus' joy, we can ask what it would have been about Jesus that would have made the eyewitness think he was joyful. We ordinarily know first-hand that people are joyful by hearing the tone of their voice or observing their physical appearance – a pleasure may show in their faces that circumstances allow us to perceive specifically as joy. Here we have an example of *redundantia* in the physical aspect of the sensory effect of intellectual joy. Presumably joy was sometimes written in the face of Christ and was resonant in his voice, and so those who were with him knew him to be joyful. Now on the one hand, one might suppose that all this would be caused by a temporary suspension of the suspension of the *redundantia* of beatific joy, something akin to what Aquinas thinks happened to Christ's body in the Transfiguration[66] – but for a moment the beatific vision was

---

63. Ibid., 2a.2ae., q. 59, a. 5.
64. Cf. Leeming, 'The Human Knowledge of Christ', p. 145.
65. *Summa*, 1a.2ae., q. 31, a. 3 ad 3.
66. Ibid., 3a., q. 45, a. 3.

allowed its delightful effect in the sensory appetite. On the other hand, it may be that Christ just perceived something or had thoughts of something according to the natural processes of his knowledge, by means of finite *species* formed from supernatural or natural resources, and took an intense but limited joy through these thoughts, such that it redounded onto his sensory appetite and showed in his face and voice in quite the normal way. Thinking humanly of how the Father had made his revelation not to the wise but to mere children just brought him delight, as well it might to us.

Lombardo thinks that such instances of joy would be simply impossible in a beatific Christ, just as he thinks that a beatific Christ could not have taken an interest in anything but God, as we saw in the last chapter. According to him, not only Christ's negative passions, but also his positive passions, are excluded by the beatific vision. Of Aquinas he writes: 'by the logic of his system, Christ had even less room to experience human joy than he did to experience human suffering'.[67] This means that all Christ's earthly intellectual joys would have been 'swallowed up and overwhelmed by his beatific joy'. The presupposition appears to be that the blessed are not able to experience finite joys because they would be suppressed by their overwhelming beatific joy. Again, we would appear to have an example of glory destroying nature rather than perfecting it. However, if glory does indeed perfect nature rather than destroy it, one must suspect that beatitude would enhance the saints' capacity for natural joys rather than impede it. The separated souls of the saints could take joy in the object of what natural knowledge they have apart from their bodies, and the risen will take joy in what they see through their glorified senses, namely, the risen bodies of Christ and the saints, and other contents of the new heaven and the new earth. Aquinas acknowledged the common joy of the saints in receiving their bodies at the resurrection.[68] Now when Aquinas envisioned a saint seeing an object in the new heavens and earth and giving glory to God for it, a possibility to which we adverted in Chapter 5, he also envisaged a distinct response of joy to what had been particularly perceived.[69] Such joys may seem paltry when compared with the beatific joy that arises from the vision of God, but it must be distinct joy nonetheless with its own value. Aquinas certainly allowed examples of 'accidental reward' to co-exist with the incomparable 'essential beatitude' of seeing God.[70] Perhaps it would be difficult for an earthly witness to distinguish a particular joy in the glorified face and voice of the risen saint, who would enjoy the repercussions of beatific joy throughout his whole being, but comparable acts of joy could hardly be difficult to distinguish visibly and audibly in the case of the earthly Christ, in whom this heavenly *redundantia* was not operative.

Would such examples of general repercussion of higher on lower be ruled out by Aquinas's principle that each power of Christ's humanity is allowed its

---

67. *Logic of Desire*, p. 217.
68. *Super Epistolam S. Pauli Apostoli ad Hebraeos lectura*, 11.8.
69. *Compendium*, 1.170.
70. Cf. *Summa Theologiae*, Suppl., q. 96, a. 1.

own activity? While Aquinas's opponents seem to suppose that they would be, could we interpret the principle in such a way that that need not necessarily be the case? The principle states that each power exercises its proper function. But, as Lombardo rightly points out, it is normal for there to be mutual engagement among the powers. Could we not say that it is part of what is proper to the intellectual appetite, in cases of greater intensity, that it have an impact on the sensory appetite? Can we not say that it is part of what is proper to the sensory appetite that it receive the impact of intense joy in the intellectual appetite? It seems to me that one thing the principle should definitely rule out is anything where there is an impact of one on another that is somehow unfitting for Christ. Hence the passions of the sensory appetite should arise only in tune with reason and not rise up so as to deflect reason. But why cannot the principle allow that one power can be naturally affected by another, when that is for good rather than for evil? Hence the pleasure that would come into the sensory appetite by way of a particular instance of intellectual joy in Christ would be something that would assist him at various times during his ministry. Developing the teaching of Pius XI, which we noted in Chapter 1, we could even conceive of Christ drawing from his vision of the divine essence finite *species* by which he had knowledge of the fact of future acts of reparation, and that he drew some solace from such thoughts. Of course there could be no pleasure that would be of any assistance to Christ right at the very end of his life, given that the point was for him voluntarily to assume the greatest pain and sorrow, without any relief. But that would simply mean that Christ would determine not to engage in human joyful or consoling thoughts but to hand himself over completely to suffering, giving consideration rather to his own bodily suffering and to the sins of the whole world.

What we are suggesting is that the earthly Christ would not have been entirely exceptional as regards the impact of the higher powers on the lower, because this natural interpenetration counts towards the proper working of these powers. While an exception would be made in the case of the repercussions of the beatific vision, so that Christ would be able to experience negative passions as was required for our salvation, he would not be an exception in terms of the more general working of human psychology where the higher affections redound onto the sensory appetite. Again, these repercussions could assist Christ in the carrying out of his mission, just as passions can be of help to us in our journey to God. This suggestion of a distinction between two kinds of top-down overflow, one of which is suspended and the other not, becomes more plausible when we consider that there may well be an intrinsic difference between the mode of the heavenly *redundantia* of glory and the mode of all other *redundantia* of higher onto lower powers. Aquinas does not really explain how the overflow from higher to lower ordinarily takes place, but scholars have attempted to fill out the details. Lombardo suggests that the vehemence of the will's affection leads to reason's forming of an intentional object that itself prompts a response in the sensory appetite.[71] Since Aquinas holds that our conceptual knowledge necessarily involves the use of sense

71. *Logic of Desire*, p. 90.

images, this explains how 'passions respond to concepts'. Lombardo attributes to Sherwin the following view:

> Since concepts are known through phantasms [sense images] abstracted from material objects, they are directly related to sense experience and thus the sense appetite, and so it follows naturally that the passions might respond to the apprehension of a concept.[72]

Cates likewise appeals to the close relation in Aquinas's thought between our immaterial intellectual acts and the need for them to be accompanied by the use of 'phantasms'. It is the involvement of such sensory images in the apprehension of a good that brings about the impact of intellectual joy in the sensory appetite and the body. Any such overflow, Cates says, 'must take place through the medium of sensory apprehension'.[73] This use of sensory images by the immaterial intellect is the 'pathway', we might say, by which there can be ordinary instances of *redundantia* from the intellectual affections to the sensory appetite.

When we come to the beatific vision, however, we encounter a unique case. This is because, as we saw in Chapter 4, this knowledge of the infinite divine essence cannot take place by means of any finite intelligible *species*, let alone any sensory image. Though the overflow of glory from higher to lower powers that takes place in the blessed is explained by Aquinas by reference to the natural union of soul and body, it cannot be explained in any more particular way by reference to the use of sensory images, just because there is no place for such images in the act of beatific vision itself. Thus we can distinguish two types of *redundantia* from higher to lower: that which we regularly experience through ordinary acts of knowledge where there is a turning to sense images, and that which is uniquely experienced by the blessed, where no such images are involved. What we are suggesting is that, in the case of the earthly Christ, it was divinely willed that the impact of his beatific vision on his sensory appetite be suspended, but not the impact of those other joys that were linked to ordinary acts of the intellect which make use of sense images. This would mean that Christ was very much like us in the everyday psychology of his human affectivity, sharing with us the possibility of intense acts of intellectual joy that brought pleasure in his sensory appetite and were manifested in his body. Where he would have differed from us in terms of the impact of higher powers on the lower would be in a single instance, and one we on earth do not share with the earthly Christ anyway. In this light, the extent to which he is exceptional should hardly be so great a problem that we would need to abandon the theory of his beatific vision. There is little here that can damage the authenticity of his humanity, where glory perfects nature. Even in his appearance to others there can have been nothing that would undermine the genuineness of his humanity according to their judgement, since the suspension of the overflow of higher to lower powers in a single case (which concerns something outside

---

72. Ibid., p. 91.
73. *Aquinas on the Emotions*, p. 222.

their own experience anyway) would not be visible to his contemporaries, while the negative passions this suspension allowed would have been a powerful visible testimony to his authentic human nature.

Lombardo has one final problem with Aquinas's presentation of Christ's passions, though it is not so much to do with Christ's beatific joy as with his beatific knowledge. Lombardo evidently thinks it important that Christ be able to experience fear exactly the way we do, as when we become frightened by something unknown to us. If that were not the case, he thinks, there would be an unacceptable discontinuity between Christ's affectivity and ours. This discontinuity would, however, be caused by Christ's possession of the beatific vision, which would give him knowledge of the object of his fear.[74] As we saw above, Aquinas certainly did not think Christ's fear in Gethsemene could be of the type Lombardo favours, since he certainly had knowledge of what he feared, that is, of his impending passion. Whether or not this is a problem that could only arise for Lombardo in view of Christ's beatific vision is doubtful. Even if Christ did not possess beatific knowledge of his coming passion, the Gospels clearly attribute to him some extraordinary knowledge of it, such that the removal of the beatific vision from Christ would not change the nature of his fear. Whether Aquinas thought Christ ever experienced the other kind of fear is equally doubtful, if only given the fact that he held Christ to have acquired a completed empirical knowledge during childhood. On this view, the speed of Christ's acquisition of knowledge may well have enabled him successfully to identify anything that went bump in the night. However, if we accept that Aquinas's account of the perfection of acquired knowledge is no longer viable and adopt the modified version of it suggested in Chapter 6, we could certainly allow this kind of fear in Christ, because he would not necessarily have acquired sufficient finite *species* through which to know the identity of everything that might give him a sudden fright. Of course he would have been able quickly to come to know the nature of the object, should he wish to, by supernatural means, if only because he was able to draw the pertinent *species* from the beatific vision, but that would hardly disallow the possibility of such spontaneous experiences of fear. Christ then need not be wholly unlike us in respect of fear.

Even if Aquinas's solution to the compatibility of Christ's joy and suffering does not introduce such grave problems for Christ's affectivity and the genuineness of his humanity as Lombardo supposes, there still remains the question of whether his solution is a necessity. For Torrell and Gondreau, suspension of the *redundantia* of Christ's glory, which they consider so inconvenient if logical and coherent, is totally unnecessary because Christ's beatific vision is *already* unnecessary. In other words, there is no need to make any exception of Christ in respect of the overflow from higher to lower powers, because he is no exception to the general rule that the beatific vision is received only after this life. In Chapter 2, we argued that Scripture portrays Christ in such a way that some theological explanation of his extraordinary but communicable knowledge is required, and that the beatific

---

74. *Logic of Desire*, p. 217.

vision presents itself as a possible part of the overall explanation. In contrast Torrell and Gondreau treat Aquinas's explanation as altogether unnecessary, because the descriptions of Christ's passion in the Gospels, while emphasizing the extent of his suffering, do not give any clue that Christ was experiencing intellectual joy. The fact that the beatific vision is not manifested in the Gospels' descriptions they take as evidence that it was not there. They do this despite the fact that, if Aquinas's theory of Christ's beatific vision and the suspension of its effects were true, its manifestation would be no less absent than if the vision were not there at all. It hardly seems right to expect the kind of theological reflection that leads to the theory of Christ's purely intellectual joy to be so straightforwardly represented in the descriptive narratives of the Gospels. Moreover, while we argued in Chapter 3 that there is also some very slight support for the theory of Christ's beatific vision in the Fathers, as well as good reasons for supposing the Fathers would on the whole not have had reason to think of it, Torrell without further ado simply asserts that they give it no support.[75]

Together with his view that there is nothing taught by the Magisterium to prevent the exploration of further theories, all this gives Torrell a starting point for explaining Scripture's broader picture of Christ the Teacher by his alternative theory of a prophetic light. When we examined this theory in Chapter 5, however, we saw that it runs into trouble, because it inevitably ascribes faith to Christ, which brings its own difficulties. Among these is the fact that the notion of faith is so ubiquitous in Scripture and the Fathers that one could reasonably suppose that, if Christ had had faith, they would have plainly attributed it to him. But they do not. We have argued that, in view of the problems that attributing faith to Christ brings, his beatific vision must provide the better theological explanation of the witness of the authorities of Catholic theology, so long as the objections to it can be met. In these last chapters, we have been attempting to show that not only can the objections of opponents be answered, but a beatific Christ presents us with a convincing picture of our Saviour, which should leave the Catholic theologian in no doubt that a vision of the Father in his human mind on earth is a true part of the theological explanation of his extraordinary knowledge. For the Catholic theologian, the earthly Christ's possession of the beatific vision should be a moral certainty.

There is one final objection we can put, one we can draw from Scripture itself. As we saw in Chapter 2, according to a theme running through the Bible, no one can see God and live: this mortal life and the vision of God are mutually exclusive. We concluded too how the writers of the New Testament could confidently believe in a future face to face vision of the Father, just as he is: then we shall no longer exist in our present mortal condition but rather beyond death in immortality. What, however, of the earthly Christ, since he too was mortal? How could he, who was to die for our salvation, see the Father? We might deal with this by distinguishing our own mortality, which is implicated in sin, from the mortality Christ assumed to save us from sin. Aquinas, however, explained the

75. 'S. Thomas d'Aquin et la science du Christ', p. 402.

ultimate basis of the inability of the pilgrims of this life to see God by reference to their natural mode of knowledge: while we naturally know here and now through *species* derived from sensory images, the essence of God cannot be seen through any such finite means.[76] We first saw in Chapter 4 how Aquinas interpreted Paul's being caught up to the third heaven as a transient glimpse of the divine essence. In explaining his view, he said that the apostle, as one in the pilgrim state, needed to be withdrawn from the normal workings of sensory images and from the senses.[77] Paul was thus briefly in a middle state between this life and the next, where he was still potentially in this life, though temporarily not in it with regard to act.[78] At the resurrection Paul, like all the saints, will enjoy both the vision of God and an enhanced natural knowledge, because then the body and its senses will be perfected through the overflow of glory from the soul, with the body now made immortal. At the resurrection there will be no need for Paul to be snatched from glorified senses. However, as we recalled in the last two chapters, there is a radical difference here between the earthly Paul and the earthly Christ, who, though a pilgrim in regard to his mortal body, was always a *comprehensor* with regard to his intellect. While natural knowledge belonged to Paul first, long before his rapture, Christ enjoyed the knowledge of the next life from the very first moment of his conception. Jesus was never suddenly caught up from one means of knowledge to another, from the earthly to the heavenly, but his natural knowledge developed and was nurtured within the context of an ever-present vision. Hence, the glorification of his body was not required for the perfect harmony of the knowledge of the next life and of this, and he was uniquely able both to live in this mortal life and to see the Father. Yet again he was fittingly an exception, for the purpose of our salvation.

On a deeper meaning of the Scriptural text, however, we may say in conclusion that the earthly Christ was no exception to the biblical rule at all. If no one may see God in this life and live, then this too may be said of Christ. He saw the Father, and he died. He saw the Father, and he had to die. Though more than thirty years may elapse between his being blessed with the vision of God and his death on the cross, these two are profoundly linked. In one sense it is precisely because he saw God that, humanly speaking, he opened his arms on the cross and gave up his life on our behalf, doing not his own will but the will of the Father. In his ineffable vision of the divine essence he saw all that pertained to his mission, including those for whom he must die if they were to be saved from sin and death. It was out of his immense, unsurpassable charity, which arose from his vision of the Father, that he loved us, loved me, and offered himself for our salvation, gave himself for me. It was by this beatific love that he merited the beatific vision, not for himself who already enjoyed it, but for others. Thus was he their Saviour, opening the gate of heaven and drawing them to share his own vision of the Father for all eternity.

76. *Summa*, 1a., q. 12, a. 11.
77. Ibid., 2a.2ae., q. 175, a. 4.
78. Ibid., 2a.2ae., q. 180, a. 5.

BIBLIOGRAPHY

Magisterial Documents

Papal Documents

Benedict XII, *Benedictus Deus*. DH 1000–2.
Benedict XVI, *Ad Romanam Curiam ob omina natalicia*. AAS 98 (2006), pp. 40–53.
Francis, *Lumen Fidei*. AAS 105 (2013), pp. 555–96.
Gregory the Great, *Epistula ad Eulogium, Sicut aqua frigida*. DH 474–6.
John Paul II, *Novo Millennio Ineunte*. AAS 93 (2001), pp. 266–309.
Leo the Great, *Tomus ad Flavianum, Lectis dilectionis tuae*. DH 290–5.
Pius IV, *Iniunctum Nobis*. DH 1862–70.
Pius XI, *Miserentissimus Redemptor*. AAS 20 (1928), pp. 165–78.
Pius XII, *Mystici Corporis Christi*. DH 3800-22; AAS 35 (1943), pp. 200–43.
Pius XII, *Haurietis Aquas*. AAS 48 (1956), pp. 309–53.

Conciliar Documents

First Council of Nicaea, *Symbolum Nicaenum*. DH 125–26.
Council of Chalcedon, *De duabus naturis in Christo*. DH 300–3.
Third Council of Constantinople, *Definitio de duabus in Christo voluntatibus et operationibus*. DH 553–9.
Council of Vienne, *Ad Nostrum Qui*. DH 891–9.
Council of Florence, *Laetentur Caeli*. DH 1300–8.
Council of Trent, *Decretum de iustificatione*. DH 1520–83.
First Vatican Council, *Dei Filius*. DH 3000–45.
Second Vatican Council, *Dei Verbum*. DH 4201–35.

Catechetical Documents

Catechismus Catholicae Ecclesiae (Vatican: Libreria Editrice Vaticana, 1997).

Congregation for the Doctrine of the Faith (Holy Office)

Congregation for the Doctrine of the Faith, *Notificatio de Operibus P. Jon Sobrino, S. I.* DH 5107; AAS 99 (2007), pp. 181–94.
Holy Office, *Lamentabili*. DH 3401–66.
Holy Office, *Circa Quasdam Propositiones de Scientia Animae Christi*. DH 3645–7.

Commissions

International Theological Commission, 'Select Questions on Christology' in M. Sharkey
(ed.), *International Theological Commission: Texts and Documents 1969–1985* (San
Francisco: Ignatius, 1989), pp. 185–205.
International Theological Commission, 'Theology, Christology, Anthropology' in
M. Sharkey (ed.), *International Theological Commission: Texts and Documents
1969–1985* (San Francisco: Ignatius, 1989), pp. 207–23.
International Theological Commission, 'The Consciousness of Christ concerning himself
and his mission' in M. Sharkey (ed.), *International Theological Commission: Texts and
Documents 1969–1985* (San Francisco: Ignatius, 1989), pp. 305–16.
Pontifical Biblical Commission, *Instructio de Historica Evangeliorum Veritate. AAS* 56
(1964), pp. 712–18.

Ancient Authors

Ambrose, *De Fide ad Gratianum.* CSEL 78.
Ambrose, *De Incarnationis Dominicae Sacramento.* CSEL 79, pp. 223–81.
Ambrose, *Expositio Evangelii secundum Lucam.* CCSL 14.
Anthimus, *Sermo ad Iustinianum.* Eds J. D. Mansi et al., *Sacrorum conciliorum nova et
amplissima collectio* (31 vols; Florence: Zatta, 1759–93), vol. 11, cols. 440–1.
Athanasius, *Orationes contra Arianos.* Ed. K. Metzler and K. Savvidis, *Athanasius Werke*
(Berlin: Walter De Gruyter, 1934ff.), 1.1.2–3.
Augustine, *De Genesi ad Litteram.* CSEL 28.1
Augustine, *De Libero Arbitrio.* CCSL 29, pp. 205–321.
Augustine, *Epistulae.* CSEL 34, 44, 57, 88.
Augustine, *De Civitate Dei.* CCSL 47–8.
Augustine, *De Doctrina Christiana.* Ed. R. H. P. Green (Oxford: Clarendon, 1988).
Augustine, *De Spiritu et Littera.* CSEL 60, pp. 153–300.
Augustine, *Retractationes.* CCSL 57.
Augustine, *De Sermo Domini in Monte.* CCSL 35.
Augustine, *De Trinitate.* CCSL 50.
Augustine, *De Diversis Quaestionibus LXXXIII.* CCSL 44A, pp. 1–249.
Augustine, *De Peccatorum Meritis et Remissione et de Baptismo Parvulorum.* CSEL 60.
Augustine, *Contra Maximinum Haereticum Arianorum Episcopum.* PL 42.
Augustine, *In Johannis Evangelium Tractatus.* CCSL 36, pp. 1–42.
Basil, *Contra Eunomium.* SC 299, 305.
Basil, *Epistulae.* Ed. Y. Courtonne, *Lettres* (Paris: Belles Lettres, 1957–66).
Clement of Alexandria, *Stromata.* GCS 52; 17, pp. 1–102.
Cyprian, *Epistulae.* CCSL 3B–C.
Cyril of Alexandria, *Apologeticus contra Theodoretum pro XII Capitibus.* Ed. P. E. Pusey,
*Sancti Patris Nostri Cyrilli Archiepiscopi Alexandrini Epistolae Tres Oecumenicae, Libri
Quinque contra Nestorium, XII Capitum Explanatio, XII Capitum Defensio Utraque,
Scholia de Incarnatione Unigeniti* (Oxford: Clarendon, 1875).
Cyril of Alexandria, *Epistulae Paschalis.* SC 434.
Cyril of Alexandria, *Commentarii in Ioannem.* Ed. P. E. Pusey, *Sancti Patris Nostri Cyrilli
Archiepiscopi Alexandrini in D. Joannis Evangelium* (3 vols; Oxford: Clarendon, 1872).
Cyril of Alexandria, *De Sancta et Consubstantiali Trinitate.* SC 231, 237, 246.

Cyril of Alexandria, *Thesaurus de Sancta et Consubstantiali Trinitate*. PG 75, cols. 9–656.

Didymus the Blind, *De Trinitate*. PG 39, cols. 269–992.

Dionysius the Aeropagite, *De Divinis Nominibus*. PTS 33.

Epiphanius, *Ancoratus*. GCS 25, pp. 1–149.

Fulgentius, *Ad Trasimundum Regem Vandalorum Libri Tres*. CCSL 91, pp. 95–185.

Fulgentius, *Epistula 14, Ad Ferrandum Diaconum de Quinque Quaestionbus*. CCSL 91, pp. 387–444.

Gregory the Great, *Moralia in Job*. CCSL 148–148B.

Gregory of Nazianzus, *Orationes*. SC 247, 309, 405, 270, 284, 250, 318, 358, 384.

Gregory of Nyssa, *De Vita Moysis*. H. Musurillo in W. Jaeger and H. Langerbeck (eds), *Gregorii Nysseni Opera* (Leiden: Brill, 1952ff.), 7.1.

Gregory of Nyssa, *De Beatitudinibus*. Ed. J. F. Callahan in *Gregorii Nysseni Opera*, 7.2.

Gregory of Nyssa, *Antirrheticus Adversus Apollinarium*. Ed. F. Mueller in *Gregorii Nysseni Opera*, 3.1, pp. 129–233.

Irenaeus, *Adversus Haereses*. SC 263, 293, 210, 211, 100, 152, 153.

Jerome, *Tractatus in Marci Evangelium*. CCSL 78, pp. 449–500.

Jerome, *Epistulae*. CSEL 54–6.

John Chrysostom, *De Incomprehensibili Dei Natura*. SC 28bis.

John Chrysostom, *Homiliae in Matthaeum*. Eds. F. Field et al., *Sancti Patris Nostri Joannis Chrysostomi Archiepiscopi Constantinopolitani Homiliae in Matthaeum* (3 vols; Cambridge: In Officina Academica, 1839).

John Chrysostom, *Homiliae in Epistolam ad Hebraeos. Sancti Patris Nostri Joannis Chrysostomi Archiepiscopi Constantinopolitani in Divi Pauli Epistolam ad Hebraeos Homiliae XXXIV* (Oxford: Wright, 1862).

John of Damascus, *Expositio Fidei*. PTS 12.

Leontius of Byzantium, *Contra Nestorianos et Eutychianos*. PG 86, cols. 1267–396.

Leontius the Scholastic, *De Sectis*. PG 86, cols. 1193–268.

Maximus the Confessor, *Centuriae de Caritate*. SC 9.

Maximus the Confessor, *Quaestiones et Dubia*. CCSG 10.

Origen, *De Principiis*. GCS 22.

Origen, *Commentarii ad Romanos*. PG 14, cols. 833–1292.

Origen, *Commentarii in Matthaeum*. GCS 38, 40–1.

Origen, *Commentarii in Ioannem*. SC 120, 157, 222, 290, 385.

Photius, *Bibliotheca*. Ed. R. Henry, *Bibliothèque* (9 vols; Paris: Belles Lettres, 1959–91).

Severus of Antioch, *Liber Contra Impium Grammaticum*. Latin tr. CSCO 102.

Theodoret of Cyrus, *Interpretatio Epistolae ad Ephesios*. PG 82, cols. 505–58.

Theodosius, *Tomus ad Theodoram Augustam*. Latin tr. OLA 56, pp. 42–56.

Theophilus, *Ad Autolycum* (ed. R. M. Grant; Oxford Early Christian Texts; Oxford: Clarendon, 1970).

Medieval and Early Modern Authors

Abelard, P., *Sententie*. CCCM 14.

Alcuin, *De Fide Sanctae Trinitatis et de Incarnatione Christi*. CCCM 249.

Alexander of Hales, *Glossa in Quatuor Libros Sententiarum* (4 vols; Florence: Quaracchi, 1951–7).

Alexander of Hales, *Summa Theologica* (4 vols; Florence: Ad Claras Aquas, 1924–48).

Anselm of Canterbury, *Cur Deus Homo. S. Anselmi Cantuariensis Archiepiscopi Opera Omnia* (ed. F. S. Schmitt; 6 vols; Edinburgh: Nelson, 1946–61), vol. 2, pp. 37–133.

Anselm of Canterbury, *De Libertate Arbitrii. Opera Omnia*, vol. 1, pp. 207–26.

Bonaventure, *Commentaria in Quatuor Libros Sententiarum* (Opera Theologica Selecta; ed. L. M. Bello, 4 vols; Florence: Ad Claras Aquas, 1934–49).

Candidus [Hwita/Wizo], *Epistola num Christus Corporeis Oculis Deum Videre Potuerit.* PL 106, cols. 103–8.

Candidus, *Opusculum de Passione Domini.* PL 106, cols. 57–104.

Cano, M., *De Locis Theologicis.* Ed. J. P. Migne, *Theologiae Cursus Completus*, vol. 1 (Paris: Migne, 1839), cols. 59–716.

Duns Scotus, *Ordinatio. Opera Omnia* (eds C. Balić et al.; Vatican: Vatican, 1950–), vol. 1.

Pétau, D. [Dionysius Petavius], *Opus de Theologicis Dogmatibus*, vol. 6: *De Incarnatione Verbi* (Barri-Ducis: Guerin, 1869).

Peter Lombard, *Sententiae in IV Libris Distinctae* (Spicilegium Bonaventurianum, 4–5; Grottaferrata: Ad Claras Aquas, 1971–81).

Poinsot, J. [John of St Thomas], *Cursus Theologicus in Summam Theologicam D. Thomae* (10 vols; Paris: Vivès, 1883–86).

Salmanticenses, *Collegii Salmanticensi Cursus Theologicus Summam d. Thomae Complectens* (20 vols; Paris: Palmé, 1870–83).

Suárez, F. *De divina substantia et ejusque attributis. Opera Omnia* (28 vols; Paris: Vivès, 1856–78), vol. 1, pp. 1–234.

Thomas Aquinas, *Catena aurea in quatuor Evangelia* (ed. A. Guarenti; 2 vols; Rome and Turin: Marietti, 1953).

Thomas Aquinas, *Compendium Theologiae seu brevis compilatio theologiae ad fratrem Raynaldum.* LC 42, pp. 83–205.

Thomas Aquinas, *Lectura super Ioannem.* Ed. R. Cai, *Super Evangelium S. Ioannis Lectura* (5th rev. edn; Turin and Rome: Marietti, 1952).

Thomas Aquinas, *Quaestiones Disputatae de Anima.* LC 24/1.

Thomas Aquinas, *Quaestiones Disputatae de Veritate.* LC 22/1–3.

Thomas Aquinas, *Scriptum super Sententiis magistri Petri Lombardi* (eds P. Mandonnet and M. F. Moos; 4 vols; Paris: Lethielleux, 1929–47).

Thomas Aquinas, *Summa contra Gentiles.* LC 13–15.

Thomas Aquinas, *Summa Theologiae* (ed. T. Gilby; 61 vols; London: Eyre & Spottiswoode, 1964–81).

Thomas Aquinas, *Super Epistolam S. Pauli Apostoli ad Hebraeos lectura* (Turin: Marietti, 1929).

Modern Authors

Adam, K., *The Christ of Faith* (London: Burns, Oates & Washbourne, 1957).

Adams, M. M., *Christ and Horrors: The Coherence of Christology* (Cambridge: CUP, 2006).

Allen, R. M., *The Christ's Faith: A Dogmatic Account* (London and New York: T&T Clark, 2009).

Allison, D., *Jesus of Nazareth: Millenarian Prophet* (Minneapolis, MN: Fortress, 1998).

Anderson, G. A., 'To See Where God Dwells: The Tabernacle, the Temple, and the Origins of the Christian Mystical Tradition', *LS* 4 (2008): 13–45.

Ashley, B. M., 'The Extent of Jesus' Human Knowledge According to the Fourth Gospel' in M. Dauphinais and M. Levering (eds), *Reading John with St. Thomas Aquinas: Theological Exegesis and Speculative Theology* (Washington, DC: CUA, 2005), pp. 241–53.

Attridge, H. W., *The Epistle to the Hebrews: A Commentary on the Epistle to the Hebrews* (Hermeneia – A Critical and Historical Commentary on the Bible; Philadelphia: Fortress, 1989).

Ayres, L., *Nicaea and its Legacy: An Approach to Fourth-Century Trinitarian Theology* (Oxford: OUP, 2004).

Barnes, C. L., *Christ's Two Wills in Scholastic Thought: The Christology of Aquinas and its Historical Contexts* (Toronto: PIMS, 2012).

Barrett, C. K., *A Commentary on the First Epistle to the Corinthians* (Black's New Testament Commentaries; London: Black, 2nd edn, 1971).

Barton, J., *Oracles of God: Perceptions of Ancient Prophecy in Israel after the Exile* (Oxford: OUP, new edn, 2007).

Bathrellos, D., *The Byzantine Christ: Person, Nature, and Will in the Christology of Saint Maximus the Confessor* (Oxford and New York: OUP, 2004).

Bauckham, R., *Jesus and the Eyewitnesses: The Gospels as Eyewitness Testimony* (Grand Rapids, MI and Cambridge: Eerdmans, 2006).

Billot, L., *De Verbo Incarnato* (Rome: Gregorian, 7th edn, 1927).

Bird, M. and Sprinkle, P. M., *The Faith of Jesus Christ: Exegetical, Biblical, and Theological Studies* (Milton Keynes: Paternoster; Colorado Springs and Hyderabad: Hendrickson, 2009).

Bogliolo, L., 'Strutture Antropologiche e visione beatifica dell'anima di Cristo', *DC* 36 (1983): 331–46.

Boland, V., *St Thomas Aquinas* (Continuum Library of Educational Thought, vol. 1; London and New York: Continuum, 2007).

Boxall, I., *The Revelation of Saint John* (Black's New Testament Commentaries; London and New York: Continuum, 2006).

Brown, R. E., *New Testament Reading Guide: The Gospel of St. John and the Johannine Epistles* (Collegeville, MN: Liturgical, 1960).

Brown, R. E., *The Gospel According to John* (New York: Doubleday, 1966).

Brown, R. E., *Jesus, God and Man* (London and Dublin: Chapman, 1968).

Brown, R. E., *The Critical Meaning of the Bible* (London: Cassell, 1982).

Brown, R. E., *An Introduction to New Testament Christology* (New York: Doubleday, 1997).

Brownsberger, W. L., *Jesus the Mediator* (Washington, DC: CUA, 2013).

Bultmann, R., *The Johannine Epistles: A Commentary on the Johannine Epistles* (trans. R. P. O'Hara, L. C. McGaughy and R. Funk; Hermeneia – A Critical and Historical Commentary on the Bible; Philadephia: Fortress, 1973).

Byrskog, S., *Jesus the Only Teacher: Didactic Authority and Transmission in Ancient Israel, Ancient Judaism and the Matthean Community* (Stockholm: Almqvist & Wiksell International, 1994).

Byrskog, S., *Story as History – History as Story: The Gospel Tradition in the Context of Ancient Oral History* (Leiden: Brill, 2002).

Cates, D. F., *Aquinas on the Emotions: A Religious-Ethical Enquiry* (Washington, DC: Georgetown, 2009).

Cessario R., 'Incarnate Wisdom and the Immediacy of Christ's Salvific Knowledge' in *Problemi Teologici Alla Luce dell'Aquinate* (Studi Tomistici, 44:5; Vatican: Vaticana, 1991), pp. 334–40.

Clayton, Jr., P. B., *The Christology of Theodoret of Cyrus: Antiochene Christology from the Council of Ephesus (431) to the Council of Chalcedon (451)* (Oxford and New York: OUP, 2007).

Colish, M., *Peter Lombard* (2 vols; Leiden: Brill, 1994).

Collins, R. F., *First Corinthians* (Sacra Pagina, 7; Collegeville, MN: Liturgical, 1999).

Congar, Y., *Jesus Christ* (trans. L. O'Neill; Chapman: London, 1966).

Conzelmann, H., *1 Corinthians: A Commentary on the First Epistle to the Corinthians* (trans. J. W. Leitch; Hermeneia – A Critical and Historical Commentary on the Bible; Philadelphia: Fortress, 1975).

Corvez, M., 'Le Christ voyait-il l'essence de Dieu pendant sa vie mortelle?', *DC* 36 (1983): 406–11.

Cross, R., 'Incarnation' in T. Flint and M. Rea (eds), *The Oxford Handbook of Philosophical Theology* (Oxford: OUP, 2009), pp. 452–75.

Crouzel, H., *Origen* (trans. A. S. Worrall; Edinburgh: T. & T. Clark, 1989).

Crowe, F. E., 'The Mind of Jesus', *Communio* 1 (1974): 365–84.

Crowe, F. E., 'Eschaton and Worldly Mission in the Mind and Heart of Jesus' in *Appropriating the Lonergan Idea* (Buffalo TOR and London: University of Toronto, 2006), pp. 193–234.

Davies, W. D. and Allison, D. C., *A Critical and Exegetical Commentary on the Gospel According to Saint Matthew* (International Critical Commentary on the Holy Scriptures of the Old and New Testaments; 3 vols; Edinburgh: T&T Clark, 1988).

De la Taille, M., *The Mystery of Faith Regarding the Most August Sacrament and Sacrifice of the Body and Blood of Christ* (2 vols; New York: Sheed & Ward, 1940–50).

De Lavalette, H., 'Candide, Théologien Méconnu de la Vision Béatifique du Christ', *RSR* 49 (1961): 426–9.

De Margerie, B., *The Human Knowledge of Christ: The Knowledge, Fore-knowledge and Consciousness, Even in the Pre-paschal Period, of Christ the Redeemer* (Boston, MA: St Paul's, 1980).

Donahue, J. R. and Harrington, D. J., *The Gospel of Mark* (Collegeville, MN: Liturgical, 2002).

Dubarle, A.-M., 'La connaissance humaine du Christ', *RSPT* 29 (1940): 244–63.

Dubarle, A.-M., 'La connaissance humaine du Christ d'après Saint Augustin', *ETL* 18 (1941): 5–25.

Dulles, A., *The Assurance of the Things Hoped For: A Theology of Christian Faith* (New York and Oxford: OUP, 1994).

Dulles, A., 'Jesus and Faith', in D. Kendall and S. T. Davis, *The Convergence of Theology: A Festschrift Honoring Gerald O'Collins, S.J.* (New York and Mahwah, NJ: Paulist, 2001), pp. 273–84.

Duquoc, C., *Christologie: Essai Dogmatique*: vol.1: *L'homme Jésus* (Paris: Cerf, 1968).

Durand, A., 'La science du Christ', *NRT* 71 (1949): 497–503.

Durand, E., *L'Offre universelle du salut en Christ* (Paris: Cerf, 2012).

Elliott, M. W., 'Πίστις Χριστοῦ in the Church Fathers and Beyond' in M. Bird and P. M. Sprinkle, *The Faith of Jesus Christ: Exegetical, Biblical, and Theological Studies* (Milton Keynes: Paternoster; Colorado Springs and Hyderabad: Hendrickson, 2009), pp. 277–89.

Emery, G., *The Trinitarian Theology of St Thomas Aquinas* (Oxford and New York: OUP, 2007).

Ernst, J. T., *Die Lehre der Hochmittelalterlichen Theologen von der Vollkommenen Erkenntnis Christi: Ein Versuch zur Auslegung der klassischen Dreiteilung: Visio Beata, Scientia Infusa und Scientia Acquisita* (Freiburg etc.: Herder, 1971).

Evans, C. A., 'Patristic Interpretations of Mark 2:26: "When Abiathar was High Priest"', *VC* 40 (1986): 183–86.

Farrell, J. P., *Free Choice in St. Maximus the Confessor* (South Canaan, PA: St Tikhon's, 1989).

Fee, G. D., *The First Epistle to the Corinthians* (Grand Rapids, MI: Eerdmans, 1987).

Feuillet, A., 'La science de vision de Jésus et les Évangiles. Recherche exégétique', *DC* 36 (1983): 158–79.

Foster, P., 'Πίστις Χριστοῦ Terminology in Philippians and Ephesians' in M. Bird and P. M. Sprinkle, *The Faith of Jesus Christ: Exegetical, Biblical, and Theological Studies* (Milton Keynes: Paternoster; Colorado Springs and Hyderabad: Hendrickson, 2009), pp. 91–109.

France, R. T., *The Gospel of Matthew* (New International Commentary on the New Testament; Grand Rapids, MI and Cambridge: Eerdmans, 2007).

Friedrich, G. (ed.), *Theological Dictionary of the New Testament* (trans. G. W. Bromiley, 10 vols; Grand Rapids, MI: Eerdmans, 1964–76).

Gaine, S. F., *Will there be Free Will in Heaven?: Freedom, Impeccability and Beatitude* (London and New York: T&T Clark, 2003).

Gaine, S. F., 'Christ's Acquired Knowledge according to Thomas Aquinas: How Aquinas's Philosophy Helped and Hindered his Account', *NB* 96 (2015): 255–68.

Galot J., *Who is Christ?: A Theology of the Incarnation* (trans. M. A. Bouchard; Chicago: Franciscan Herald, 1981).

Galot J., 'Le Christ terrestre et la vision', *Gregorianum* 67 (1986): 429–50.

Galtier, P., 'L'enseignement des Pères sur la vision béatifique dans le Christ', *RSR* 15 (1925): 54–68.

Galtier, P., *De Incarnatione ac Redemptione* (9th edn, Paris: Beauchesne, 1947).

Galtier, P., 'La conscience humaine du Christ', *Gregorianum* 35 (1954): 225–46.

Garrigou-Lagrange, R., *Our Savior and His Love for Us* (trans. A Bouchard; St Louis and London: Herder, 1951).

Gondreau, P., *The Passions of Christ's Soul in the Theology of St. Thomas Aquinas* (Beiträge zur Geschichte der Philosophie und Theologie des Mittelalters, Neue Folge 61; Münster: Aschendorff, 2002).

Gondreau, P., 'The Passions and the Moral Life: Appreciating the Originality of Aquinas', *TTh* 71 (2007): 419–50.

Gondreau, P., 'Aquinas, the Communication of Idioms, and the Suffering of Christ' in J. F. Keating and T. J. White (eds), *Divine Impassibility and the Mystery of Human Suffering* (Grand Rapids, MI and Cambridge: Eerdmans, 2009), pp. 214–45.

Grillmeier, A. and Hainthaler, T., *Christ in Christian Tradition*, vol. 2/2 (trans. J. Cawte and P. Allen; London: Mowbray; Louisville, KY: WJK, 1995).

Gumerlock, F. X., 'Mark 13:32 and Christ's Supposed Ignorance: Four Patristic Solutions', *TJ* 28 (2007): 205–13.

Gutwenger, E., 'Das menschliche Wissen des irdischen Christus', *ZKT* 76 (1954): 170–86.

Gutwenger, E., *Bewusstsein und Wissen Christi: Eine dogmatische Studie* (Innsbruck: Felizian Rauch, 1960).

Gutwenger, E., 'The Problem of Christ's Knowledge', *Concilium* 1 (1966): 48–55.

Hagner, D. A., *Matthew 1–13* (Word Biblical Commentary, 33A; Dallas, TX: Word, 1993).

Hanby, M., 'These Three Abide: Augustine and the Eschatological Non-Obsolescence of Faith', *PE* 13 (2005): 340–60.

Hanson, A. T., 'Two Consciousnesses: The Modern Version of Chalcedon', *SJT* 37 (1984): 471–83.

Harrington, D. J., *The Gospel of Matthew* (Sacra Pagina, 1; Collegeville, MN: Liturgical, 1991).

Harrison, C., *Beauty and Revelation in the Thought of St. Augustine* (Oxford: Clarendon, 1992).

Harrisville, R. A., 'ΠΙΣΤΙΣ ΧΡΙΣΤΟΥ: Witness of the Fathers', *NT* 36 (1994): 233–41.

Harrisville, R. A., 'Before ΠΙΣΤΙΣ ΧΡΙΣΤΟΥ: The Objective Genitive as Good Greek', *NT* 48 (2006): 353–8.

Haubst, R., 'Die Gottesanschauung und das natürliche Erkenntniswachstum Christi', *TQ* 137 (1957): 385–412.

Hayes, Z. (ed.), *Works of St. Bonaventure*, vol. 5: *Disputed Questions on the Knowledge of Christ* (Bonaventure Texts in Translation Series; St Bonaventure, NY: Franciscan Institute: 2005).

Hays, R. B., 'ΠΙΣΤΙΣ ΧΡΙΣΤΟΥ and Pauline Christology', in E. E. Johnson and D. M. Hay, *Pauline Theology*, vol. 4: *Looking Back, Pressing On* (Atlanta: Scholars, 1997), pp. 35–60.

Healy Jr., N. J. 'The Filial Mode of Christ's Knowledge', *NV* 11 (2013): 341–55.

Hiebert, T., 'Theophany in the OT' in D. N. Freedman et al. (eds), *The Anchor Bible Dictionary* (6 vols; New York and London: Doubleday, 1992), vol. 6, pp. 505–11.

Hill, W., *Proper Relations to the Indwelling Divine Persons* (Washington, DC: Thomist, 1955).

Hooker, M., 'ΠΙΣΤΙΣ ΧΡΙΣΤΟΥ', *NTS* 35 (1989): 321–42.

Houlden, J. L., *A Commentary on the Johannine Epistles* (Black's New Testament Commentaries; London: Black, 2nd edn, 1994).

Howard, G., 'Faith of Christ' in D. N. Freedman et al., *The Anchor Bible Dictionary* (New York, London etc.: Doubleday, 1992), vol. 2, pp. 758–60.

Hunn, D., 'Debating the Faithfulness of Jesus Christ in Twentieth-Century Scholarship' in M. Bird and P. M. Sprinkle, *The Faith of Jesus Christ: Exegetical, Biblical, and Theological Studies* (Milton Keynes: Paternoster; Colorado Springs and Hyderabad: Hendrickson, 2009), pp. 15–31.

Iammarrone, L., 'La visione beatifica di Cristo Viatore nel pensiero di San Tommaso', *DC* 36 (1983): 287–30.

Jedwab, J., 'The Incarnation and Unity of Consciousness' in A. Marmodoro and J. Hill (eds), *The Metaphysics of the Incarnation* (Oxford: OUP, 2011), pp. 168–85.

Jugie, A. M., 'La béatitude et la science parfaite de l'âme de Jésus Viateur d'après Léonce de Byzance et quelques autres théologiens byzantins', *RSPT* 10 (1921): 548–59.

Kasper, W., *Jesus the Christ* (London: Burns & Oates; New York: Paulist, 1976).

Klimczak, P., *Christus Magister: Le Christ Maître dans les commentaires évangeliques de saint Thomas d'Aquin* (Fribourg: Academic, 2013).

Kromholtz, B., *On the Last Day: The Time of the Resurrection of the Dead according to Thomas Aquinas* (Fribourg: Academic, 2010).

Lagrange, M.-J., *Évangile selon Saint Jean* (Paris: Victor Lecoffre, 1927).

Lagrange, M.-J., *Évangile selon Saint Marc* (Paris: Victor Lecoffre, 1929).

Lane, W. L., *The Gospel of Mark* (The New International Commentary on the New Testament; Grand Rapids, MI: Eerdmans, 1974).

Lebreton, J., *History of the Dogma of the Trinity From its Origins to the Council of Nicaea*, vol. 1: *The Origins* (London: Burns, Oates & Washbourne, 1939).

Leeming, B., 'The Human Knowledge of Christ', *ITQ* 19 (1952): 135–47, 234–53.

Leget, C., *Living with God: Thomas Aquinas on the Relation between Life on Earth and 'Life' after Death* (Leuven: Peeters, 1997).

Levering, M., *Christ's Fulfillment of Torah and Temple: Salvation According to Thomas Aquinas* (Notre Dame: University of Notre Dame Press, 2002).

Levering, M., *Jesus and the Demise of Death: Resurrection, Afterlife, and the Fate of the Christian* (Waco, TX: Baylor, 2012).

Lévy, A., *Le créé et l'incréé: Maxime le confesseur et Thomas d'Aquin* (Bibliothèque Thomiste 59; Paris: Vrin, 2006).

Loisy, A., 'L'Apocalypse Synoptique', *RB* 5 (1896): 173–98, 335–59.

Loke, A., 'The Incarnation and Jesus' Apparent Limitation in Knowledge', *NB* 94 (2013): 583–602.

Lombardo, N. E., *The Logic of Desire: Aquinas on Emotion* (Washington, DC: CUA, 2011).

Lonergan, B., *De Verbo Incarnato* (Rome: Gregorian, 3rd edn, 1964).

Lonergan, B., *The Ontological and Psychological Constitution of Christ* (Ontario and London: University of Toronto, 2002).

Lossky, V., *The Vision of God* (trans. A. Moorhouse; 2nd edn; Crestwood, NY: St Vladimir's, 1983).

Ludlow, M., 'Divine Infinity and Eschatology: The Limits and Dynamics of Human Knowledge according to Gregory of Nyssa (*CE* II 67–170)' in L. Karfíková, S. Douglass and J. Zacchuber (eds), *Gregory of Nyssa: Contra Eunomium II: An English Version with Supporting Studies* (Supplements to Vigiliae Christianae, 82; Leiden and Boston: Brill, 2007), pp. 217–37.

Lupieri, E. F., *A Commentary on the Apocalypse* (trans. M. P. Johnson and A. Kamesar; Italian Texts and Studies on Religion and Society; Grand Rapids, MI and Cambridge: Eerdmans, 2006).

Lyons, E., 'His Own Person or Divine Puppet?' in M. A. Hayes and L. Gearon, *Contemporary Catholic Theology: A Reader* (Leominster: Gracewing, 1998), pp. 251–8.

Madigan, K., *The Passions of Christ in High-Medieval Thought: An Essay on Christological Development* (Oxford and New York: OUP, 2007).

Maillard, P.-Y., *La Vision de Dieu chez Thomas d'Aquin: Une lecture de l' "In Ioannem" à la lumière de ses sources augustiniennes* (Paris: Vrin, 2001).

Mansini, G., 'Understanding St. Thomas on Christ's Immediate Knowledge of God', *TTh* 59 (1995): 91–124.

Marenbon, J., 'Candidus' in H. C. G. Matthew and B. H. Harrison (eds), *Oxford Dictionary of National Biography from the Earliest Times to the Year 2000* (60 vols; Oxford: OUP, 2004), vol. 9, pp. 888–9.

Maritain, J., *On the Grace and Humanity of Jesus* (trans. J. W. Evans; New York: Herder, 1969).

Marshall, I. H., *New Testament Theology: Many Witnesses, One Gospel* (Downers Grove, IL: Intervarsity, 2004).

Matlock, R. B., '"Even the Demons Believe": Paul and πίστις Χριστοῦ', *CBQ* 64 (2002): 300–18.

McCabe, H., *God Matters* (London: Chapman, 1987).

McCool, G. A., *Nineteenth-Century Scholasticism: The Search for a Unitary Method* (New York: Fordham, 1989).

McDermott, J. M., 'How Did Jesus Know He Was God? The Ontological Psychology of Mark 10:17–22', *ITQ* 74 (2009): 272–97.

Michel, A. 'Science de Jésus-Christ', *DTC* 14 (1941), cols. 1628–65.

Milner, R., *Thomas Aquinas on the Passions* (Cambridge: CUP, 2009).

Moloney, F. J., *The Gospel of John* (Sacra Pagina, 4; Collegeville, MN: Liturgical, 1998).

Moloney, R., 'The Mind of Christ in Transcendental Theology: Rahner, Lonergan and Crowe', *HJ* 25 (1984): 288–300.

Moloney, R., 'Approaches to Christ's Knowledge in the Patristic Era' in T. Finan and V. Twomey (eds), *Studies in Patristic Christology* (Dublin: Four Courts, 1998), pp. 37–66.

Moloney, R., *The Knowledge of Christ* (London, and New York: Continuum, 1999).

Mongeau, G., 'The Human and Divine Knowing of the Incarnate Word', *JJT* 12 (2005): 30–42.

Morris, T. V., *The Logic of God Incarnate* (Ithaca and London: Cornell, 1986).

Most, W. G., *The Consciousness of Christ* (Front Royal, VA: Christendom, 1980).

Nicolas, M. J., 'Voir Dieu dans la "condition charnelle"', *DC* 36 (1983): 384–94.

O'Callaghan, J. P., 'Imago Dei: A Test Case for St. Thomas's Augustinianism' in M. Dauphinais, B. David and M. Levering (eds), *Aquinas the Augustinian* (Washington, DC: CUA, 2001).

O'Callaghan, J. P., *Thomist Realism and the Linguistic Turn: Toward a More Perfect Form of Existence* (Notre Dame, IN: University of Notre Dame Press, 2003).

O'Collins, G., *Incarnation* (London and New York: Continuum, 2002).

O'Collins, G., *Christology: A Biblical, Historical, and Systematic Study of Jesus* (2nd edn, Oxford: OUP, 2009).

O'Collins, G. and Kendall, D., 'The Faith of Jesus', *TS* 53 (1992): 403–23.

O'Neill, J. C., *The Puzzle of 1 John* (London: SPCK, 1966).

Oakes, E. T., *Infinity Dwindled to Infancy: A Catholic and Evangelical Christology* (Grand Rapids, MI and Cambridge: Eerdmans, 2011).

Ols, D., 'Réflexions sur l'actualité de la Christologie de Saint Thomas', *DC* 34 (1981): 58–71.

Ols, D., A propos de la vision béatifique du Christ viateur', *DC* 36 (1983): 395–405.

Ols, D., *Le cristologie contemporànee e le lóro posizióni fondamentali al vaglio della dottrina di S. Tommaso* (Studi Tomistici, 39; Vatican: Libreria Editrice Vaticana, 1991).

Patfoort, A., 'Vision béatifique et théologie de l'âme du Christ: Á propos d'un ouvrage récent', *RT* 93 (1993): 635–9.

Pinckaers, S., *The Sources of Christian Ethics* (Edinburgh: T&T Clark, 1995).

Pitstick, A. L., *Light in Darkness: Hans Urs von Balthasar and the Catholic Doctrine of Christ's Descent into Hell* (Grand Rapids, MI and Cambridge: Eerdmans, 2007).

Pomplun, T., 'Impassibility in St. Hilary of Poitiers's *De Trinitate*', in J. F. Keating and T. J. White, *Divine Impassibility and the Mystery of Human Suffering* (Grand Rapids, MI and Cambridge: Eerdmans, 2009).

Porter, S. E. and Pitts, A. W., 'Πίστις with a Preposition and Genitive Modifier: Lexical, Semantic, and Syntactic Considerations in the πίστις Χριστοῦ Discussion' in M. Bird and P. M. Sprinkle, *The Faith of Jesus Christ: Exegetical, Biblical, and Theological Studies* (Milton Keynes: Paternoster; Colorado Springs and Hyderabad: Hendrickson, 2009), pp. 33–53.

Rahner, K., 'Current Problems in Christology' in *Theological Investigations*, vol. 1: *God, Christ, Mary and Grace* (trans. C. Ernst; London: Darton, Longman & Todd; New York: Seabury, 1961), pp. 149–200.

Rahner, K., 'Some Implications of the Scholastic Concept of Uncreated Grace' in *Theological Investigations*, vol. 1: *God, Christ, Mary and Grace* (trans. C. Ernst; London: Darton, Longman & Todd; New York: Seabury, 1961), pp. 319–46.

Rahner, K., 'Dogmatic Reflections on the Knowledge and Self-Consciousness of Christ' in

Theological Investigations, vol. 5: *Later Writings* (trans. K.-H. Kruger; London: Darton, Longman & Todd; Baltimore: Helicon, 1966), pp. 193–215.

Rahner, K., 'The Eternal Significance of the Humanity of Jesus for our Relationship with God', *Theological Investigations*, vol. 3: *The Theology of the Spiritual Life* (trans. K.-H. and B. Kruger; London: Darton, Longman & Todd; Baltimore: Helicon, 1967), pp. 35–46.

Rahner, K., *The Trinity* (London: Burns & Oates, 1970).

Rahner, K., *Foundations of Christian Faith: An Introduction to the Idea of Christianity* (London: Darton, Longman & Todd, 1978).

Rahner, K., 'An Investigation of the Incomprehensibility of God in St Thomas Aquinas' in *Theological Investigations*, vol. 16: *Experience of the Spirit: Source of Theology* (trans. D. Morland; London: Darton, Longman & Todd, 1979), pp. 244–54.

Ratzinger, J., 'Bewusstsein und Wissen Christi', *MTZ* 12 (1961): 78–81.

Richard, L., 'Une texte de saint Augustin sur la vision intuitive du Christ', *RSR* 12 (1922): 85–7.

Riedlinger, H., *Geschichtlichkeit und Vollendung des Wissens Christi* (Quaestiones Disputatae, 32; Freiburg, Basel and Vienna: Herder, 1966).

Riestra, J. A., 'La scienza di Cristo nel concilio Vaticano II: Ebrei 4, 15 nella Costituzione Dogmatica "Dei Verbum"', *AT* 2 (1988): 99–119.

Rivière, J., 'Le problème de la science humaine du Christ: Positions classiques et nouvelles tendances', *BLE* 7 (1915–16): 241–61, 289–314, 337–64.

Rocca, G. P., *Speaking the Incomprehensible God: Thomas Aquinas on the Interplay of Positive and Negative Theology* (Washington, DC: CUA, 2004).

Rosenberg, R. S., 'Christ's Human Knowledge: A Conversation with Lonergan and Balthasar', *TS* 71 (2010): 817–45.

Rowland, C., *The Open Heaven: A Study of Apocalpytic in Judaism and Early Christianity* (London: SPCK, 1982).

Salgado, J.-M., 'La science du Fils de Dieu fait homme prises de position des Pères et de la Préscolastique (IIè-XIIè siècle', *DC* 36 (1983): 180–286.

Sarrasin, C., *Plein de grâce et de verité: Théologie de l'âme du Christ selon Thomas d'Aquin* (Vénasque: Carmel, 1992).

Saward, J., *Cradle of Redeeming Love: The Theology of the Christmas Mystery* (San Francisco: Ignatius, 2002).

Scheeben, M. J., *The Mysteries of Christianity* (trans. C. Vollert; St Louis, MO and London: Herder, 1947).

Schell, H., *Katholische Dogmatik: Kritische Ausgabe*: vol. 3: *Menschwerdung und Erlösung, Heiligung und Vollendung* (eds H. Petri and P.-W. Scheele; Paderborn etc.: Schöningh, 1994).

Schmitz, R. M., 'Christus Comprehensor. Die "Vision Beatifica Christi Viatoris" bei M. J. Scheeben', *DC* 36 (1983): 347–59.

Schnackenburg, R., *The Johannine Epistles: Introduction and Commentary* (trans. R. and I. Fuller; London: Burns & Oates, 1992).

Schoonenberg, P., *The Christ* (London and Sydney: Sheed & Ward, 1972).

Schüssler Fiorenza, F. and Galvin, J. P. (eds), *Systematic Theology: Roman Catholic Perspectives* (Dublin: Gill and Macmilliam, 1992).

Sharkey, M. (ed.), *International Theological Commission: Texts and Documents 1969-1985* (San Francisco: Ignatius, 1989).

Sherwin, M. S., *By Knowledge and By Love: Charity and Knowledge in the Moral Theology of St. Thomas Aquinas* (Washington, DC: CUA, 2005).

Silva, M., *Philippians* (Grand Rapids, MI: Baker Academic, 2005).

Smalley, S. S., *1, 2, 3 John* (Word Biblical Commentary, 51; Nashville: Nelson, 1984).

Sobrino, J., *Christology at the Crossroads* (trans. J. Drury; London: SCM, 1978).

Sobrino, J., *Jesus the Liberator: A Historical-Theological Reading of Jesus of Nazareth* (trans. P. Burns and F. McDonagh; Tunbridge Wells and New York: Burns & Oates, 1994).

Sobrino, J., *Christ the Liberator: A View from the Victims* (trans. P. Burns; Maryknoll, NY: Orbis, 2001).

Stump, E., *Aquinas* (London and New York: Routledge, 2003).

Sumruld, W. A., *Augustine and the Arians: The Bishop of Hippo's Encounters with Ulfilan Arianism* (Cranbury, NJ and London: Associated, 1994).

Swinburne, R., *The Christian God* (Oxford: Clarendon, 1994).

Tekippe, T. J., 'Towards a Systematic Understanding of the Vision of Christ', *MJLS* 11 (1993): 77–101.

Terrien, J.-B., *La grâce et la gloire ou la filiation adoptive des enfants de Dieu étudiée dans sa réalité, ses principes, son perfectionnement et son couronnement final* (Paris: Lethielleux, new edn, 1901).

Thistleton, A. C., *The First Epistle to the Corinthians: A Commentary on the Greek Text* (Grand Rapid, MI and Cambridge: Eerdmans, 2000).

Thüsing, W., 'New Testament Approaches to a Transcendental Christology' in K. Rahner and W. Thüsing, *A New Christology* (London: Burns & Oates, 1980), pp. 44–211.

Torrell, J.-P., 'S. Thomas d'Aquin et la science du Christ: Une Relecture des questions 9–12 de la "Tertia pars" de la Somme de Théologie' in S.-T. Bonino (ed.), *Saint Thomas au XXe siècle: Actes du colloque du centenaire de la "Revue Thomiste" 25–28 mars 1993 – Toulouse* (Paris: St Paul, 1994), pp. 394–409.

Torrell, J.-P., *Le Christ en ses Mystères*, vol. 2 (Paris: Desclée, 1999).

Torrell, J.-P., *Recherches thomasiennes. Études revues et augmentées* (Paris: Vrin, 2000).

Tremblay, R., *La manifestation et la vision de Dieu selon saint Irénéé de Lyon* (Münsterische Beiträge zur Theologie, 41; Münster: Aschendorff, 1978).

Trottmann, C., *La Vision Béatifique: Des disputes scolastiques à sa définition par Benoît XII* (Bibliothèque des Écoles Françaises d'Athenès et de Rome, 289; Rome: École Française, 1995).

van Bavel, T. J., *Recherches sur la Christologie de saint Augustin: L'humain et le divin dans le Christ d'après saint Augustin* (Fribourg: Éditions Universitaires, 1951).

van Fleteren, F., 'Per Speculum et in Aenigmitate: 1 Corinthians 13:12 in the Writings of St. Augustine', *AS* 23 (1992): 69–102.

Vögtle, A., 'Exegetische Erwägungen über das Wissen und Selbstbewusstsein Jesu' in J. B. Metz, W. Kern, A. Darlapp and H. Vorgrimler (eds), *Gott in Welt: Festgabe für Karl Rahner* (2 vols; Freiburg, Basel and Vienna: Herder, 1964), vol. 1, pp. 608–67.

Von Balthasar, H. U., *The Glory of the Lord: A Theological Aesthetics*, vol. 1: *Seeing the Form* (trans. E. Leiva-Merikakis; Edinburgh: T&T Clark, 1982).

Von Balthasar, H. U., *Theo-Drama: Theological Dramatic Theory*, vol. III: *Dramatis Personae: Persons in Christ* (trans. G. Harrison; San Francisco: Ignatius, 1987).

Von Balthasar, H. U., 'Fides Christi: An Essay on the Consciousness of Christ' in *Explorations in Theology*, vol. 2: *Spouse of the Word* (San Francisco: Ignatius, 1991), pp. 43–79

Von Balthasar, H. U., *Theo-Drama: Theological Dramatic Theory*, vol. V: *The Final Act* (trans. G. Harrison; San Francisco: Ignatius, 1998).

Wallis, I. G., *The Faith of Jesus Christ in Early Christian Tradition* (Cambridge: CUP, 1995).

Weinandy, T. G., *Does God Change? The Word's Becoming in the Incarnation* (Still Rivers, MA: St. Bede's, 1985).

Weinandy, T. G., 'Jesus' Filial Vision of the Father', *PE* 13 (2004): 189–201.

Weinandy, T. G., 'The Beatific Vision and the Incarnate Son: Furthering the Discussion', *TTh* 70 (2006): 605–15.

White, T. J., 'The Voluntary Action of the Earthly Christ and the Necessity of the Beatific Vision', *TTh* 69 (2005): 497–534.

White, T. J., 'Dyotheletism and the Instrumental Human Consciousness of Jesus', *PE* 17 (2008): 396–422.

Wickham, L. R., 'The Ignorance of Christ: A Problem for the Ancient Theology' in L. R. Wickham and C. P. Bammel (eds), *Christian Faith and Greek Philosophy in Late Antiquity: Essays in Tribute to George Christopher Stead* (Supplements to Vigiliae Christianae, vol. 19; New York: Brill, 1993), pp. 213–26.

Wiles, M., *The Spiritual Gospel: The Interpretation of the Fourth Gospel in the Early Church* (Cambridge: CUP, 1960).

Wilkins, J., 'Love and Knowledge of God in the Human Life of Christ', *PE* 21 (2012): 77–99.

Winandy, J., 'Le logion de l'ignorance (Mc XIII, 32; Mt XXIV, 36)', *RB* 75 (1968): 63–79.

Wright, N. T., *The New Testament and the People of God* (Christian Origins and Questions and the Question of God, vol. 2; London: SPCK, 1996).

INDEX OF ANCIENT, MEDIEVAL AND EARLY MODERN AUTHORS

INDEX OF MODERN AUTHORS

Lightning Source UK Ltd.
Milton Keynes UK
UKHW020626300519
343585UK00003B/52/P

9 780567 682130